THE DREAM
AND THE
NIGHTMARE

Also by Myron Magnet

Dickens and the Social Order

THE DREAM AND THE NIGHTMARE

THE SIXTIES' LEGACY TO THE UNDERCLASS

MYRON MAGNET

ENCOUNTER BOOKS
SAN FRANCISCO, CALIFORNIA

First paperback edition published in 2000 by Encounter Books, an activity of Encounter for Culture and Education, Inc., a nonprofit tax exempt corporation.

First published in 1993 by William Morrow and Company, Inc.

Encounter Books website address: www.encounterbooks.com

Cover and text design by Andrea DuFlon.
Composition by Catherine Campaigne.

Manufactured in the United States and printed on acid-free paper.

Library of Congress Cataloging-in-Publication Data

Magnet, Myron.
    The dream and the nightmare: the sixties' legacy to the underclass / Myron Magnet—with a new introduction by the author.
     p. cm.
    Includes bibliographical references and index.
    1. United States—Social conditions—1960–1980.   2. United States—Social conditions—1980–.   3. United States—Social policy—1980–.   4. Poor—United States.   5. Social values.   6. Subculture.   I. Title.
HN59.M25   2000
305.5'69'0973-dc20   92-23260 CIP
ISBN 1-893554-02-3 (pb)

10 9 8 7 6

For
Julia and Alec

CONTENTS

PREFACE

The *Dream and the Nightmare* was the first book to argue that culture, not racism or lack of jobs or the welfare system, was the cause of the underclass. I didn't mean that the culprit was some "culture of poverty" or "ghetto culture." The problem, I contended, lay in the majority culture. Led by its elite institutions—the universities, the judiciary, the press, the great charitable foundations, even the mainstream churches—American culture underwent a revolution in the 1960s, which transformed some of its most basic beliefs and values, including its beliefs about the causes of poverty. When these new attitudes reached the poor, and particularly the urban, minority poor, the result was catastrophic: many of the new culture's beliefs downplayed the personal responsibility, self-control, and deferral of gratification that it takes to succeed. At the same time, the new culture celebrated an "if it feels good, do it" self-indulgence that for the poor, whose lives have less margin for error than the prosperous, too often proved disastrous. The social policy that these ideas engendered compounded the disaster.

In 1993, this was a hotly controversial idea. Thinkers on both the political left and right believed, understandably, that intergenerational poverty, being an economic condition, must have an economic cause. But in the intervening years, my cultural argument has won converts—most notably presidential aspirant George W. Bush, whose political strategist recently told the press that *The Dream and the Nightmare* is "a road map to

1

the governor's attitudes on the role of government." Even the proponents of the two main economic theories against which *The Dream and the Nightmare* argued—Charles Murray and William Julius Wilson—have begun to see how powerful a force culture has been in forming the underclass.

One particularly instructive convert is Doe Fund president George McDonald, who in 1993 was as strident an advocate for the homeless as you could find. We had a vituperative television debate back then, in which he preached the ascendant gospel that the homeless were victims of a heartless society, needing only "housing, housing, housing" to solve their problems. But closer acquaintance with the homeless in the intervening years caused him to revise his views: surveys of residents of the homeless shelter he ran showed that four out of five of his charges were chronic drug users, whose problem wasn't unaffordable housing but self-destructive behavior—enabled by a culture that showered them with housing, handouts, and sympathy. What the homeless needed, he came to believe, was a strong message of work, sobriety, and personal responsibility from the surrounding culture, and the success of his "Ready, Willing & Able" program in rehabilitating the homeless according to those principles (which he had so vehemently rejected in our TV debate) bears out that belief.

I had assumed as I wrote *The Dream and the Nightmare* that, because elite culture had caused the problems I described there, that same elite culture would be the likeliest source of a solution. In this I was mistaken. Social learning takes place much closer to the ground, right up against concrete social reality, in the manner of George McDonald's change of heart. America tried its grand experiment with the elite cultural values of the 1960s. It loosened its crime and welfare policies, it had its fling with the sexual revolution, it remade its mores from top to bottom, it instituted affirmative action, it turned its universities into academies of the new culture. In due course all this produced real-world consequences, plain to see: cities made unlivable by the crime, incivility, and squalor generated by the underclass and the homeless; children damaged when the "If it feels good, do it" ethos broke up their families and provided them with so little help in solving the problems of life.

In the 1990s, in a pragmatic fashion without much talk about theory, the nation began to address not the cultural revolution itself but some of its most destructive consequences related to the underclass. The work of repair—effected less by intellectuals than by public officials—has had two main milestones so far. The first is New York mayor Rudolph Giuliani's campaign, beginning in 1994, to slash crime in what had come to be thought of as the murder capital of the world; the second is the federal Welfare Reform Act of 1996. Both these reforms, as it turned out, had the effect of utterly disproving some of the most cherished tenets of the cultural revolution, and thus they may be seen as the beginning of the latest chapter of the story *The Dream and the Nightmare* tells.

The year before Giuliani took office, New York had 2,240 murders, public housing projects crackled with gunfire nightly, car theft was epidemic, and New Yorkers famously barricaded themselves into triple-locked apartments, after walking home past open-air madhouses and drug supermarkets in the parks or on the streets. Giuliani at once instituted a new style of activist policing that enforced the laws against such quality-of-life offenses as excessive noise, graffiti, prostitution, low-level drug dealing, and aggressive panhandling—crimes that, when unpunished, make public places seem disorderly and threatening, scaring away the law-abiding and emboldening potential criminals to attempt worse crimes, since no authority seems to be in charge. Giuliani's police force also dismantled entire drug gangs, destroyed the infrastructure of fences and chop shops without which criminals can't operate, and pushed hard to get illegal guns off the streets.

The result by 1999: overall felonies fell by half; murder dropped 68 percent; New York became the nation's safest big city. Freed from fear, New Yorkers came out at night and flocked into the theaters and restaurants, joined by hordes of tourists, who crowded into the city once it lost the reputation for violence and disorder that had previously kept them away. And this concrete, real-world success left in tatters the cultural revolution's orthodoxy that society can't cut crime without curing its "root causes" of inequality and racism. New Yorkers, who saw their own quality of life improve and their city revive and flourish because of the restoration of public order, found it hard to keep alive the orthodox belief that "the system" rather than the criminal was responsible for crime. They lost their faith that the criminal might himself be a victim, whom it would be doubly unjust to blame or punish.

Welfare reform had a similar disintegrating effect on prevailing wisdom. When the new law passed in 1996, even such reputedly level-headed figures as Senator Daniel Patrick Moynihan apocalyptically predicted shivering women huddled on grates and children starving on the streets *en masse*. It never happened. Instead, the welfare rolls have dropped over 40 percent nationwide, as welfare mothers have entered the workforce in large (but as yet incompletely quantified) numbers and found they could support their families. Again, the received orthodoxies, like those Senator Moynihan had voiced, began to fray. Not enough jobs? Jobs too far away for inner-city dwellers to reach them? Experience proved otherwise.

To be sure, critics contend that Giuliani cut crime by "Gestapo tactics"; other naysayers are still expecting to see children starving in the streets whenever the economy turns down, and they will oppose welfare reform for the next decade and more. But for many Americans, these policy changes are turning out to produce thoroughgoing cultural changes. The majority of New Yorkers—and citizens of other cities now trying to replicate New York's anticrime success—now either flat-out disbelieve the cultural revolution's shibboleths about crime and criminals or have lost confidence in them, even if they can't bring themselves to say so. Nobody wants to go back to the days of out-of-control crime, when many believed New York had no future. Criminals and potential criminals have different attitudes, too: they know that the cops are out to catch them, with growing support from the citizenry. They are hearing a lot less talk about criminals as poor victims or manly rebels—and so it becomes a little harder to hold these ideas themselves, though many popular singers are working as hard as they can to keep gangster outlawry glamorous. Underclass people, like anyone else, shape their behavior according to the ideas that are in their minds, and the improving crime statistics reflect changed attitudes.

So too with welfare. Increasingly during the nineties, as welfare clearly had become a way of life for the underclass—and a way of life shot through with dismaying social pathology—Americans came to dislike it, especially since the work ethic was the one traditional value that emerged from the cultural revolution largely intact in mainstream America. But there was always that specter of children starving on the streets. The experience of seeing welfare recipients successfully entering the workforce—and of reading press accounts of how optimistic many of them say they are as a result—casts a new light on welfare and welfare recipients, on poverty and on compassion. The new message coming from the larger culture to the underclass—that you are expected to work, that work is dignified while idleness is not, that there can be no benefits without reciprocal obligations— looks from anecdotal evidence to be starting, though only very tentatively as yet, a liberating change in the worldview of the inner city communities, particularly among young women.

This whole progression—from cultural revolution, to efforts to clean up its worst consequences, to new changes in attitudes—underscores a well-worn truth about the dialectical relationship between ideas and reality: ideas have real-world consequences, which in their turn alter consciousness. And it underscores another equally old truth: that reality—especially the reality of human nature—is not infinitely malleable but rather has its own laws. Therefore, there is a right life for man, a life in accord with our nature, a life that most fully realizes our potential for freedom, dignity, happiness—indeed, for humanity. We have three or four millennia of philosophers and poets trying to tell us what that right life is, three or four millennia of history to see how our predecessors tried to accomplish it: and, while there isn't unanimity of opinion, there are vast areas of agreement on such matters as the need for social order, for personal responsibility, for sexual restraint, for moderation and sobriety, for families that nurture children, for truthfulness and honesty, for liberty under law.

Any number of what John Stuart Mill called "experiments in living" have tried to organize human existence in disregard of these principles, and the historical landscape is littered with their failures and the appalling human casualties they caused, from the self-immolation of antinomian sects in the Middle Ages down to the collapse of Communism in our own time. It's to our nation's credit that our cities didn't have to disintegrate entirely before we admitted the failure of some of the experiments we began in the sixties and brought our practices more into conformity with what human nature requires. But a lot of people were murdered, and a lot of underclass lives ruined, before that happened.

I think that we will look back on the heinous April 1999 rampage at Columbine High School, in which two upper middle class teenagers with attack weapons murdered a teacher and 12 of their fellow students—and would have blown up the entire school with all its nearly 2,000 pupils in it had their plans succeeded—as another turning point in our culture. As American culture went awry in the sixties—as its beliefs fell out of alignment with human reality and stopped giving a clear and persuasive account of right and wrong, and of how we should live our lives—those at the margins of society suffered first. Early on, poor, mostly black, inner city residents, with few skills and little education, declined into an underclass. But as our cultural revolution advanced beyond the 1960s, as what colleges inculcated and what primary and secondary schools taught, what TV shows dramatized and popular music celebrated, what the press broadcast from almost every organ, and what shaped the relations between parents and children and men and women all became more extreme, the circle of damage widened. The mores and values of an earlier age would have led disturbed young people like the two Columbine murderers (and the unprecedented rash of school shooters who preceded them during the nineties) to act out their disordered fantasies in less apocalyptic ways. Those same earlier mores would have led school authorities to intervene sooner and perhaps—though this is mere speculation—might have made their families better able to deal with such disturbance or less likely to give rise to it in the first place.

This is the conclusion most Americans reached in the wake of the rampage, and they reached it with anxiety and dismay. As more than one horrified observer put it to the press right after Columbine: "What kind of culture have we created?" Everybody knows that our culture changed radically in the last decades, but only now are people beginning fully to gauge its real-world consequences for the next generation of Americans of all classes—and therefore for the future of American society at large.

I pointed to these consequences in the concluding chapters of *The Dream and the Nightmare*. I had argued throughout the book that the cultural revolution had two distinct, though intertwined and mutually reinforcing strands: a political one that admirably sought to bring blacks into full equality, and another strand that sought the personal liberation of the individual, especially his or her sexual liberation. Both these strands, I noted, were leading to wilder and wilder extremes, producing a culture that could provide young people with little to nourish their souls or make sense of their lives. These trends have only intensified in the intervening years, with increasingly baleful effects on the young.

The political strand of the cultural revolution has led, in a misguided campaign to sweep away traditional standards of excellence and value that blacks and other designated victim groups might find invidious, to a cultural and moral relativism so sweeping that it provides young people with only the flimsiest guides to the good, the true, and the beautiful that should be the goal and measure of human striving. On the personal side, the sexual revolution has so weakened the American family—the fundamental social institution in which character is forged and strengthened—that too many kids grow up with a fundamental insecurity and a weak sense of self, all exacerbated when the parents (or parent or step-parent) participate in the prevailing relativism and so provide little in the way of moral guidance that gives order to the world. Moreover, as young people enter adolescence and then young adulthood, they find that the same strand of the cultural revolution has so confused relations between the sexes that this traditional arena of human fulfillment is now problematic in the extreme. The revolution that promised greater human happiness on balance produced much less.

In 1993, I sympathized with the plight of those who had entered adulthood at the start of the 1980s, with the cultural revolution in full swing. I observed that the cultural trends that produced their plight were even more pronounced at the start of the 1990s, and I took it for granted that the toll on the young would be ever greater. Even so, the nihilism of so many kids of the nineties, with their nightmare-image tee-shirts and their popular songs of death and violence, takes me aback. Especially in the wake of Columbine, it takes most Americans aback—enough aback to ask the questions at the center of *The Dream and the Nightmare,* "What kind of culture have we created?" and what are its consequences? With that explicit critical consciousness, the work of repair might begin in earnest.

It's possible that elected officials may be the agents of this change, as they have been with changes in attitudes toward crime and welfare. *The Dream and the Nightmare* appeared at the beginning of Bill Clinton's pants-down presidency, and Clinton has been a caricature-like embodiment of the values of the cultural revolution, with his exaggerated I-feel-your-pain display of "compassion" for the "victimized" and "oppressed," accompanied by his never-ending, utterly irresponsible sexual soap-opera. In accord with the principles of the cultural revolution, he has behaved as if the moral authority that flows from his compassion—the value that trumps all else—cancels or justifies his unprincipled conduct in so many departments of life. Presidents both reflect and shape our national culture, and no tenet of the cultural revolution has failed to get a boost from an almost daily dose of presidential exemplification from this Chief Executive. It may be, though, that widening exasperation with Clinton in the wake of his impeachment may hasten our national rejection of the sixties' values he represents.

I write this just as the campaign for the 2000 presidential election gets under way, and right now that election looks like it will be a referendum on the values of the cultural revolution. George W. Bush has already begun explicitly attacking the "if it feels good, do it" culture of the sixties. He's told me that he deeply believes that the cultural revolution turned out to be a national calamity and that the family breakdown it has produced stands at the top of our national problems. From what he's told me, and from his public statements so far, I believe he will run and govern as the anti-Clinton and the un-sixties: a committed family man devoted to traditional values and traditional beliefs, after his youthful fling with the culture of the sixties led him to reject it emphatically from firsthand knowledge of its destructiveness. I am hopeful that the national debate he will spark, the personal-responsibility-based policies he promises to champion, and the personal example he will set will all together move the culture in the right direction, so that—for starters—we will no longer pick up the morning paper and read of America's privileged children massacring their schoolmates.

No one should minimize how Herculean a task this change will be for the nation. So many forces in the elite culture are still moving powerfully in the wrong direction. In the universities, the dogma that all cultures and values are equal, but that Western culture and its traditional values are less equal than others, is more entrenched than ever, and has spread into the law schools, the schools of education, even the schools of public health. The Supreme Court is still capable of a decision like *Romer* v. *Evans,* which "impos[ed] upon all Americans" the pro-sexual revolution, anti-traditional morality views of "the elite class" to which the judges belong, as Justice Scalia's dissent put it. *The New York Times,* the Ford Foundation, the National Council of Churches—all still march in lockstep to the ever more discordant beat of the cultural revolution's drummer.

In the middle and lower reaches of the culture, the beat sounds almost as loudly. A New York high school teaches a course in how to do grafitti—as an art form purportedly no less worthy than that Michelangelo practiced—while a gifted third-grader in New York's best public primary school, which even in *math* class teaches that Columbus was a genocidal villain, hasn't heard of George Washington and thinks his questioner must mean George Washington *Carver.* The fact that popular culture keeps pushing the limits of the sexual revolution ever further is too familiar to need any comment; while in real life the divorce rate remains very high, and the marriage rate has declined by a third between the sixties and the nineties.

Even so, no one should think that this worldview and the mores that spring from it are eternal and immutable. Cultural changes can happen very quickly, like the cultural revolution itself or, to take a more recent (if much more modest) example, the successful campaign to stigmatize smoking, which turned cigarettes from glamorous to disgusting almost overnight. Though Cassandras may believe that cultures only ratchet downward in an inexorable process of decline, the example of Victorian England proves otherwise: in a single generation, an elite of writers, social reformers, philanthropists, and clergymen—backed by an exemplary head of state—turned a gin-swilling nation addicted to cockfights and bull-baiting, with soaring illegitimacy and crime rates and a degraded urban poor living in squalor, into a law-abiding, sober, upright country, with strong families and rising health and prosperity widely diffused among the population. At the turn of a new century in America, changes beginning to flow within our own culture offer hope for the underclass and more signs of hope for a larger renewal than we've seen in decades.

INTRODUCTION

What's Gone Wrong?

Weren't dizzying contrasts of wealth and poverty supposed to have gone out with Dickensian London? What are they doing flagrantly alive again, deeply ingrained in the basic texture of today's American cities?

The daily juxtapositions are so bizarre that they strain belief, however numbingly familiar they grow. In New York City, directly under the windows of the treasure-crammed five-million-dollar apartments that loom over glittering Fifth Avenue, for instance, sleep the homeless, one and sometimes two to a park bench, haggard, usually ill, huddled in rags turned dead gray with dirt and wear. In a gentrified neighborhood across town, bustling with upper-middle-class professionals, only a thickness of brick separates a building where staid burghers have paid upwards of three quarters of a million dollars for an apartment from the squalid crack house next door.

Not far away, for the last few Christmas seasons, the line of fur-coated holidaymakers jovially filing into a luxury food store to buy caviar advertised at "only" $260 a pound has adjoined the sullen line of ravaged paupers waiting for the soup kitchen to open at the church around the corner. Downtown, in the suave, postmodern towers that house health clubs, power lunches, and automated teller machines, grimy derelicts looking like leftovers from the Depression haunt the gleaming atriums for warmth and safety, while above sit dapper investment bankers, some of whom made seven-figure incomes rearranging the industrial order before they were forty. As for the urban parks and pillared train stations that speak of a once-confident civic pride and prosperity, how often are they now—graffitied, vandalized, reeking of human waste—but dreary gauntlets of beggary?

Or worse: think of the savage 1989 rape of a twenty-eight-year-old jogger by a "wilding" pack of Harlem teenagers in New York's Central Park. What starker contrast of Haves and Have-Nots could be found than between the victim, a Wall Street investment banker ambitious to excel in every pursuit, and her brutal attackers, unregenerate beneficiaries of a wide array of social programs designed to uplift the "disadvantaged"?

Like Death interrupting the dumbstruck banquet, the poverty and vice that pervade America's cities appall the prosperous. What's wrong with the country, they worry, that such problems are everywhere? Does the same system that enriches the Haves simultaneously degrade the Have-Nots? Does the comfort of the prosperous somehow rest upon the debasement of their poorest fellow citizens, the homeless and the underclass? Are the prosperous *responsible* for the condition of the poor?

When the Haves think about their relation to the poor, the images that come to mind feed their anxiety and sense of guilt: their brother's keeper ... the biblical grandee Dives with the beggar Lazarus at his mansion gates ... the religious duty to aid the poor. They think of Dickens's *Christmas Carol* or of "Good King Wenceslas," embodiments of that Victorian paternalist ethic that holds masters responsible for the condition of their dependents. Who doesn't remember how utterly a hard Scrooge devastates exploited Bob Cratchit and his family; how a reformed Scrooge, with the administration of a timely dose of paternalist generosity, gives Tiny Tim life? Exemplifying right treatment of the poor, Good King Wenceslas, his charity stronger than the fury of wild nature, carries a feast to his needy subject through a blizzard, proving himself worthy of God's blessing by blessing the poor.

But happily, modern society isn't hierarchical, in Victorian fashion. Today's Haves aren't the "betters" or the "masters" of the Have-Nots, and today's worst-off poor are nobody's mistreated dependents or exploited employees: they are radically disconnected from the larger society, and they don't work. Victorian philanthropy isn't equal to their plight.

Impersonal and economic, rather than intimate and moral like the Victorian notions, modern theories hold the prosperous, as a class, responsible for the condition of the poor, as a class. Take Jesse Jackson's much-trumpeted theory of "economic violence," holding that the Reagan administration mind-set that unfettered the rich simultaneously immiserated the poor by unraveling the social safety net. The rich got a tax break, leaving less revenue to go to the poor. A more sophisticated formulation holds that in the eighties the Haves created a world economy that handsomely rewards themselves while constricting opportunity for the Have-Nots.

The eloquent fact that means-tested federal welfare spending rose 44 percent between 1980 and 1987, however, explodes a theory like Jackson's. And further refuting this whole line of thought, the eighties boom that enriched the tycoons created an astonishing 18.4 million new jobs, both skilled and unskilled, offering a way out of poverty to almost any poor person with the willingness and discipline to work.

So even if the economic developments of the eighties did increase the disparity in income between the rich and the poor, I will argue in Chapter Two that those developments don't explain why we have an underclass or why the homeless haunt the streets. Since low-skill jobs exist in profusion, since work today will normally lift people above the poverty line, and since opportunity for further advancement is open to those with the ambition and energy to seize it, for the able-bodied poverty in America is no longer an utterly ineluctable fate: one can choose to try to escape, by legitimate rather than criminal paths, with a good chance of success.

But in that case, America's deepest-rooted poverty starts to look more than a little mysterious. If jobs do exist, as they did throughout the eighties, why do large numbers of very poor people remain in poverty? The emblem of this mystery, ubiquitous in big cities, is the panhandler begging outside McDonald's, right under the *Help Wanted* sign.

This book will suggest that the key to the mystery of why, despite opportunity, the poorest poor don't work is that their poverty is less an economic matter than a cultural one. In many cases, as Chapters Two through Five will argue, the Have-Nots lack the inner resources to seize their chance, and they pass on to their children a self-defeating set of values and attitudes, along with an impoverished intellectual and emotional development, that generally imprisons them in failure as well. Three, sometimes four generations have made the pathology that locks them in—school-leaving, nonwork, welfare dependency, crime, drug abuse, and the like—drearily familiar.

But the underclass culture they live in is far from being wholly of their own invention. Underclass culture has its own very distinct inflection, to be sure; but for all its idiosyncratic peculiarity it is a dialect, so to speak, shaped more by the culture as a whole, and by the singular history of underclass communities within that culture, than by any independent, internal dynamic.

That's why the prosperous are indeed implicated in the poverty of the poor, even though they don't extract their BMWs from the hides of the underclass the way mine owners squeezed profits out of abused children in the early days of the Industrial Revolution, when "economic violence" was more than rhetoric. This book's central argument is that the Haves are implicated because over the last thirty years they radically remade American culture, turning it inside out and upside down to accomplish a cultural revolution whose most mangled victims turned out to be the Have-Nots.

This was the precise opposite of what was supposed to happen. For when the Haves began their cultural revolution a generation ago, they acted in the name of two related liberations. Above all, impelled by the fervor of the civil rights movement, they sought the political and economic liberation of the Have-Nots, the poor and the black. The ideal that guided them was a vision of democracy; their honorable aim was to complete democracy's work, to realize democratic values fully by making American society more open and inclusive. Out of this democratic impulse sprang the War on Poverty, welfare benefit increases, court-ordered school busing, more public housing projects, affirmative action, job-training programs, drug treatment programs, special education, *The Other America,* Archie

Bunker, *Roots,* countless editorials and magazine articles and TV specials, black studies programs, multicultural curricula, new textbooks, all-black college dorms, sensitivity courses, minority set-asides, Martin Luther King Day, and the political correctness movement at colleges, to name only some of the almost endless manifestations.

The deep changes in the majority culture's beliefs about the nature of democratic society and the poor's place within it had momentous consequences for the worst-off, as the ensuing chapters will show. But in addition to trying to liberate the poor and excluded from their marginality, the cultural revolution sought a second, even more spectacular liberation, which also shaped the fate of the poor, indirectly but far-reachingly.

This was the personal liberation that the Haves sought for themselves. Chafing against what the avant-garde writers and "sick" comedians of the fifties lambasted, only sometimes correctly, as that era's life-denying repression and conventionality, the Haves yearned to free themselves from a sense of anxious, stifling conformity, to claim a larger, more fulfilling life than that of an Organization Man or Man in the Gray Flannel Suit, or as a faceless atom in a Lonely Crowd, as titles of some of the era's influential texts had it.

That longing found two epochal expressions. The first was the sexual revolution, whose attitudes, diffused throughout the culture by advertising, movies, popular music, and television, so transformed values and behavior that they ultimately reshaped family life, increasing divorce, illegitimacy, and female-headed families on all levels of society.

The second manifestation was the sixties counterculture. As its name announced, the counterculture rejected traditional bourgeois culture as sick, repressive, and destructive. Bourgeois culture's sexual mores, based on guilt, marriage, and the perverse belief that present gratification should be deferred to achieve future goals, were symptoms of its pathology.

Its sobriety and decorum were mere slavish, hypocritical conformism; its industriousness betokened an upside-down, materialistic value system; its family life was yet another arena of coercion and guilt. This culture went hand in hand with an inherently unjust capitalist economic order, and a political order whose murderousness was plainly revealed by "Amerika's" war in Vietnam.

By contrast, "letting it all hang out," expressing yourself, acting upon what you really feel, "doing it"—all this constituted authentic, liberated selfhood, healthy and life-affirming. Such free expressiveness would get you closer to the counterculture's cherished ideal of a guilt-free, undivided selfhood, described in the therapeutic language of psychoanalysis as filtered through counterculture gurus like Norman O. Brown and Herbert Marcuse.

Consistent with that ideal, you didn't have to live by the disciplines of work and family and citizenship but could drop out from one or all, forging your own "alternative life-style," as the phrase went, more valid and authentic, and certainly more communitarian, than the conventional one. Moreover, you would get closer to authentic selfhood by kicking free of mechanical rationality and opening yourself to altered states of consciousness—drug-induced or not—that would let you behold truths deeper than reason reveals.

Just as you didn't have to frequent singles bars to be affected by the sexual revolution, you didn't have to live in a commune and eat mushrooms to be affected by the counterculture's quest for personal liberation. The new adversary stance toward conventional beliefs and ideals, breathlessly reported by the press and diffused almost instantly among the young, quickly put traditional values on the defensive, making them newly problematic even for those who continued to hold them.

And because the counterculture belonged to the young, its influence has persisted into the present, as the original Aquarians have matured into middle age and assumed positions of influence. That's what accounts for the dreams of so many Silicon Valley entrepreneurs that they'll drop out before long, and for the widespread use of cocaine in Hollywood and on Wall Street until recently. What you believe at twenty, as one historian has remarked, has a way of leaving its stamp on your worldview for life.

The cultural revolution's yoking together of personal and political liberations had a curious effect. It dignified the purely personal, making self-cherishing seem unselfish, almost civic-minded. Conversely, the irresponsibility that could mark the quest for personal liberation sometimes got carried over into social policy, too. The career of Senator Edward Kennedy exaggeratedly, almost parodically, exemplifies this process: as columnist Joe Klein has observed, the no-fault way in which he has conducted his personal life is mirrored by his no-fault social policy, all rights and entitlements without responsibilities.

Partly because of this confusion of the selfish and the civic, the cultural revolution failed in devastating ways in both of its two large intentions. Instead of ending poverty for the Have-Nots—despite the civil rights movement, despite the War on Poverty—the new cultural order fostered, in the underclass and the homeless, a new, intractable poverty that shocked and dismayed, that seemed to belong more to the era of ragged chimney sweeps than to modern America, that went beyond the economic realm into the realm of pathology. Poverty turned pathological, this book will argue, because the new culture that the Haves invented—their remade system of beliefs, norms, and institutions—permitted, even celebrated, behavior that, when poor people practice it, will imprison them inextricably in poverty. It's hard to persuade ghetto fifteen-year-olds not to get pregnant, for instance, when the entire culture, from rock music to upscale perfume commercials to highbrow books, is intoxicated with the joy of what before AIDS was called "recreational" sex.

Worse, during the sixties and seventies, the new culture of the Haves, in its quest for personal liberation, withdrew respect from the behavior and attitudes that have traditionally boosted people up the economic ladder—deferral of gratification, sobriety, thrift, dogged industry, and so on through the whole catalogue of antique-sounding bourgeois virtues. As social thinker Irving Kristol puts it, "It's hard to rise above poverty if society keeps deriding the human qualities that allow you to escape from it."

Moreover, as I will suggest in Chapters Six through Eight, the new culture held the poor back from advancement by robbing them of responsibility for their fate and thus further squelching their initiative and energy. Instead of telling them to take wholehearted advantage of opportunities that were rapidly opening, the new culture told the Have-Nots that they were victims of an unjust society and, if they were black, that they were entitled to restitution, including advancement on the basis of racial preference rather than mere personal striving and merit. It told them that the traditional standards of the larger community, already under attack by the counterculture, often didn't apply to them, that their wrongdoing might well be justified rebellion or the expression of yet another legitimate "alternative life-style." It told them that, if they were mentally ill, they were really just marching to a different drummer and should be free to do their marching in the streets—which is where many of them ended up, homeless.

The new culture, Chapters Eight and Nine will contend, allowed the neighborhoods of the Have-Nots to turn into anarchy, and it ruined the Have-Nots' schools by making racial balance, students' rights, and a "multicultural" curriculum more important than the genuine education vitally needed to rise. In all this, too, the new culture hinted to the Have-Nots that they must be slightly defective, or they wouldn't need such extraordinary measures. Otherwise—went the implication—if the Have-Nots hadn't been truly damaged by their deprivation, a simple opening of opportunity would have been enough to liberate them.

It wasn't only that the new cultural program failed the Have-Nots in important ways, as evidenced by the increase of the underclass and the homeless. The Haves harmed themselves with the new cultural order they brought into being. It was supposed to make their lives happier, more meaningful, more just. The personal liberation aspect of it was supposed to allow them to live more authentically, more intensely, with a larger area of pleasure and spontaneity in their lives. Instead, the personal freedom they claimed weakened families and communities, diluting the authority they had once had to invest individual life with meaning and solidity.

Even the aspect of the cultural revolution aiming to liberate the Have-Nots was also intended to increase the pleasure the Haves took in their own lives. It gave them an ennobling cause, larger than themselves and worth fighting for. They would make good on the long-imperfect American promise of doing

justice to the poor and most especially by righting the historic
wrongs done to blacks, finally creating the fully just, fully democratic society. Surely that part of the effort would allow the
Haves to feel that their lives had moral substance and dignity.
Were they inclined to use the language of religion, they might
say it would show that they were justified. For the revolution
was a kind of secular crusade, with the most elevated, sincere
moral aims, for which the appropriate marching music might
be "The Battle Hymn of the Republic."

For a generation, the moral intensity of these worthy aims
gave social policy questions something of the aspect of faith.
It invested policies designed to achieve these aims with the zeal
that charged the aims themselves. Yet however creditable, that
zeal made it hard to argue against the wisdom or efficacy of the
specific policies. How could one argue against benevolence and
goodwill? And if one asked if the policies were really working,
the faith that can look beyond the mere appearances of things—
the faith that is proof against the doubts of reason—would
reply: how could they fail?

But very often they did fail, not merely leaving conditions for
the Have-Nots unimproved but making them worse. And failure
was the harder to confront because, beyond liberating the Have-
Nots, the policies had the additional, unspoken aim of confirm-
ing the Haves in their sense of self-worth and moral excellence.

It was the harder to confront because of the price the Haves
had been willing to pay to achieve success. For paradoxically,
in the name of more perfect democracy, the cultural revolution
trampled underfoot key democratic values. In order to gain
laudable ethical ends, the Haves acquiesced in dubious and ultimately destructive measures such as the parceling out of rewards
on the basis of race, as Chapter Nine will consider, or the excusing of criminals as themselves victims, as Chapter Eight dis-
cusses, or, as Chapters Six and Seven will examine, the lifetime
public support of able-bodied women whose only career was
the production of illegitimate and mostly ill-parented children.

Countenancing these measures, as I will argue in Chapter
Nine, subverted the fundamental democratic principles from
which Americans derive their strongest sense of national identity
and unity. However temporary, for however good a purpose,

what most Americans knew to be wrong—imposing racial quotas, say, or freeing violent criminals on trivial technicalities—became officially right in the service of a supposedly higher value. When the evidence of their senses proclaimed the inevitable bad results of these measures, many even came to mistrust their senses.

No wonder that their heads swam, that their ethical judgments became guarded and tentative, that they came to view moral assertions with wary cynicism. No wonder that so many complain that America is undergoing a crisis of values. That crisis—real enough—is not caused by greed, contrary to what is often alleged. As Chapters Ten and Eleven will suggest, it is the unsurprising result of three decades of holding basic beliefs in abeyance and using questionable means to try to achieve a worthy social end. It is the result of making a democratic cultural revolution that ended—tragically—by making a travesty of the democratic values it had set out to uphold.

Before examining how waves of change in the elite culture rippled outward across American life and thought and engulfed the underclass, we need to focus, in Chapter One, on the power of cultural forces to shape the material and institutional reality in which people live their lives. Then we need to examine the underclass and the homeless more precisely. Determining who they are—and why—will be the task of Chapters Two through Five. But first, to conclude these introductory remarks, let me add two brief general observations.

First, the cultural revolution was made by an elite of opinion makers, policymakers, and mythmakers—lawyers, judges, professors, political staffers, journalists, writers, TV and movie honchos, clergymen—and it was overwhelmingly a liberal, left-of-center elite. Thus for the last thirty years, the dominant American culture has been liberal culture; notwithstanding Republican presidents in the White House, the ideas and values that have come to Americans from their newspapers and network news programs, their university (and increasingly their grammar and high school) classrooms, their pulpits, their novels and movies and television sitcoms, their magazines and advertisements and popular music, their courtrooms and their Congress, have added up to a liberal, left-of-center worldview.

By no means did everyone embrace this culture, but it became the norm for a generation, and it formed the set of assumptions out of which social policy sprang. It became powerful enough to put those who didn't endorse it on the defensive. They came to look upon their own opposing views, however strongly held, as old-fashioned, no longer in the cultural mainstream, no longer utterable with the same intellectual and moral authority.

Most of those who did buy into the new culture, of course, didn't adopt it after careful study and analysis. Participating in a *Zeitgeist* is more a matter of sympathy, unexamined assumption, fashion, and political correctness. As a result, many of the Haves who bought into the new culture did so only partially, with reservations, in some cases without relinquishing diametrically opposed ideas. Consequently, at its farthest reaches the new culture was beset with strains; it wasn't a unitary system. When it came to such extreme practical embodiments of the cultural revolution as busing and especially affirmative action, many Haves grew restive and uncomfortable. But such was the power of the new culture that dissent became hard to express. Often enough, doubt manifested itself as a willful suspension of disbelief.

Second, when the Haves ask what responsibility they bear for the plight of the poor, they ask because they earnestly want to help. It would debase their lives, they feel, to be implicated in degradation they didn't try to relieve. What more, they wonder, should they be doing? "The emotional problem for the middle class is very real," political scientist Charles Murray once remarked, "but unrelated to the actual problem."

The bitter paradox that is so hard to face is that most of what the Haves have already done to help the poor—out of decent and generous motives—is part of the problem. Like gas pumped into a flooded engine, the more help they bestow, the less able do the poor become to help themselves. The problem isn't that the Haves haven't done enough but that they've done the diametrically wrong thing. "If people could just stop making things worse," concludes economist Thomas Sowell ruefully, "it would be an enormously greater contribution than they're likely to make any other way."

CHAPTER ONE

The Power of Culture

Before explaining how our remade culture has unintentionally worked to keep the poor in their poverty, I ought to say
a more general word about how cultural changes can have large
consequences in other key areas of life. For much modern
thought, including today's most up-to-date social history and
deconstructionist literary criticism, dismisses the notion that
the values and beliefs that make up culture can determine the
kinds of lives people lead by shaping their behavior and the
institutions that surround them.

Once only Marxists scoffed at that idea. What's *really* real,
they used to argue, are economic relations. Beliefs and values
just float above, like insubstantial froth on the economic waves.
Change the economic relations and you automatically change
the beliefs and values that passively "reflect" them.

Today, though, Marxism has many intellectual offspring,
and thinkers of various stripes have bought the view that ideas,
beliefs, and values don't create social reality but only reflect it.
Sociologist William Julius Wilson in his influential book, *The
Truly Disadvantaged,* advances several arguments that are up-to-
the-minute cases in point. To take only one: underclass women
have babies out of wedlock because underclass men, unable to
find jobs, aren't "marriageable" from an economic point of view.
If you want to change that custom, he asserts, the *only* way to
do it is to change the economic circumstances and give the men
jobs.

But the relationship between culture and social and economic reality works more powerfully the other way. Consider these instances. On the grandest level, if you believe that human choices and actions, rather than blind, impersonal forces, determine the shape of history, then the ideas and visions impelling the human actors become crucial causes of the reality that unfolds. Men don't simply have their environment handed to them from on high; they collectively make and remake it from the cultural and material resources that lie ready at hand. And great men augment those resources by inventing new techniques and new ideas.

Developments in the cultural sphere can produce momentous consequences for the economy and society. For example, the spread of Methodism in England in the eighteenth century, as a result of John Wesley's preaching, seems a peripheral enough happening. But according to the historian Elie Halévy, it imbued the English lower-middle class and respectable working class with a conservative orderliness that explains why England, of all the nations of Europe, has been the most free from revolutionary violence or upheaval. To take another example, sociologist E. Digby Baltzell ascribes the more august national leadership role played by Boston's elite by comparison with Philadelphia's elite to differences between the hierarchical, authoritarian Puritanism of Boston and the egalitarian, antiauthoritarian Quaker tradition of the City of Brotherly Love. In other words, "freedom" or "Islam" or "equality" or "honor" or other such emanations from the realm of culture are by no means mere froth on the waves.

The cultural values and aspirations that individuals and groups hold go a long way to determining their economic condition. The sociologist Max Weber explained how the Protestant ethic powerfully promotes success in a free economy, given Protestantism's emphasis on the individual and his works, along with the Protestant willingness to see in worldly prosperity a sign of inner grace. More recently, several commentators have ascribed Britain's economic decline in this century to cultural developments in the nineteenth century that made disdain for industry and trade a common attitude among the British educated classes. The great contemporary novelist V. S. Naipaul looks to the quietism and otherworldliness of India's religious culture to explain the tardiness of that nation's political and economic development.

The main theme of Thomas Sowell's *Ethnic America* is that cultural differences account in large measure for the differing kinds, degrees, and rates of success among the various ethnic groups that have peopled America. For example, Italian-Americans valued schooling less than work in the first part of this century, Sowell says. As a result, as late as 1969 Italian Americans over thirty-five had on average less schooling than other Americans of the same age and were underrepresented in professional and other high-level positions that require education. The spectacular flourishing of America's Asian immigrants—including many who arrived destitute—is the most recent illustration of the powerful influence of culture on economic success.

Economic opportunity is meaningful only if individuals are culturally equipped to seize it. Cultural values such as neatness, punctuality, thoroughness, and dependability are the causes, not the results, of economic mobility. The same is even more true of such cultural traits as ambition, entrepreneurialism, respect for education, or pushing one's children to succeed.

Both liberals and conservatives often resist seeing culture as a central cause of underclass poverty and pathology. Liberals balk because such a way of thinking tends to hold individuals and their beliefs and outlook personally responsible for their objective economic fate. Liberals prefer to fix the responsibility for poverty on society at large, which in turn is shaped by vast, impersonal economic forces that can be modified by well-intentioned social policy changes.

Conservatives—particularly those of a libertarian cast—also prefer economic explanations to cultural ones. Do the chronic poor vegetate on welfare or commit crimes when work is available to them? If so, it's a simple matter of economic calculation, conservatives might reply: welfare or crime net a better economic package than the available low-pay work. Underclass criminals and welfare mothers represent nothing more than rational responses, such as any reasonable person might make, to economic incentives.

Though the reasoning is different, in each case it never comes to grips with fundamental truths that lie, unspoken, beneath all theorizing about social policy. In the ongoing debate over the misery index, the illegitimacy rate, the income distribution, the labor market, the true number of the homeless, or the fit between jobs and job seekers—generally framed in sociological, even statistical, language—the most basic question is never so much as raised, much less examined.

What is society for? Why do we need it? Without this large question as a beacon, how is it possible to judge whether policies are aimed in the right direction, directed to producing the good society?

The profoundest answer to these basic questions comes from a tradition in political philosophy that arises from *philosophe* Jean-Jacques Rousseau and ultimately from Aristotle: society is the medium in which individual selves get turned into fully human creatures, with all the characteristically human excellences. As Victorian thinker Matthew Arnold summed it up: "Civilization is the humanization of man in society."

All that is finest and most distinctively human in mankind, this tradition holds, doesn't come from nature. The arts and sciences, morality and conscience, self-consciousness and even individuality itself—all these are the product of man's development in society. The commonplace social rituals provide a model of the transformation society works on the raw material of human nature: from weddings and funerals to ordinary dinner parties, they convert such animal realities as procreation, death, and eating into assertions that men are higher than beasts impelled by natural instinct alone.

Further, this transformation isn't something that happened only in mankind's historical evolution. Society works it in each individual life. Without nurture and cultivation in society— starting with nurture in that elemental social unit, the family— the human potentialities that are latent in individuals at birth are doomed to be withered or stunted. Each person undergoes in childhood a development analogous to the evolution of civilization: his upbringing provides him with the cultural inheritance that turns little more than a wild animal into a fully human being with human aspirations and a human conscience.

Sigmund Freud's idea of the superego is the latest formulation of the idea that society, not nature, endows individuals, in the deepest part of their being, with their most characteristically human attributes.

In this sense, it is hardly an exaggeration to speak of state-craft as soulcraft, in George Will's fashion. Social policy's ultimate goal should be a social order that nurtures the fullest develop-ment in individuals of the qualities that define humanity—rea-son, conscience, selfhood, individuality, creativity, judgment, the ability to impose order upon the world and meaning upon life. In the deepest sense, that is what society is for, and it is the fundamental measure of a good society. It is more than a mat-ter of free institutions alone; the crucial element is the intan-gible cultural spirit, the values and ideals, animating the whole and nourishing each individual.

By basing social policy on a vision of the individual self that is so utterly the creation of material forces, the liberal view makes the self so passive and shrunken as to deprive it of moral significance or dignity or even individuality. In doing so, lib-eralism ignores and devalues the entity that social policy's proper object is to promote. From this point of view, selves could be corn or alfalfa, automatically flourishing or languishing with a greater or lesser supply of sunshine, rain, and nitrogen, rather than human creatures with individual human souls.

This isn't to say that identity is independent of circum-stance: everyone is a creature of this time, of that place, as Lionel Trilling put it. But individuals affect circumstances no less than circumstances affect individuals. It is in creatively acting upon circumstances—altering them, turning them to account, accord-ing to the vision in your own mind developed out of materials you have chosen from the cultural stock available to you—that individual selves are forged.

By contrast with the liberal assumption that makes selves nothing but emanations of circumstance, the conservative view I have in mind misses the fundamental truth that should under-lie social policy by imagining selves to be essentially indepen-dent of their social milieu. The rationally calculating man, able to weigh costs and benefits with admirable nicety, is assumed to be the spontaneous creation of nature rather than the triumphant product of a long, laborious cultural development. Such conservatives would therefore be hard-pressed to say what society is for.

But it isn't a given of nature that people restrain their aggression, beget and nurture their offspring in marriage, exercise foresight, calculate rationally, or work to improve their condition. The wonder is not that people *don't* do it, but that they do. So instead of looking for economic incentives that make people prefer theft to labor and single parenthood to wedlock, it makes more sense to ask the opposite question first—to ask how society fosters selves that dependably work and marry and are capable of rational calculation; how culture takes the aggressive, impulsive, egotistical raw material of human nature each of us is born with and develops in it conscience, reason, and duty.

The answer brings us back to the cultural issue that social-policy thinkers shun, and it brings us, as well, to the crux of the underclass problem. What chiefly ails the individuals who compose the underclass is that the cultural inheritance essential to generate fully developed, fully humanized, fully individualized selves is not getting transmitted adequately to them. They are deprived of the basic socialization in early childhood that awakens and develops the conscience and fosters the beliefs, values, and habits of thought and feeling that constitute civility and that impose meaning and direction on individual life. Because of this deprivation, they are also poor in basic knowledge and in the skills of reasoning, analysis, and judgment needed to master the world.

For this impoverishment, blame the revolutionized culture of the Haves. The face that culture presents to the underclass, under the aspect of benevolence, is so meretricious and degraded, so shot through with falsehood, that it lacks adequate nurturing power. The beliefs and values it transmits to the underclass are all the wrong ones, retarding rather than promoting self-development: you've been marred by victimization, you can't succeed without special treatment, your success or failure is really not in your own hands, the values that allow us Haves to succeed have no application to you Have-Nots and will only oppress you, your own self-destructive behavior is a legitimate expression of your history and your oppression. Add to this the schools inadvertently ruined by the Haves' quest for racial liberation, the families subverted by the well-intentioned contagion of welfare, and the neighborhoods reduced to savage anarchy thanks to failed order-keeping masquerading as enlightened justice, and you can hardly wonder at the dismal harvest of pathology that imprisons the underclass.

In the name of benevolence, the culture of the Haves holds out a quite separate standard to the worst-off. For itself, some key bourgeois values—especially work, career, ambition, striving, competence, and foresight—remain alive, notwithstanding the Haves' continued fascination with certain yearnings of the counterculture. What remains of the bourgeois ethic protects the Haves when they experiment with the self-liberation aspect of the cultural revolution, but the Have-Nots enjoy no such protection when they come under the spell of that part of our remade culture. The Haves may pay a price for experimenting with sexual liberation or drugs or dropping out (almost always temporarily), but it is usually not a catastrophic price, nothing like the price the Have-Nots pay in ruined lives.

Only the force of culture can explain one of the most dramatic singularities of the underclass problem: the fact that suddenly all the indicators of social pathology among the poorest poor went wrong *together.* So though there may be considerable explanatory power in the conservative notion of economic incentives to go on welfare or to choose crime over low-wage work—"incentives to fail," as Charles Murray called them in his brilliant, highly influential *Losing Ground*—those incentives, however real, ultimately don't explain enough. They don't explain why crime, welfare dependency, illegitimacy, school-leaving, nonparticipation in the labor force, and drug abuse *all* took off for the stratosphere in tandem, beginning in the mid-1960s and accelerating in the early 1970s. They don't explain why men and women become degraded into the underclass at exactly the same time, even though the incentives to fail were different for women than for men. Indeed, why did so many of the incentives to fail, such as judicial leniency or welfare generosity, fall into place at the same time?

The answer is that all these manifestations were emanations of the same spirit of the age, of that great cultural shift that transvalued values and transformed the way the Haves, and soon the Have-Nots, conceived of authority, equality, justice, law, merit, morality, poverty, race, and the social order. What turned poverty pathological, in other words, wasn't just a series of institutional changes, but the cultural revolution that informed those changes and that conveyed to the poor a new and destructive set of norms and values.

I am not arguing that the problem is a "culture of poverty" as described by earlier writers like Michael Harrington or Oscar Lewis—a set of defeatist expectations arising within the ghetto itself in response to overwhelmingly unfavorable economic conditions. I am suggesting, instead, that the trouble started with elite, mainstream culture, which underwent a series of convulsions that left it communicating to the poor exactly the wrong message and the most self-destructive values.

In America, the problem of poverty is inseparable from the problem of race. The underclass is overwhelmingly a minority population. Most estimates agree that around 60 percent of those who compose it are black; 20 percent or so are Hispanic. Most of the homeless are minorities too, with the proportion varying from as many as 89 percent in a metropolis like New York to around 23 percent in a smaller city like Portland, Oregon.

The new culture created by the Haves has been cruel to the minority poor, especially to poor blacks. In the sixties, just when the successes of the civil rights movement were removing racial barriers to mainstream opportunities, the mainstream values that poor blacks needed to seize those chances, values such as hard work and self-denial, came under sharp attack. Poor blacks needed all the support and encouragement that mainstream culture could give them to stand up and make their own fates. But mainstream culture let them down. Issuing the opposite of a call to responsibility and self-reliance, the larger culture told blacks in particular, and the poor in general, that they were victims, and that society, not they themselves, was responsible for not only their present but their future condition.

Except for America's original European settlers, all ethnic groups have found their passage into mainstream culture difficult and sometimes painful. But even more than Irishmen fleeing famine and political oppression or Jews fleeing pogroms, blacks wronged by slavery have faced particular disadvantages in making that transition. Their historical experience in America includes a wealth of possible causes: a system that intentionally kept slaves in deep ignorance, especially of self-reliance; a sharecropping system that to some degree encouraged dependency and helped form the forebears of the underclass in Chicago's ghettos, according to Nicholas Lemann's absorbing, if highly controversial, bestseller, *The Promised Land.* Add to that the cultural residue of long years of racist exclusion and suppression: simmering resentment; the inclination to believe that one is the passive plaything of capricious chance rather than the master of one's fate; a repression of entrepreneurial impulses; a streak of messianism focusing on future salvation rather than gradual, partial improvement in the here and now; and a strain of separatism that reemerged in the sixties with uncompromising virulence in the Black Power movement, with its sweeping rejection of white norms. Other, more advantageous legacies permitted many blacks to flow out of the ghettos and into the middle class in the sixties and seventies. But as a residue of a painful history, black culture preserved tendencies potentially unhelpful to some blacks in mastering—or sometimes even in *seeing*—opportunities that called for initiative, perseverance, a regard for education, and an integrative impulse.

In the face of all this, when it behooved mainstream culture to assert traditional mainstream values with conviction, the Haves refused to assert to the poor and the black the most fundamental of those values: the worth of the respectable working life, however humble. When it is pointed out that jobs are widely available to the low-skilled, many Haves contemptuously ask, almost by reflex, why anyone would or should be willing to flip hamburgers for not much more than the minimum wage. Even so sophisticated an observer as investment banker Felix Rohatyn—longtime chairman of New York City's Municipal Assistance Corporation, sometime writer for the respected, liberal *New York Review of Books,* oft-mentioned candidate for secretary of the treasury under a Democratic administration, preeminent representative of the new culture of the Haves—can sometimes strike this note. In an interview, for example, he spoke to me of "the man and his wife slogging away in menial jobs that are dead-end jobs, with three kids, trying to deal with an environment that is very depressing" as "people who are living dead-end lives."

Think about that judgment. Suppose that the man spends his working life as a short-order cook or janitor while his wife makes beds at the motel or cleans up at the nursing home. If both earned only the minimum wage, they could together support their family of five just above the poverty line. But in fact a big-city short-order cook would make two to three times the minimum wage, and an urban nursing-home cleaner perhaps 50 percent more than it. From a material point of view, with an annual income between $31,000 and $40,000, their lives would be threadbare but adequate.

But you do not judge people's lives only from the material point of view. Suppose that these two have brought up their children to respect the parents' hard work, to be curious about the world, to study in school, to take pleasure in family and community life, to consider themselves worthwhile people, to work hard and think about the future, to become skilled tradesmen or even professionals as adults, and to bring grandchildren to visit.

If this is a dead end rather than a human accomplishment worthy of honor and admiration, then it is hard to know what human life is about. And what makes it not a dead end is the cultural tissue of beliefs, values, and relationships that make family life meaningful and sustaining and that permit the rise of the next generation. Change that cultural dimension, without changing the economic circumstances one iota, and you've changed everything.

Dead-end lives. Yet these are people who have gotten married and stayed married. Who have gotten jobs and kept them. Who support and foster their children. What message are they to get if, white or black, they are described as sloggers going nowhere? That they are chumps and jerks—that their achievement isn't to be valued and indeed is sneered at and dispraised? That they aren't as good as a millionaire investment banker and a far stretch better than someone who sells dope or vegetates on welfare, producing illegitimate progeny at the cost of the state?

What message are members of the underclass to get? That at least they are not dumb enough to make a dead-end choice like a low-pay job? Certainly they can't help learning that virtually no way exists for them ever to *earn* respect, for the first step they once could have taken toward achieving that—putting a foot firmly on the bottom rung of the job ladder—has had respectability withdrawn from it by such a mainstream attitude as Felix Rohatyn voices, symptomatic of the cultural change this book tries to describe.

How radically the great American cultural revolution changed values, assumptions, and institutions is a story that subsequent chapters will explore more fully. For the present, it is enough to say that even though it took place in the sixties and seventies, it was long in the making. It was foreshadowed a century ago, when writers and artists first started thinking of themselves as an avant-garde dedicated to dumbfounding the bourgeoisie and dancing upon its straitlaced values.

Just over a generation ago, more than a decade before the Summer of Love, a young and promising Norman Mailer proclaimed in an essay, "The White Negro," a new kind of man. He was the hipster, who knew from the atom bomb and the Nazi concentration camps that societies and states were murderous, and that under the shadow of mass annihilation one should learn what ghetto blacks already knew. One should learn from ghetto culture, Mailer said, to give up "the sophisticated inhibitions of civilization," to live in the moment, to follow the body and not the mind, "to divorce oneself from society" and "follow the rebellious imperative of the self," to forget "the single mate, the solid family, and the respectable love life," to choose a life of "Saturday night kicks," especially orgasm and marijuana. For 1957, this was prophetic: it contained in a nutshell much of the self-liberation part of the cultural program of the sixties. As political scientist Lawrence Mead has remarked, "It's precisely the more anarchic aspects of black culture that became popularized as white culture in the sixties."

True, the sixties were a quarter of a century ago and more, and yes, belaboring them now might seem like flogging a dead horse. But large, ingrained, intergenerational social pathologies such as homelessness and underclass culture don't spring up overnight from trivial causes. They are the mature harvest of seed sown by the Haves and rooted years ago. We can't hope to cure them without knowing what caused and furthered them—and continues to further them even now.

Moreover, while culture does evolve by gradual steps, the really important shifts often occur in wholesale leaps that change the entire game rather than only a rule or two. In certain important cultural respects, America is still living under the sign of Aquarius, however tattered and faded after the eras of hyperinflation and Reagan.

If you doubt it, take a walk through the encampments of the homeless in America's western cities—in Phoenix, say, or Santa Barbara—and look at the crowds of young men, mostly white, in their twenties, dressed like refugees from the Summer of Love: calico headbands, shoulder-length hair, torn jeans, black T-shirts emblazoned with Harley-Davidson or Grateful Dead logos.

Many of them are homeless because they are enslaved by the specious liberation whose troops have worn that uniform for the past quarter century. When middle-class college kids began their fling with "protest," drugs, sexual experimentation, and dropping out in the sixties, they had a margin of safety because of their class. Working-class kids who today enlist under that washed-out banner, now *démodé,* run a bigger risk. Once they drop out, some may never get back in, like these young men in the homeless encampments, devoid of skills, discipline, or direction, and most of them—along with many of the homeless nationwide—dependent on drugs, alcohol, or both.

Many have apparently been neglected or abused by families whose disturbance or breakup is part of the general cultural unraveling. Deprived of family support and guidance, these young people feel they have little to turn to in the larger culture beyond the "freedom" that has landed them here, with such petulantly angry looks understandably on their faces. As sociologist Christopher Jencks remarked in an interview, "One way to read the sixties is to say it was a failed experiment whose price was paid by the Have-Nots. The rest of us landed on our feet."

Leave the poor of these sunny, open-air encampments for the ghetto underclass and you come upon a nightmare parody of liberated sixties culture. Sexual liberation? In urban ghettos like New York's central Harlem, around 80 percent of all babies are born out of wedlock, many to girls still in their teens. In the late eighties, Calvin Watkins, then thirty-one and liberated with a vengeance, boasted to reporters that he had nineteen children by four women, two of whom were living with him in a Brooklyn welfare hotel with nine of the kids—a tax-supported commune.

Drugs? Just when college kids started turning on with marijuana, the heroin epidemic overwhelmed the ghetto: Harlem and Newark after 1966, Detroit not until after 1970. Today, with crack cheap and all-pervasive, the drug epidemic and the criminality that attends it have nightmarishly made anarchy more than a metaphor in ghetto life, as thirteen-year-old dealers strut the streets with automatic weapons they don't hesitate to use. In the age of AIDS, the needle-sharing of heroin addicts and the licentious sexuality of crack addicts have turned at least part of the ghetto underworld into a macabre orgy of self-destruction that Bosch or Hogarth scarcely could have depicted. Crack is one of the main roads to big-city homeless shelters, the sub-basement of underclass life, where you find pathology much more often than innocent misfortune. And as turf wars and the petty criminality of addicts looking to finance the next dose spill beyond the confines of the ghetto, mainstream society increasingly—and properly—has come to view not just this aspect but all aspects of underclass pathology as subversive of the larger social order.

"Turn on, tune in, drop out" was the slogan of the sixties counterculture, and the underclass duly turned on. As for dropping out: only one student in three who entered such inner city New York high schools as Theodore Roosevelt in the Bronx, Thomas Jefferson in East New York, or Bushwick in Brooklyn in 1984 had managed to earn a diploma or a GED certificate seven years later—and New York's dropout rate is not as bad as those of Chicago and Los Angeles. As adults, a large but unknown proportion do not work. What is known is that in 1991, only 59.5 percent of the black males aged twenty to twenty-four who were not in the armed forces, in jail, or in some other institution were employed. Of black males aged eighteen and nineteen, less than one in three had a job.

But while the cultural revolution included experimentation with drugs and sexual liberation, it was also propelled by deep misgivings about the justice of the entire American social and moral order, misgivings born out of the civil rights movement and the Vietnam War. As a result, the cultural revolution didn't merely give the poor the wrong messages about sex and drugs. It also reached out to change radically the character of central American institutions—the universities, the law, the public schools, the welfare system, and the mental health system—through all of which, as we'll see, it reached out to affect the lives of the poor in concrete ways.

But first, who are the poor?

CHAPTER TWO

The Underclass

onsider the poor, and your first thought tends to be "There but for the grace of God go I." True enough in one sense. But that's not to say that the underclass—the poor at the very bottom of American society—are what you would be if you suddenly were plunged into destitution.

For poverty is not the defining feature of this troubling, highly visible subgroup of the poor. What makes the underclass different not just from you but also from the majority of the poor both today and in the past is its self-defeating behavior and the worldview from which that behavior springs. Among the urban poor, the underclass includes only those shackled in poverty and dependence, often from generation to generation, by what social psychologist Kenneth Clark deplored twenty-five years ago as a "self-perpetuating pathology"—chronic lawlessness, drug use, out-of-wedlock births, nonwork, welfare dependency, and school failure.

This group's inner reality, its entire outlook on life, is distinctive, not just its outer circumstances. It faces the climb out of poverty without the internal, cultural tools you would bring to the struggle—your values, your ambitions, your perseverance, your social skills, your basic literacy and numeracy, your sense of affiliation to the larger society. In place of all this, which you would still possess even if you were stripped naked of every external advantage, the underclass is equipped with different, and sparser, mental and emotional furniture, unhelpful for taking advantage of the economic opportunities that American life offers.

Listen to the voices of the underclass, if only overheard on the street or reported in the press, and you will find yourself inside an unsettling worldview:

"Man, you go two, three years not working, and hanging around and smoking reefer or drinking, and then you get a job—you can't handle it. You say, 'I don't want to get up in the morning, get pushed and shoved. I'm gonna get on welfare.'"

"What's open to me? McDonald's and Burger King? I can't deal with that."

"People don't realize that hustling's hard work. You got your police, and your enemies, and kids trying to take your dope. You're tense every day."

"I get pissed off when I go to all the trouble to rob someone, and they don't got nuttin'.... I cut his neck from here to here. I don't know if he's dead or what."

"Society is set up so that black people can't get ahead. I'm not supposed to have the American dream and all that. I'm supposed to be in jail."

"By having a baby so young, when I'm older I can have more time to party."

"You get a baby by these guys, and the next day they don't know your name."

"This is the pits—Harlem, U.S.A. You have to hustle to survive. People are walking around here like zombies. They've had a foot on their necks so long they don't know what to do."

Whether their tone is bravado or self-pity, nihilism or defeatism, these voices resonate with the hopelessness, degradation, and menace of life in underclass communities. They speak of a poverty more profound than lack of money—a poverty social, moral, and spiritual. "Underclass," these voices testify, describes a state of mind and a way of life—a cultural rather than an economic condition.

After all, it is not impossibly hard to rise out of poverty in late twentieth-century America. That's why the vast majority of people whom the census counts as poor—most of the non-underclass poor—don't stay poor long. Statistics suggest that the recipe for escaping long-term poverty is straightforward:

finish high school, get and keep *any* full-time, full-year job (even at the minimum wage), get married as an adult and stay married, even if it takes more than one try. "These are demanding, although not superhuman, tasks," dryly remarks the report of the Working Seminar on the Family and American Welfare Policy, a group of scholars and former government officials.

From an analysis of a uniquely comprehensive tracking of the incomes of a wide array of people throughout the seventies, seminar member Charles Murray concluded that just earning a high school diploma alone was an almost sufficient antidote to poverty in itself. In the study, only 0.6 percent of adult men with four years of high school and only 2 percent of adult women fell below the poverty line. Against this background of success, no wonder poverty experts have singled out the underclass with a special name: a population whose poverty remains chronic, even intergenerational, and whose behavior doesn't include the commonplace first steps toward upward mobility, demands scrutiny and explanation.

Who are the individuals who compose the underclass? Start with a typical representative: Preston Simmons of the Bronx, known as Little Man. He rises above anonymity because he was blasted away on Thanksgiving Day 1989, by eleven bullets from a nine-millimeter automatic pistol. His age: fourteen.

He was the fourth of seven illegitimate children, the youngest of whom was fifteen months old at the time of Little Man's murder. His mother had been on welfare for two decades, ever since first getting pregnant as an eleventh grader and dropping out of high school in 1969. His angry, drug-using father had lived off and on with the boy's mother for two tumultuous years, sometimes returning from his strayings by smashing in the door or window. The mother says that he beat her and her children: finally she got a court order to keep him away.

Home was the Castle Hill Houses, an East Bronx public housing project of bleakly utilitarian red-brick high rises, at once massive and flimsy. The dank stink of urine in the elevators and the halls vandalized with crude wriggles of graffiti proclaim the pervasive incivility that keeps the spirit of community from taking root there. Worse still is the sound of gunfire that has become commonplace in this housing project as in many others.

As one teenage resident told Kevin Sack of *The New York Times*: "People are dying over jackets, drugs, money, even the way you look at people. For $5, they'll shoot you in your head."

Before they moved to Castle Hill in the summer of 1988, Little Man's family had briefly lived in a homeless shelter. Before that, they were shoehorned into the two-bedroom apartment of Little Man's grandmother. Like his mother, she too had begun having babies as a teenager.

Education hadn't done much for Little Man. His school had put him in a special-education class, deeming him hyperactive, a neurological condition making it hard to learn in an ordinary situation. Epidemic among underclass schoolchildren, this condition can be caused by mothers who drink or take drugs or are ill nourished when pregnant.

Little Man had two main extracurricular activities. The first was selling five-dollar bags of marijuana in a playground at the project for a profit of up to forty-five dollars a day. In a photo taken not long before his murder, he looks out with a cool, challenging, sidewise gaze from a lumpy parka worn over a sweatshirt with the hood pulled up. He had threatened to go into competition with his drug supplier; his family and friends believe that's what got him killed.

His second interest was his girlfriend, seventeen and pregnant with Little Man's child when he died, making the third illegitimate generation in his family. Evidently Little Man lived much of his short life by the cartoonlike ideal of masculinity that had given him his macho nickname from the time he was a burly, remote little boy.

A sad coda to Little Man's sad history is the unruffled matter-of-factness with which his family and friends accepted not only the grimness of his life and death but also the virtual certainty of a future just as bleak for his child. As his girlfriend's brother explained to *The New York Times,* Little Man of course sold dope "for the reason all the young dudes do it: young people like to keep up with the styles, and it's expensive to keep up." It cost him his life, as he doubtless knew it could, and it made his child fatherless as well as illegitimate.

"We hope it's a boy, so he can keep his name," Little Man's mother summed up. "We loved Little Man a lot. Since he's not here any longer, we all will have something to remember him by." What one hears vibrating in this talk is not a sense of the tragic evanescence of human life but of its cheapness and meaninglessness. As for the baby who will be a souvenir of Little Man, Little Man's girlfriend prophesies thus: "If he's still living around here, I guess he'll be selling drugs—will be forced to sell drugs—or will have a lot of bad habits."

It might seem preternatural that Little Man's history should contain, like a textbook, almost every cliché of underclass pathology: illegitimate teen pregnancy, single parenthood, school dropout, perpetual welfare dependency, parental abusiveness, blunted feelings, school behavior problems of either physiological or emotional origin, a remedial program that remedies little, a spell in a homeless shelter, a public housing project careening into anarchy, puffed-up macho, drugs, violent crime, early death, and generation after generation of the same problems. But underclass pathology is always a tangled multitude of the same disturbing mutual reinforcements.

The statistics on underclass pathology tell a coherent and dismaying tale. Members of the underclass are a minority of the roughly thirty-two million Americans with incomes below the official poverty line, though they may be a bare majority of the ten million citizens estimated as being chronically, rather than transiently, poor. Estimates of their exact number vary widely, from one to twenty million, since they are notoriously difficult to count. But the most plausible number seems to be that produced by researchers who, in somewhat rough-and-ready fashion, subtracted the elderly and disabled from reliable estimates of the chronically poor and counted the remaining five million or so Americans—just over 2 percent of the United States population—as underclass.

The speed with which the underclass jumped into existence and proliferated is only one of its startling attributes. The poor we have had always with us; but the underclass, with its distinctive pathology, didn't begin to crystallize as a major American problem until the mid-1960s. During the seventies, Urban Institute data suggest, it tripled in size. In the 1980s—the statistical evidence is still sketchy, but the evidence of one's senses is fairly unequivocal—it appears to have continued to proliferate, though much more slowly, as it seems to be doing even now. Observing underclass neighborhoods as they spread out and swallow larger and larger tracts of old central cities, watching the concentration and intensification of pathology within them, one can't help being grimly reminded of the spread of an epidemic. It is as if a contagion of disorder, an infectious overthrowing of basic social norms, were inexorably tightening its grip.

The underclass is almost wholly an urban population, concentrated in crumbling ghetto neighborhoods and prisonous public housing projects. Only five cities—Chicago, Los Angeles, Philadelphia, Detroit, and above all New York—house perhaps half the nation's underclass.

It is overwhelmingly a minority population. Though only 12 percent of Americans are black, blacks account for at least 60 percent of the underclass. Hispanics, primarily Puerto Ricans, account for perhaps 20 percent.

But this circumstance raises one final problem about statistics on the underclass. It would be nice if there were hard-and-fast numbers on many aspects of underclass behavior. But there aren't. In their absence, most social scientists—black and white alike—have cited statistics on blacks as rough guidelines. They are well aware that, even though the majority of the underclass is black, only a minority of black Americans—perhaps one in nine or ten—belongs to the underclass. But the black members of the underclass form a sizable enough group of individuals to make a significant impact on the statistics for blacks in general and to explain in great measure why those statistics show so much social pathology. In other words, much of the abundant social pathology one finds in the statistics for blacks is underclass pathology, and the startling statistical increase in black social pathology in the last quarter century reflects, above all, the rise of the underclass.

Such a statistical procedure moves onto very touchy ground, however, since white racists have seized on numbers like these as evidence of some inherent black defect. In the face of such vilification, who can be surprised that blacks and some whites regard the very mention of these matters as a slur? It's little wonder that some blacks are unwilling so much as to admit the existence of a definable underclass. Do not Italian Americans bristle at mention of the Mafia, or Jews cringe at talk of how many Wall Street insider traders were Jewish? Don't all groups stormily reject theorizing by outsiders about how their history and culture might have given a recognizable twist to the character of the malefactors or failures of the group? One almost can't help feeling, however mistaken that feeling often is, that the deepest criticism is being made of oneself and of the innermost nature of one's entire group.

Simple politeness prompts silence on most of these issues. Yet the underclass is so disruptive a problem in American life that, despite the understandable touchiness of some blacks on this matter, it demands forthright public discussion. Not, however, without this preamble: though a majority of the underclass is black, only a minority of blacks are underclass. The central fact of the black experience in the last decade—the rise of so many blacks into the middle class and the doubling of black families with incomes over $50,000 to one million—testifies eloquently to the contrary.

But would it not have been better if black and liberal outrage and charges of racism had not instantly stifled all discussion of this issue when Daniel Patrick Moynihan first raised it in his 1965 report on *The Negro Family*? Here was an alarm being sounded about the formation of the underclass at the dawn of its existence. Imagine if the nation had squarely confronted the problem then, before so much damage had been done, so many lives marred.

I am not speaking here only of those who fell into the underclass. For blacks are beyond all other groups the victims of the underclass, and coming to grips with the issue would have benefited most of all those hardworking blacks who live in ghettos where underclass disorder and danger blighted and still blight their lives. Surely the fate of these strivers, who do not get to enjoy in full measure what they so laboriously earn, ought to be the first concern of any friend to blacks.

With these caveats in mind then, consider the starkly troubling statistics. For example, though free public education is the traditional vehicle of American upward mobility, 40 to 60 percent of high school students in inner cities drop out before graduation. Though an income from full-time, full-year work at the minimum wage is enough to support a single person above the poverty line, the underclass works little.

All through the fifties, black and white men participated in the labor force, as workers or as active job seekers, at the same rate. But in the mid-sixties, black men suddenly, startlingly, and in ever-increasing numbers began to drop out. By the late seventies, when the underclass had emerged as an obdurate fact, black participation was 8.4 percentage points lower than white participation, a difference that statisticians find colossal. For young men aged sixteen to twenty-four, the difference between black and white participation was an even more huge 15.4 percentage points. Only a minority of black men in that age group, 43 percent, had jobs. In the late eighties, notwithstanding almost a decade of economic expansion, labor force participation of black men remained virtually unchanged, and still only a minority of sixteen- to twenty-four-year-old black men went to work. A 1988 Louis Harris survey found, depressingly, that 82 percent of the ghetto households that contained at least one grown man contained at least one grown man with no regular job.

In a few cities this may be in part because jobs are scarce, as the conventional explanation has it. But however ferocious the debate on this issue, the statistics on participation in the labor force make a powerful argument that this cannot be the prime reason for such extensive joblessness. The arresting fact is that blacks dropped out of the labor force not when times were bad and jobs scarce, but rather in the economically expansive sixties—and precisely in that part of the decade when jobs were most plentiful. Just at that moment, too, the civil rights movement was expanding opportunity for blacks.

An up-to-the-minute explanation attributes current underclass nonwork to changes in the economy since the mid-seventies. Certainly changes occurred with a vengeance. Foreign competitors and hard-eyed raiders pounced on torpid corporations like packs of hounds and shook them in the last decade, precipitating a vast, still uncompleted transformation of American industry. Had the economy remained static, East European style, instead of dynamically meeting changed global realities, Americans would have watched their standard of living erode. Instead, manufacturing productivity rose at an annual rate of 2.9 percent during the eighties (with the strongest growth in the most restructured industries), per capita money income rose 16.5 percent in real terms from 1980 to 1990 while per capita money income for blacks rose an even stronger 28.9 percent, and by the end of the decade unemployment was at its lowest point in fifteen years. Yet however necessary to keep American industry competitive, the restructuring undeniably swept away jobs, including many unionized unskilled or semi-skilled jobs paying over ten dollars an hour.

The result is that the real earnings of unskilled young working men dropped: down 18.8 percent between 1979 and 1988 for white males aged twenty-five to thirty-four lacking a high school diploma. The pay of a young, white, male high school dropout, which averaged 68 percent of his college-grad counterpart's in 1979, averaged only 54 percent of a college grad's pay by 1988. But this doesn't say that the low-skilled can't make a living—only that, more than ever, education pays.

More to the point, it certainly doesn't say that the evolution of the U.S. economy is making low-skill jobs extinct, as one current theory about the relation of the rich to the poor holds. This theory waves aside the new jobs created in the eighties, arguing that they benefited only the well-off. Global economic changes produced richly rewarded high-skill jobs for the Haves, this view holds; but the same changes impoverished the Have-Nots by sending low-skill jobs abroad or abolishing them altogether. If the poor had the requisite skills to match the existing employment opportunities, there would be no problem. But they don't. "We're creating a two-tier society," says one prominent corporate elder statesman and civic leader. "The educational requirement for jobs is going up rapidly, and we're not giving the poor the kind of education required to handle the jobs that are around today."

True, well-paid jobs needing more than basic skills did mushroom in the eighties and will keep proliferating in the nineties. But around two out of five of the millions of jobs created between 1983 and 1990, by an unprecedentedly powerful surge of job growth that resulted in a larger proportion of Americans working than ever before, were unskilled or low-skill. Of the employment categories that in absolute numbers produced the most new jobs in the eighties, clerks, cashiers, cooks, and light truck drivers ranked third, fourth, fifth, and sixth respectively. Laborers and machine operators ranked tenth and eleventh, and child care workers ranked fourteenth. Missing from these statistics are the off-the-books jobs held by a significant but unknown number of domestic servants and illegal aliens concentrated in the lower-skill employment categories. These developments in the labor market suggest no shortage of opportunity to find employment, despite low skills, and—with ambition and energy enough to get trained—to advance further.

Putting all this aside, though, how can structural changes in the economy be blamed for the existence of the underclass if the changes happened well *after* the underclass was fully formed and sizable? This isn't to say that you won't find men fired in the industrial restructuring now marooned on ghetto street corners, wasted by drugs or drink; changes of this magnitude can indeed overwhelm individuals and produce casualties. But Rust Belt factory workers who speak of such sad cases hasten to add that they are few. Nor are these stories at all congruent with those of the underclass, in anything but the unhappy ending.

For the underclass, the crucial story about economic opportunity in the eighties is the red-hot job creation, not the demise of Rust Belt factory jobs. But in cities where the economy was good, the job creation failed to draw additional young black males into the labor force. Only in those few cities where not just good but extraordinary economic growth sent the overall unemployment rate down under 5 percent did labor force participation increase among young black males. Even then, in a then-booming city like Boston, one fifth of young black males still chose not to work. And who were these young nonworkers? They were high school dropouts who lived in ghetto public housing projects and who had been born to teenage single mothers with low incomes and little education—in other words, the underclass.

The testimony of underclass youths themselves contradicts the conventional explanations of job scarcity. Over 70 percent of the out-of-work inner-city black youths whom Harvard economist Richard Freeman surveyed in 1980—and nearly 75 percent of those he surveyed in 1989—said they could easily find a job. But they generally disdained the readily available hamburger flipper or checkout clerk jobs as low-paid or leading nowhere, even though over the last decade up to a million or more immigrants, from Asians to West Indians, have been finding in menial jobs their gateway to the American dream— and even though, despite Felix Rohatyn's disparagement, "dead-end" jobs flipping hamburgers are good at teaching what underclass kids lacking basic skills need first to learn about managing the world of work: how to show up on time, look presentable, be efficient, and deal pleasantly with customers and bosses.

It is sad enough to see, as I recently saw, one ghetto youth jeering through the window of an urban supermarket at his embarrassed acquaintance who was manning the cash register inside. But sadder still, not long ago a ghetto renovation project in Newark, New Jersey, a city with a large underclass population, couldn't attract local workers at five to six dollars an hour and ended up importing union labor from the suburbs. These were jobs paying well over the minimum wage, were right in the neighborhood, and were teaching skills that clearly could lead somewhere.

You would think that an economy that creates not only a sufficiency of low-skill jobs but also a growing abundance of higher-skilled, higher-paying jobs would cause celebration as an opportunity for upward mobility rather than occasion for anxiety. Sure, change entails upheaval and dislocation, but the flexibility of Americans, their readiness to reinvent themselves and remake their circumstances, is a key element both of the American national character and of American economic success. And what more archetypal American ideal is there than the poor kid who studies and works hard, seizes his opportunity, and rises? Were the economy producing not enough high-skill jobs to permit such mobility, *that* would be cause for alarm.

Even if individuals couldn't take advantage of these opportunities for themselves, they ought to see them as a boon for their children. Surely the children and grandchildren of the original members of the underclass could hardly be harmed rather than advanced by the creation of higher-skill jobs for which they could qualify in many cases simply by paying attention through high school.

After all, in this context "higher skill" does not mean neurosurgery. For instance, the higher skills that one steel mill not far from Chicago needed recently to fill jobs that were going begging for lack of qualified applicants amounted to little more than being able to divide one hundred by four and, going one step further, to understand the concept of 75 percent. It generally takes only basic math for a worker to handle the statistical process control that is one of the key recent technological advances in manufacturing. One didn't think of secretarial skills as being particularly elevated until recently, when corporations in big cities found that increasing numbers of applicants lacked them. Now anxious companies pay their employees bounties for bringing in qualified applicants for secretarial jobs. Anyone who wants her children not only to escape poverty but to cross the line into the middle class needs only to make sure they learn basic literacy, computer typing, and polite, businesslike demeanor in high school. How can a scarcity of unskilled jobs in steel mills explain why ghetto mothers don't do this?

Not least of the many boons the recent wave of immigration has brought America is that it highlights economic realities that have been obfuscated. When you see immigrant families living from cab-driving jobs, fast-food jobs, janitor jobs, busboy and dishwasher jobs, child care jobs, how can anyone contemptuously dismiss the income from such "dead end" employment as "chump change," as so many activists, journalists, and politicians are accustomed to do? These assiduous immigrants are hardly chumps.

Take an example offered by novelist Amy Tan. In an interview, Tan spoke of her half-sister and her brother-in-law, both now in their mid-forties, who arrived from China in 1983. After only four years in America, they owned a car, three televisions, and a house. They had two children in college. They accomplished all this with dead-end jobs: he washed dishes; she helped manage a take-out restaurant. They worked constantly, six days a week, with no vacations, imposing on themselves an unwavering thrift and frugality.

Their own assessment of what they have achieved is without illusion. Says Tan: "These accomplishments were important to them as a sign that they had succeeded and had taken advantage of an opportunity they wouldn't have in China." But still, adds Tan, "My sister said, 'I know I'll never get ahead that far. I'm working hard. We're doing fine. But it's my children who are going to do well, for us.'" Surely, this is what America is for. And it shows how decent a life, how hopeful a future, can be made of dead-end jobs. The key is not in the job but in the motivation, aspiration, and realism of expectation the worker brings to it.

No one argues that it is easy. The difficulty goes beyond the grubby work and long hours. The whole effort imposes a psychic cost, too. Tan's relatives, for example, live within a social isolation as deep as the apartness from mainstream society that ghetto blacks often feel. After all these years, Tan's sister still doesn't speak English. A friend who has lived even longer in America and similarly hasn't learned English still knows only one way to get home and had to direct Tan ten miles out of the way to drive her there. "That to me was a perfect metaphor for her lack of assimilation," Tan concludes.

Like previous immigrant groups, recent immigrants strive for success with less assurance and confidence than at first appears. They are even harried by ambivalence about the mainstream success they wish for their children. In becoming American, will the children not become less Chinese, Mexican, Jewish—fill in the blank—and therefore less able to understand the values that support the parents' sense of their own worth? No doubt an array of psychic and social difficulties does hold back the underclass from regular employment, but immigrants who are succeeding by means of low-skill jobs face similar barriers and overcome them.

The statistics also show, somberly, that men in underclass communities often choose crime instead of work, and crime is the most attention-grabbing element of underclass social pathology. Just as underclass nonwork springs not out of lack of opportunity but out of the lack of inner motivation, so underclass crime is impelled more by cultural than economic causes.

The explosion of hard-core crime in the sixties and seventies gave early and ever more emphatic evidence of the underclass problem. Robbery rates nearly quadrupled between 1963 and 1980; burglary and assault rates roughly tripled; the murder rate more than doubled. By 1970 a baby born and raised in a big city had a greater chance of being murdered than a World War II GI had of dying in battle. Today, a twelve-year-old American boy has an 89 percent chance of becoming a victim of violent crime in his lifetime, and an urban household has a 93 percent chance of being burgled sometime during the next twenty years. No less grim, in mid-1989, one out of every four young black American males was either in jail or on probation—a larger proportion than was in college. And a recent report claims that on any given day in 1991, 42 percent of Washington, D.C.'s black men between the ages of eighteen and thirty-five were either in jail, on probation or parole, awaiting trial, or sought by police with warrants for their arrest.

The crime boom changed the quality of urban life, afflicting urbanites with that characteristic caution verging on paranoia that they didn't have in the decades before the sixties. Today young city dwellers listen almost incredulously when older neighbors reminisce about sitting in the parks till past midnight on hot nights in the forties or fifties. Very different from the cities they know now, with double locks on every apartment door, with buildings and even street signs vandalized by graffiti, with metal detectors at high school entrances, with cars outfitted with ever-wailing alarms, removable radios, and testily worded "No Radio" signs, and with gutters sometimes glittering like a polar fantasy not with ice but with little cubes of smashed safety glass from the windows of cars unprotected by antiburglary measures.

True, highwaymen preyed upon Londoners crossing Hampstead Heath in the eighteenth century, and *Oliver Twist*'s pickpockets and housebreakers are reminders of an ugly nineteenth-century urban reality; but in late-twentieth-century American cities, increased crime spawned by the underclass surely represents a step backward in the development of civilization.

In ghettos it's more like two or three steps backward. Poor blacks get robbed four times as often as middle-class whites, and notoriously the leading cause of death among young black men is murder. No wonder fear pervades underclass areas, smothering the spirit of community and keeping some law-abiding residents from getting ahead by working the night shift or going to night school.

The fate of John Wiggers, sixty-nine, a retired hospital porter in the Bronx, crystallizes what they fear. To protect his wife, a night-shift hospital housekeeper, from muggers, he met her at the subway stop each midnight to walk her home. Stepping off the train at 12:15 A.M. one winter night in 1989, Mrs. Wiggers saw a crowd and went to see what was going on, only to discover her husband in the middle of it, dead. A mugger in a stocking cap, tall, young, and black, had just shot him point-blank in the face for trying to resist being robbed.

The thug who blasted away this decent citizen almost certainly was part of the infestation of crackheads who made Wiggers's neighborhood so dangerous. Criminals like this murderer are hardly men driven to desperation by hunger and the cries of their suffering children, as in the Depression. Pondering this slaughter, one can't help remembering Aristotle's judgment that intoxication, far from excusing crime, makes the criminal guiltier, for besides committing his crime he has willfully deprived himself of the human reason that distinguishes right from wrong and makes him more than a beast. So with drugs: to create a craving that snuffs out your powers of reason and leads you to prey on the innocent for money to satisfy that craving is doubly evil.

Doubtless some fraction of underclass crime is a rational economic response to underclass poverty and supposed lack of opportunity. But before completely embracing this often asserted economic explanation, please look squarely at the brutal unreason of the murder of Wiggers and of so much underclass crime. Like most underclass pathology, it is the fruit not of economic deprivation but of inner defect.

Why has violence become so casually gratuitous, hand in hand with the rise of the underclass? What possible reason can today's robbers have for killing their victims so much more frequently than in the past? Why do underclass quarrels, even the most trivial ones, so often conclude with gunshots? A recent argument between two Manhattan high school students over a cookie thrown in the cafeteria ended with one youth catching the other later on the packed Lexington Avenue subway and pumping five fatal shots into him.

Some months earlier, an oft-arrested eighteen-year-old walked into a crowded Brooklyn McDonald's at dinnertime and saw someone with whom he'd been feuding. Seizing his opportunity, he blazed away with his nine-millimeter, missing his target but snuffing out the life of a bystander, eighteen-year-old Tondelayo Alfred, a pretty and promising young woman in a special course for talented minority students at Brooklyn College. "You've heard Martin Luther King talk about the dream?" the victim's former English teacher remarked of her. "She *was* the dream."

While the robbery rate quadrupled between 1963 and 1980, so did the rape rate. Ravaging someone else is hard to present as having anything to do with rationality or economic condition. Rita Kramer, in *At a Tender Age: Violent Youth and Juvenile Justice,* recounts in heart-chilling detail the 1984 rape and murder of a fifty-one-year-old bag lady in Central Park by three underclass boys, ages sixteen, fourteen, and twelve. Finding the woman sleeping on a bench in a part of the park peopled during the day by the children and nannies of the rich, the three boys dragged her behind the boathouse and took turns raping and sodomizing her while the others held her down. To silence her cries, they beat her with their fists and stuffed a plastic bag in her mouth, later found still there and soaked with blood. They then broke into the boathouse and took out a golf club and a stick, with which they beat the woman to death. They covered her body with sticks and tried unsuccessfully to incinerate her. In the police photographs, Kramer says, her blood-splattered body looks like a rag doll a careless child has dropped.

Only savage malice drove these boys. In a less violent vein, nothing but resentful malice impelled a pack of underclass teenage girls who terrorized a stretch of Broadway for an autumn week in 1989 by stabbing white women from behind with pins or needles. The aim, it seems, was to make the victims fear they'd been infected with AIDS. *Were* these women infected, forcibly made blood-sisters with underclass pathology? Probably not.

Probably they were "only" pricked, in a viciously cruel hoax. But they will have plenty of time to wonder.

If members of the underclass don't succeed at the first two steps of the formula for avoiding poverty—finishing high school and working regularly—the statistics show that they succeed no better at the third and last part—getting married and staying married. The breakdown of the black family that Senator Moynihan deplored a generation ago has sharply worsened for the underclass. Whereas 25 percent of black families were headed by a woman when Moynihan wrote, the proportion had soared to 43 percent by 1984 and to 48 percent in 1990. In 1960 three quarters of young black men said they'd never been married; 93 percent say so today.

Nevertheless, they go on making babies—so one can hardly argue that nonmarriage is a response to the economic impossibility of supporting a family. While around one black child in six was born illegitimate in 1950, more than half—57 percent—were born illegitimate by 1982, and by 1989 the number had risen to about two thirds. Today, in ghettos like New York's central Harlem, four out of every five black babies are illegitimate. Worse, two out of every five of those illegitimate babies have teenage mothers, some scarcely able to take care of themselves, much less a child.

Time and again, underclass single-parent families are dysfunctional families. However hard it is for anyone to bring up children without a mate, it can be almost hopelessly so for underclass women. That's not just because families headed by women are on average significantly poorer than two-parent families, with a median income totaling only 42 percent of the median for two-parent families in 1990, and for blacks an even paltrier 36 percent of the median two-parent black family's income. The dysfunction of single-parent underclass families goes far beyond the economic realm.

The worst of it is that many underclass children, already deprived of a father, also suffer bad mothering from harried, ignorant, isolated, poor, and sometimes drug-dependent women. That's why so many underclass children arrive in school unable to understand cause and effect, to label and classify, to see how things are the same or different, to ask a question and trust that an adult will answer it helpfully, instead of pushing it aside. That's why underclass children are so frequently injured, burned, unimmunized; why their mothers so routinely hit them and threaten them; why four out of five families reported for child abuse are welfare families. And as studies show, abused children, even severely neglected children, end up with lower intelligence and a greater tendency toward crime and drug use than other children.

The mothers of underclass children are as far removed from the mainstream world of work and citizenship as the fathers are. Their alternative of choice is not crime but dependency. Most of them live on Aid to Families with Dependent Children, the nation's principal welfare program. Started during the New Deal with the modest mission of helping widows and orphans, primarily of coal miners, the program swelled hugely to include families lacking male heads because of divorce or illegitimacy.

The average divorced woman who goes on AFDC gets off in under five years. But *never-married* welfare mothers, on average, stay on welfare 9.3 years. Over a quarter of AFDC recipients stay on welfare for ten years or more, and these long-termers consume almost two thirds of all welfare payments. Two out of every five single mothers under twenty-five years old who go on welfare end up staying on the rolls for over a decade. Almost by definition, the vast majority of these dependent women are underclass mothers raising underclass children—sheltered by public housing projects, fed by food stamps, doctored by Medicaid, and taught by Head Start, by Title I programs, by GED programs, by job-training programs, generally to little avail.

Underclass women have babies for a web of reasons, among which ignorance about birth control plays almost no part, even for teenagers. A sixteen-year-old Washington ghetto girl told reporter Leon Dash in an interview for a *Washington Post* series on pregnancies among young blacks: "When girls get pregnant, it's either because they want something to hold on to, because of circumstances at home, or because they don't really have anyone to go to. And some of them do it because they resent their parents. None of that is an accident. Every teenage girl knows about birth control pills. Even when they 12, they know what it is."

This comment goes to the heart of one of the two competing explanations for the origin and growth of the underclass that currently divide the field, one from the left and one from the right. Each is powerful, arresting, and well worth examining. But each focuses primarily on economic forces; and the most important reason for stopping to consider them is to see how neither sufficiently explains the phenomenon of the underclass. When all that can be said about economic causation has eloquently been said, a gaping hole remains at the very center of the picture. The shape of that hole makes clear that the key missing element in the reasoning—the element without which nothing finally adds up or makes sense—is a matter of culture, not economics.

CHAPTER THREE

The Hole in the Theory

If the two major explanations for the rise of the underclass, the one brought to mind by the Washington sixteen-year-old quoted in the last chapter is that put forward by Charles Murray's brilliant *Losing Ground.* The most dazzling part of Murray's powerful argument is his analysis of how changes in the nation's welfare system in the 1960s inflamed the epidemic of illegitimacy central to underclass pathology.

Since the mid-sixties, Murray shows, welfare has been a particularly insidious snare. Since then, a combination of AFDC, food stamps, Medicaid, and other benefits has provided welfare mothers in the big urban states where the underclass is concentrated with more purchasing power than they'd get from a minimum-wage job. Even in less free-spending states, the benefit package is enough to support these mothers and their children fully if meanly.

If an income they can get by on is the consequence of having a baby, observes Murray, why should poor women worry about getting pregnant? Since welfare fosters the kind of passivity that makes it hard to see alternatives to the admittedly marginal existence it provides, what would impel them to seek work instead of having another illegitimate baby? And why should these women get married? A welfare mother's child, says Murray, "provides her with the economic insurance that a husband used to represent."

There is no need to invoke a breakdown of the work ethic or the development of a culture of poverty among the underclass, says Murray, though these may operate also. The welfare system by itself is enough to account for the nonmarriage, bastardy, and some of the nonwork that make up the pathology ailing the underclass. It even explains the casual attachment to work that these women's boyfriends usually have: they need work only fitfully to supplement the women's welfare payments. Welfare provides an utterly perverse set of "incentives to fail," in Murray's somber phrase.

Murray notes that other incentives changed at the same time and in the same direction. Crime was met so much less often with punishment that its benefits generally came to outweigh its cost to the criminal. Discipline and educational standards collapsed catastrophically in the public schools, subverting incentives to work hard and sanctions against disruptive behavior. Increasingly, mainstream society withdrew "status rewards" from hardworking poor people who resisted the "incentives to fail." Mainstream society did this by erasing the distinction between the respectable poor and the irresponsible, disorderly, dependent poor. Once society began to see the poor who didn't work and who neglected their families as "victims" of "the system" rather than as personally responsible for their fate and actions, then how could these poor be seen as morally inferior to the industrious poor? These simultaneous changes in the incentive structure of American society reinforced each other powerfully, Murray says, and they fostered the social pathology out of which, mushroomlike, the underclass sprang.

Following a direction set by the path-breaking sociologist of crime James Q. Wilson, Murray focuses quite narrowly on social policy and the power its incentives and disincentives have to shape the behavior of individuals. Whereas the deeper social influences on human action, the "root causes," are resistant to change, Wilson had argued, specific policies can be altered readily, and so they provide a real handle for regulating behavior. In this policy-making spirit, Murray couches his argument in the language of economic calculation, of an individual's rational balancing of costs and benefits within the altered structure of incentives and disincentives that any policy change produces. With extraordinary wisdom and originality, however, Murray demonstrates how the powerful effects policymakers achieve are often dismayingly different from those they intended. Modifying human behavior, it turns out, is a highly inexact science, given the perversely protean elasticity of people in chasing after their own goals.

Though Murray is the profoundest of all commentators on the underclass, his economic language finally pulls him up short. His discussion of "status rewards" reveals most clearly the limitations his language imposes upon him. The very term "status rewards" transforms the deepest issues of how we judge and value each other, of what we take to be the sources of dignity and of meaning in human life, into the jargon of social science, and thereby blunts and trivializes them. *Losing Ground,* a reader feels, wants to break through into the large realm of values, and Murray's subsequent work has tried to do so. But *Losing Ground* is held back by language that can only calculate the value of this or that incentive weighed against this or that disincentive, a paltrier matter altogether.

In the end, the world Murray paints, with its heartlessly mechanical interplay of incentives, seems aridly devoid of values. Its inhabitants seem mere passive responders to external incentives, not free moral agents with lives and fates that have moral significance. In this value-free universe, what else can you expect these women to do? Wouldn't any choice other than this rational one be incorrect?

So when Murray asks why, given the welfare system, an unmarried underclass girl should regret getting pregnant, or why she should marry the child's father and so lose the financial autonomy welfare gives her, one wants to cry out, "Because it is right!" What used to prevent such behavior were deeply rooted community standards and values, in terms of which people who made such choices met with condemnation not just from others but also from themselves. Before an individual could dream of engaging in such calculations as Murray imagines, a momentous sea change in values must first have occurred. Before one can focus so exclusively on the question of what the reward or penalty of this act will be, one must no longer be interested in, or troubled by, the larger question of what kind of person will I be—who will I become—if I do this.

Behavior is influenced not just by considerations of outside sanctions or rewards like jail or money, but also by what others do and think, by what is customary and accepted in terms of the culture of the community. The rational-calculation school gives short shrift to such forces, or to the vast power of conscience, in which the values of our culture are internalized and made a part of ourselves. The truth is that when underclass women decide to have illegitimate children, they don't sit down and do a cost-benefit analysis of the welfare package. What they say to themselves is what one typical young welfare mother told *The Washington Post*: "Everybody else I knew was having babies, so I just went along."

Nothing tells these young women that getting pregnant without being married and having illegitimate babies they can't support and aren't equipped to nurture well is wrong. The culture they live in, both the larger culture and the culture of the underclass, tells them that a life on welfare is perfectly acceptable and, arguably, just as good as any other kind of life. Under those circumstances, who can wonder that no inner voice condemns them for choosing such a fate? With such an outlook on the world and on themselves, it's a short step to embracing welfare.

The puzzling—and crucial—question is how they got that outlook in the first place, not where it led them once they had it. After all, by the start of the sixties, reports were already beginning to circulate of families that had been on welfare for two and sometimes even three generations, indicating that such dependency was economically feasible even before the War on Poverty made its dramatic changes in the economics of AFDC. Those reports are only anecdotal evidence, but they do suggest that the key ingredient necessary to ignite the ensuing explosion in welfare dependency was not so much the enrichment of welfare's economic lure—a lure that already existed—as it was the cultural changes that made swallowing the lure acceptable.

In fact, the policy changes that sweetened the welfare package or lessened the criminal's odds of being punished were themselves emanations of the vast cultural change the sixties accomplished. The policy changes couldn't have occurred if the cultural changes hadn't happened first. Made and applied with moral fervor by people whom a new set of cultural values had deeply persuaded of their rightness, as Murray himself notes in *Losing Ground,* these new policies emphatically conveyed to those whose lives they affected the cultural values that gave rise to the policies. And though James Q. Wilson may be right in general that policies are easier to change than root causes, that's hardly the case with policies forged, as antipoverty policy was forged, with crusading, almost religious zeal and venerated as testaments to the moral excellence of the culture.

The idea that moral choices are made primarily by economic rationality is itself an expression of the cultural unraveling that this book is talking about. That notion is a distant cousin of the idea that only the economic realm is real, while the cultural realm floats insubstantially above it, passively reflecting it. Both these ideas embody a mechanistic materialism that allows no room for the human spirit and the realm of value and meaning it creates.

Unquestionably valuable in its proper sphere, cost-benefit thinking nevertheless often turns a blind eye to that realm, sometimes producing absurd distortions. For example, such thinking led the nineteenth-century utilitarian philosopher Jeremy Bentham to the conclusion that the child's game of push-pin, since it produced an equivalent quantity of pleasure, was as valuable as poetry. Some of *Losing Ground*'s critics, who take this sort of economic calculation much further than Murray himself, end up at conclusions as absurd as Bentham's. If changes in the level of welfare benefits really did figure large in the creation of the underclass, they say, why don't the differences in welfare enrollment among states exactly mirror the variations in benefits? Why don't enrollments change precisely in line with changes in the real value of benefits, adjusted for inflation? Since they don't, these critics sum up with a flourish, *Losing Ground* is all wrong.

It's hard to imagine a more mechanical, even robotic, conception of human nature than these rigidly statistical critics seem to hold. For in truth, though I have highlighted the flaws of *Losing Ground* to show how Murray's focus on policy leads him, mistakenly, into giving primacy to economic rationality, his superb book surely is resoundingly right in its fundamental insight that raising welfare benefits above the purchasing power of the lowest-level job powerfully furthered the growth of the underclass.

The other major explanation for the underclass phenomenon, which University of Chicago sociologist William Julius Wilson expounds in his influential work *The Truly Disadvantaged,* is a more problematic matter, less compelling than Murray's argument. Journalists love to cite Wilson, so much so that his argument routinely appears in the national newsweeklies and newspapers as the universally accepted explanation of the origin of the underclass. Part of his argument, at least: for to Wilson's annoyance, reporters are prone to getting him wrong or giving only a partial account of his thought. That may happen as regularly as it does, I suspect, because journalists are instinctively trying to separate the kernels of real insight in Wilson's work from the chaff in which they are embedded. His prose may account for the problem too; by contrast with the elegant precision of Murray's writing, Wilson's style is academically flatfooted, clotted with statistics, endlessly repetitious in assertion rather than finely spun and coherently persuasive in argument.

Wilson is a principal exponent of the view that economic change caused the formation of what he calls the "ghetto underclass." Combed free of its knots and tangles, his basic argument looks like this. In the seventies and eighties, a structural shift occurred in the economies of the old northern cities, where blacks were concentrated. Well-paid factory jobs that required few skills sharply declined, to be replaced by jobs in the service industries, such as the financial services business or the health care business. Because these jobs required higher educational attainment, they left low-skill blacks out in the cold.

At the same time, racism waned, partially but nonetheless significantly. Opportunity in education, employment, and housing opened to blacks. The black middle class vigorously expanded, and middle- and solid working-class blacks streamed into suburbs and formerly all-white urban neighborhoods. Left behind in the old, central-city ghettos after the industrious and the upwardly mobile had fled was a residue of the unskilled—the truly disadvantaged—who faced the stark reality of a transformed, "deindustrialized" urban economy offering no employment for which they were qualified. So they didn't work.

Moreover, those who had left the ghettos were the stable people who formerly breathed vitality into the institutions—churches, schools, community centers—that knit a collection of separate individuals into a community. As those institutions languished, they lost their power to enforce standards of conduct. In addition, the citizens who left took with them their personal moral authority: these were the kind of people who uphold community norms by a sharp word or censorious look at the unruly young when necessary. They were the people who exemplified the connection between prosperity and education, marriage, and work. Plugged into the world of work, they also used to help young people find jobs. Now these young people have no connection to the informal networks through which people get wind of job openings and get recommended for them.

Without economic opportunity, driven by a desperate economic rationale to the only choices that existed for them, inner-city dwellers understandably turned to welfare dependency, crime, and the familiar brew of underclass disorder. As already mentioned, Wilson attributes illegitimacy to the chronic joblessness that allegedly made inner-city men economically "unmarriageable"; inner-city women accordingly didn't marry them. The pathological behavior economic disadvantage bred was intensified by the "social isolation," as Wilson calls it, that resulted from the rapid decampment of the stable and stabilizing members of ghetto communities. It was intensified further by the "concentration effects" inevitable when so much disadvantage and pathology is squeezed together and left to fester on its own, like mold and mildew in the dark, beyond the bounds of the normal community.

The result is a quite distinctive underclass culture. But it would be incorrect to call it a "culture of poverty," says Wilson, because that would imply that culture has an autonomous power to shape lives and determine circumstances. It has no such power, Wilson vigorously asserts. On the contrary. "Cultural values emerge from specific circumstances and life chances and reflect an individual's position in the class structure," he writes in *The Truly Disadvantaged*. "They therefore do not ultimately determine behavior. If ghetto underclass minorities have limited aspirations, a hedonistic orientation toward life, or lack of plans for the future, such outlooks ultimately are the result of restricted opportunities and feelings of resignation originating from bitter personal experiences and a bleak future."

Therefore, even though the pathology may *appear* to come out of the cultural realm, one can't try to cure it by looking to that realm. Rather, one must ameliorate the economic circumstances that produce the pathology, and in response the values will regain their health, albeit with a lag in time. And so Wilson puts forth a vast program of centralized economic planning aimed at energizing the economies of the central cities—a program that, at a time when even Russia and Eastern Europe have confessed the bankruptcy of central planning and command economies, looks as quaintly antique as the Copernican cosmology.

Though in the end Wilson's argument is deeply mistaken, it contains much of real value. To begin with, he exhaustively documents that there *is* an underclass, that it is defined by its pathological behavior, that most of its members are black. At a time when so many blacks and liberals deny even the existence of a definable underclass, it makes a difference that Wilson, a widely respected black who describes his politics as social democratic, authoritatively upholds the opposite view. It matters, too, that Wilson roundly confutes the idea that racism caused the underclass. How can discrimination be a cause, he asks, when the underclass arose *after* racism had abated enough to permit a surge of blacks into the middle class? Indeed, the recent opening of the American economy and society to blacks in a sense created the underclass by allowing so many to escape from the ghetto, leaving behind the least skilled to congeal into the underclass. And Wilson is right to observe that underclass behavior comes out of the realm of culture, even though he surely is wrong in seeing culture as no more than the passive reflection of economic circumstances. He is right, too, in seeing that the concentration and homogeneity of underclass communities only intensify the cultural disturbance.

But he is wrong in ascribing the underclass phenomenon to lack of economic opportunity. I won't rehash the arguments already set forth against the economic explanation for the birth of the underclass—that plenty of low-skill jobs exist, that despite the low wages immigrants are finding those jobs an adequate first step up the ladder, that no economic reason can explain why generation after generation of the underclass fails to get the skills needed to take the higher-skill jobs that are plentiful. (Generations are short when mothers can be fifteen and grandmothers thirty-two.) The point, I hope, is amply made; and if it is true that economic opportunity does exist, then Wilson's fundamental argument crumbles.

So does some of his logic. For example, following his argument that cultural values merely reflect economic reality but do not create it, you would expect to see a hunger for education and a blossoming of ambitious self-discipline among the young in underclass neighborhoods, "reflecting" the same plentiful availability of higher-skill jobs that has permitted so many of the motivated to escape the ghetto. And putting aside the debatable question of whether unemployment makes underclass men unmarriageable, how can unemployment explain the epidemic of illegitimacy that is at the core of underclass pathology? Even if unemployment makes people unable to marry, in an age of ubiquitous birth control it surely doesn't force them to have children.

It seems an additional inconsistency that Wilson should propose his vast program of central economic planning to bring the economic reality into line with the culture of the ghetto, rather than wait for ghetto culture to adjust to the economic opportunities that exist, as his theory contends it will. Such a program, almost certainly, would succeed in radically slowing the engine of economic expansion and job creation that helped propel the exodus from the ghetto into the middle class. For if one incontestable lesson is to be learned from the experience of the eighties from Peru to Poland to the Soviet Union, it is that free, flexible economies work vastly better in every respect than centrally planned ones.

At the bottom of Wilson's theory is the erroneous assumption that people are basically passive. To take the largest example, his idea that culture merely reflects economic circumstances is a passive conception of man's relation to the material world.

And as I've said, it isn't true only that circumstances make people; people in turn rework and transform the circumstances that are given to them. Within Wilson's conception of economic opportunity is a similarly troubling streak of passivity. For Wilson, opportunity is something that the ghetto population passively awaits, utterly dependent on outside circumstances either to present or withhold it. But in the same way that the real roots of wealth are less in material resources than in people—in their skill and imaginativeness and daring in deploying those resources—opportunity too can be found, or created, in the most apparently barren circumstances.

That is the lesson of Korean economic success in ghetto neighborhoods. No opportunity? Then why do Korean greengrocers flourish in Harlem and Bedford-Stuyvesant, where no such business has flourished for years? Why do newly opened Korean-owned liquor stores prosper in the Los Angeles ghettos? It doesn't take arcane skills to run a vegetable stand, only hard work, long hours, determination, rudimentary entrepreneurialism, and family cooperation. These are skills that you learn from home and community; they are skills that are nothing but the reflection of cultural values.

What limits economic opportunity for the underclass above all is the lack of such skills—skills like being able to show up on time dependably, to be conscientious and have manners, to treat customers well enough so they'll come back, to stick to something unpleasant and arduous, to attend to details. So when William Julius Wilson says that a lack of skills debars the underclass from economic opportunity, he is inadvertently describing—despite his protestations to the contrary—a cultural, not an economic, problem. You couldn't make the lesson more luminously clear if you inscribed it in big letters upon every Korean vegetable stand: in today's America, cultural values make economic opportunities.

Film director Spike Lee ruminates upon that lesson in *Do the Right Thing,* in which a Korean greengrocery in the heart of an underclass neighborhood is a sphinxlike mystery, the subject of endless puzzlement and speculation. Maybe the greengrocers succeed because the Reverend Sun Myung Moon secretly bankrolls them, one nonworking ghetto dweller theorizes, voicing a view widely held in such neighborhoods. The grain of truth behind this zany hypothesis is that Korean greengrocers do have a mechanism—a rotating credit association called the *gae*—for raising capital without collateral from friends or relatives. The twenty or thirty members of such a club each contribute three hundred or five hundred dollars or more to a monthly pot, and every month the total pot is loaned to a different member, beginning with the neediest. So that makes enough to pay a landlord his rent and to buy and stock the shelves and refrigerated cases.

But capital isn't what makes the difference—and in fact enterprising black or Hispanic ghetto dwellers aren't barred from access to capital, since they are eligible for start-up loans from an array of state-run programs or from the Small Business Administration's direct loan and loan guarantee programs. Culture, not capital, is the key ingredient in Korean business success in the ghettos. Indeed the *gae* itself, a traditional way of organizing people for mutual self-help, is nothing but a manifestation of culture. The same can be said of the sense of cooperation, loyalty, and obligation that makes such an institution of mutual trust viable. It can be said yet again of the tradition of close-knit families whose members willingly defer gratification, toil at menial jobs, and save fervidly to raise the monthly payments required for membership in a *gae*. No external bar prevents members of the underclass from doing the same thing. The economic opportunity that Koreans have taken in the ghetto was there for anyone to take, as Spike Lee's movie ruefully concludes.

But by no means all blacks who have commented publicly on this subject have agreed with Lee. Resentment of Asian economic success in underclass neighborhoods runs high, as evidenced by the widespread destruction of Korean-owned businesses in the 1992 Los Angeles riots and by ugly boycotts and threats of boycott across the nation. The public statement of a black local legislator representing Washington's Anacostia ghetto typifies the tone: "The day of the Asian community occupying or getting the majority of business in a [black] neighborhood is over. . . . We are not going to burn down our community. . . . We are going to use our clout in city hall."

The anger is understandable as well as deplorable: Asian business success in urban ghettos tears away the myth that the underclass is imprisoned in its penurious, pathological idleness by an utter absence of economic opportunity. Asian entrepreneurs have uncovered robust economic opportunity and decent livings right in the blighted and supposedly barren heart of the ghettos. Instead of allowing the underclass the solace of seeing themselves as victims, their fate not their own responsibility but forced upon them, Asian success contains an implicit reproach: *What's the matter with the underclass that they couldn't do what immigrant Asians, starting at the bottom and scarcely able to speak English, have so swiftly accomplished?* The answer is to be found in underclass culture—not, as William Julius Wilson and many others claim with increasing hollowness, in the economy.

However striking Wilson's concepts of "social isolation" and "concentration effects," the experience of Washington, D.C., suggests that neither of these forces, much less a lack of economic opportunity, is essential for the formation of the underclass. As described by sociologist James Q. Wilson, Washington's underclass emerged in the absence of virtually every condition that William Julius Wilson (no relation) deems necessary. When you look at what happened in Washington, the conclusion seems hard to avoid that forces other than those *The Truly Disadvantaged* posits are responsible for bringing the underclass into existence.

Throughout the 1960s, Washington's large black population showed strong progress by many statistical measures. Its educational level rose; its family income soared. In the high-unemployment year of 1970, the unemployment rate for Washington blacks was relatively low. Far from being a vast slum, a compressed mass of the skill-less and jobless, black Washington remained a vital middle- or lower-middle-class community. Yet within this intact community, rich in respectable role models and thriving institutions, an epidemic of drugs, crime, and welfare dependency broke out, raging through the sixties and on into the seventies.

A major reason for this explosion lies in the demographics, James Q. Wilson suggests. The growing up of the postwar baby boom children meant that Washington's sixteen- to twenty-one-year-old population increased by almost a third during the sixties. You can trace this singular generation's progress through the decade by the floodmarks of self-destructive behavior it left on a succession of institutions. In 1962, dropouts from junior high schools began to increase. In 1968, the rise in the number of senior high school dropouts reached its peak. By 1970, the unemployment rate for blacks aged sixteen to twenty-one hit 16 percent for men and 20 percent for women, while for blacks aged twenty to fifty-nine it remained a modest 4.5 percent for men and 3.6 percent for women. During the sixties, heroin addiction soared among the young; of the six thousand men who'd been born in Washington in 1953, addiction claimed over 13 percent. The number of women on AFDC tripled during the decade, with so many baby boomers added to the rolls that the average age of welfare mothers fell from thirty to twenty-three. Crime increased, with a significant but unmeasurable quantum contributed by baby boom thugs.

The young have always gotten into a disproportionate share of trouble—and with more young, more trouble was bound to ensue. But as the baby boom went through its troublemaking years, it went wrong at a startlingly higher rate than the young usually do. The rise in welfare dependency in Washington was 600 percent greater than experts would have predicted from the change in the population's age profile, for example; the rise in crime, over 1200 percent greater.

Clearly the baby boom generation made so decisive an impact not just because it was so large, but more especially because it was so different. A huge cohort grew up formed by a new culture—a new set of values, beliefs, and institutions—that was only just cooling and solidifying as the baby boom was coming to consciousness. That culture came out of the larger American community, not out of the inner city; and, as it got its distinctive twist in ghetto neighborhoods, it disposed many inner-city baby boomers to grow up underclass. The problem wasn't that the underclass was isolated from mainstream culture, but rather that it was all too powerfully influenced by it.

As the underclass version of the new culture took shape in response to the inexorable pressure of cultural forces operating in the society as a whole, it acquired an immeasurable power for ill. So potent did it grow that, far from being formed by economic circumstances, it instead often rode roughshod over them as it asserted its sway. The fact that culture, regardless of economics, is the true crucible of underclass identity is one of the key lessons of the Central Park "wilding" of 1989.

Look back for a moment on that chilling event. On the night of April 19, about a dozen and a half Harlem teenage boys, black and Hispanic, went into the northern end of Central Park, looking for trouble. Their term for this evidently familiar activity was "wilding"—pronounced, as the papers reported with punctilious respect for the niceties of underclass slang, "wil'ing." They unsuccessfully tried to mug a couple of cyclists, yelling, "Fucking white people." They beat up a drunk and attacked several male joggers, knocking one unconscious with a length of pipe and sending him to the hospital with a concussion. Then one teenager reportedly cried, "Let's get a woman jogger."

Around nine-thirty, a slim, twenty-eight-year-old woman who worked as an investment banker at Salomon Bros. had the misfortune of jogging across their path. They chased her and knocked her down, kicking and punching her as she tried to fight them off. They smashed her head and face with the pipe and a brick. They pulled off her jogging tights, and several boys held her down. Laughing, between two and four of the others took turns raping her. One sodomized her. One of the boys may have used a knife to make the deep gashes later found in her thighs.

The assailants left her for dead, bleeding and unconscious at the bottom of a muddy ravine, where she was found at one-thirty in the morning, with three quarters of her blood drained out of her and her body temperature sunk to 80 degrees. Though at first she was expected not to live, and then to live but remain badly brain-damaged, she made an extraordinary recovery and seven months after the assault returned to work part-time. "It was something to do," one of her attackers reportedly said about these events. "It was fun."

A note of puzzlement blended into the public outrage over this crime when the newspapers reported that most of the alleged assailants—the "wolf pack," as journalists called them—weren't typical underclass kids. Instead of being the offspring of teenage welfare mothers, some came from intact families, most had working parents, and around half lived in a building reported to have a doorman. One attended a private school. Could they be *middle* class? the papers fretted. But then how could they have committed such a crime, an outbreak of the anarchy and racial animosity they believed was percolating in urban ghettos? Who *were* these boys?

The six youths sentenced for the "wilding" were borderline characters in many senses of the word. Four of them lived on the very margin of Harlem, right at the corner of Central Park, overlooking but utterly separate from the world of affluence that lines most of the park's perimeter. Their building was relatively new and well kept, but its doorman, universally invoked by the newspapers as a totem of middle-classness, was only a security guard, and most of its apartments, though occupied by working people, were government-subsidized. The private school student? He'd recently enrolled in a $1,100-a-year Harlem parochial school after he'd been suspended from the public school he'd previously attended for carrying weapons.

The families of the youths ranged from a hairbreadth out of the underclass, with many underclass cultural characteristics, to full-fledged working class. Toward the underclass end of the spectrum was a fourteen-year-old living with his father and grandmother. The father, though regularly employed, paid little attention to his son. Yet he was arguably a better parent than the mother, who formerly had had charge of the boy; she reportedly had found him less interesting than drugs, drink, and sex. Another family, having the superficial appearance of stability, lacked the reality of it. The mother, described by a community center director as a "strong, caring woman," had feared when her son was twelve that she would seriously hurt him; he was placed temporarily in a group home. The father and one brother have criminal records for drugs; another brother is a transvestite. The boy failed ninth grade and, with two of the other youths involved in the rape, was suspected of being part of a gang that specialized in vandalizing a nearby housing project and beating up its residents.

Two families were intact, stable, and industrious. Yet one, headed by a postal worker who imposed a nightly curfew on his children, had produced a son who, before he was charged in the attack upon the jogger, had been the suspected leader of the housing project vandals. The other family honorably embodies the very thing that William Julius Wilson says underclass communities lack. The mother is a day-care worker, the father a parking attendant who coaches a neighborhood baseball team and is looked up to as a role model. Reportedly, their only son had started getting wild in school not long before the attack on the jogger.

Of the somber lessons in all this, the one I want to underscore is the power underclass culture has to mark even those who from an economic point of view are outside that class, albeit not far from its brink. Like a collapsing star sucking a rush of matter into its dense, dying mass, underclass culture exerts a vast gravitational force that not only sways those within it but radiates even beyond.

It wasn't the welfare system that made these six indicted youths what they turned out to be—or poverty or drugs or school-leaving. It was that they lived all their lives in an underclass community and continually drank in its values.

When they went wrong, they went wrong with a characteristic underclass ferocity and lack of restraint. Mischief for them wasn't hooky or beer drinking but, if the allegations are true, terrorizing their neighbors and vandalizing their homes. "Wilding" played a big enough part in their lives, and in their culture, to require a special name. When, doubtless following a leader gripped by a psychopathology beyond class or culture, they went crazily, catastrophically wrong, nothing in their culture pulled them up short at some intermediate atrocity instead of letting them go all the way to gang rape and—but for the timely finding of the battered jogger by unexpected passersby—murder.

Talk to any social worker or educator who deals with the poor and sooner or later you'll hear about how hard it is to "compete with the streets." This hoary cliché is a monument to the practical, gut knowledge, widespread among frontline professionals, that culture really is crucial in shaping underclass fates, that peer pressure—a key way by which culture comes to bear on individuals—carries almost all before it. Even those driven by that pressure are at least dimly conscious of what's impelling them. How else to understand the bizarre claim of one of those indicted in the attack on the jogger that he didn't really rape her but only feigned intercourse so as not to be shamed before the other thugs? Whether true or not, that claim indicates his accurate awareness of how preeminent a place the worldview of his peers holds in his imagination.

Finally, if culture rather than economics is what fundamentally makes people underclass, as I am arguing, you would expect that changes in the cultural circumstances, without any alteration in the economic ones, would successfully raise people out of that condition. Let me conclude this chapter with three dramatic examples of exactly that transformation.

The first began with a millionaire's whim. In 1981, technology entrepreneur Eugene M. Lang agreed to give the commencement speech at his old grammar school in East Harlem. Things had sure changed since he graduated in 1928, when the neighborhood was mostly Jewish and Italian. How hollow these platitudes must sound, he thought as he looked down from the podium at the bored faces eyeing him as he spoke. You need to have a dream, he exhorted. You must go to college to achieve it.

Yeah sure, these sixth graders must be thinking; fat chance. After all, in this neighborhood around three quarters of the students don't graduate from high school, and almost no one goes to college.

You *can* go, he told them; and on the spur of the moment he made them a promise that hadn't entered his mind when he first walked onstage. Finish high school, he said; get into college—and I promise I'll give you scholarships. It took a moment of stunned silence before pandemonium erupted, with bewildered mothers calling out in Spanish from the back of the auditorium: What did he say?

By June 1988 almost three quarters of the students had earned their high school diplomas; almost 90 percent had them (or the equivalent GED certificate) by June 1992. So far, almost 70 percent of the students have enrolled in post–high school education, the majority part-time. Six of the original fifty-four have earned bachelor's degrees, including B.A.'s from such elite institutions as Barnard and Swarthmore. Lang expects that ultimately around fifteen of his students will earn B.A.'s, and ten more will get community college certificates.

But note: Lang didn't spend a dime of the promised scholarship money until after he'd worked the minor miracle of getting over half his kids to graduate from high school. And by the end of the 1992 school year, Lang will have spent not much more than $200,000 keeping his promise—around $340 per kid per year, or $6.54 a week. Compared to the magnitude of the achievement, the expenditure is tiny.

For money isn't what accomplished this success. What these kids needed—what underclass kids need most—is an authoritative link to traditional values of work, study, and self-improvement, and the assurance that these values can permit them to claim full membership in the larger community. "It's important that they grow up to recognize that they are not perpetuating a life of the pariah," Lang says, "but that the resources of the community are legitimately theirs to take advantage of and contribute to and be a part of. It's a question of outlook, of self-expectations, of knowing alternatives that are available to them."

To show them what the world offered, Lang took them to restaurants, the opera, the theater. To strengthen the outlook and self-expectations part of the equation, he got involved in their lives. He made time for them to visit his midtown office, where his sober, formal manner—expressive of an old-fashioned, even antique, bourgeois ethic—conveyed its message that the work ethic pays off, even for those who started from so poor a neighborhood as he had. He hired a full-time social worker to watch over them, to help them sort out problems with school and to keep them together as a mutually supportive group, a community of shared values that endowed them all with a feeling of specialness.

The lesson took. After a men's clothing manufacturer offered to donate four suits to Lang's program as prizes to the most outstanding boys, the four winners arrived at a meeting of all the kids in the suits they had chosen. "I looked for the bright colors, the signs of youth," Lang says, "and here these four boys came in, each wearing blue or charcoal pinstripes, as though they were walking out of the training program at Morgan Stanley. I can't tell you how good I felt, because one could see what had happened *inside* these youngsters. Just that one thing alone to me was a silent justification of the program."

Programs like Lang's unfortunately can't be cloned on a grand, government-sponsored, national scale, because their success depends on intimate personal connection and intense, nonbureaucratic commitment. As Lang says: "These kids have a substitute—not an ideal substitute—for what every reasonably affluent middle-class child has. I'm to these kids the same person I was to my own children." But however particular its application, Lang's success is real; and it eloquently testifies that cultural deformation is the worst affliction underclass kids suffer. That deformation prevents them from getting what is already available for them to get. Plenty of scholarship money and lots of low-cost public institutions, after all, are already available to qualified low-income applicants.

If Lang worked his magic from outside the underclass community, the same magic gets worked from within the nation's ghettos every day. Principal Jeffrey Litt works it at the Mohegan School in a drug-ridden Bronx neighborhood, where all his students are minority, mostly from welfare-dependent, single-parent homes. In this public elementary school, Litt instituted a core curriculum based on educator E. D. Hirsch's theory that poor and marginal pupils need, even more than other kids, to be put in touch with a body of mainstream culture's common knowledge, which their family life fails to provide to them.

Accordingly, Mohegan teaches its pupils about Beethoven and Monet, *Treasure Island* and the Industrial Revolution, ancient Egypt and classical Greece. They act out what they learn: a mock trial of Long John Silver, a play about mummification, a dramatization of the life of Mozart. Litt and his teachers keep the expectations high. "Make your parents proud; make your teachers proud; make yourselves proud" is Litt's continual exhortation. When students misbehave, Litt doesn't punish them but rather tells them, "If you want to fight, you're in the wrong place: this is a place for winners." The result: four years after Litt took over, attendance is way up, no student has had to be suspended for disciplinary reasons, reading scores have risen significantly, and Mohegan students have begun winning prizes in citywide academic competitions.

Kimi Gray worked the magic on a bigger scale at the 464-unit Kenilworth-Parkside housing project in Washington. Fed up with dirt, crime, no heat, no hot water, Gray got herself elected head of the project's residents' council in 1972 as a twenty-five-year-old welfare mother with five kids. She and her council immediately organized tenants into committees, started cleanup brigades, and appointed safety officers to keep front doors locked and hall lights on. Whereas Kenilworth residents once had displayed their feelings about the police by turning over their cars, Gray and her supporters fostered cooperation and got residents and officers to view themselves as allies against criminals. After she persuaded tenants not to buy stolen goods, housebreaking plummeted, since you can only lug a hot TV so far. When drug pushers infested the neighborhood, she organized tenant marches to drive them out and told resident pushers and addicts that if they didn't quit in thirty days she'd have them evicted. "Crime is down seventy-five percent since we started," says Gray. Drug killings, formerly a more than once-a-month occurrence, have stopped entirely for the last four years.

Gray encouraged residents to take over the neighborhood PTA. As parental interest and involvement grew, the children's test scores gradually rose, and Kenilworth kids increasingly began to enroll in college. She threatened to take some residents to court for neglecting their children. Coming out of her mouth—the mouth of an impressive, Sumo-wrestler-size neighbor—ordinary standards of respectable behavior took on new force. They became the standards of one's own community, rather than alien impositions, tainted with the suspicion of racism.

From this grass roots beginning, Gray and her committee took over management of the entire project in 1982, thereby arming their efforts with the economic power of the management fee the committee received. Gray used the money to organize an employment agency to get tenants jobs outside the housing project and to start small businesses, such as a window-screen repair shop and a day-care center, which gave employment to tenants. After living on welfare, residents found themselves earning a $10,000 annual salary by working for Gray, perhaps supplemented by the $4,000 wage of their teenage child, whom Gray had encouraged to work at McDonald's. In real life, *that's* how people get out of poverty, as legions of immigrants know. One usually doesn't go straight from poverty to pinstripes.

Since 1972, welfare dependency in Kenilworth has dropped 60 percent, and some of the project's households now earn over $30,000 a year. Gray's management corporation is in the process of buying the entire project from the government, with the hope of selling individual units to tenants in the future. This amounts to a revolution in the lives of the residents, but it is a revolution that took place in the hearts of individuals and in the communal standards they set for each other. All the economic consequences flowed from that source.

At this point, my argument must seem almost self-contradictory. On one hand I hold that an infusion of mainstream, conventional respectability in outlook and actions auspiciously transforms the underclass. On the other, I argue that the culture of the Haves mightily contributed to the formation of the underclass. Am I not ascribing two diametrically opposed effects to mainstream culture?

But the paradox isn't in my argument. It is, instead, in mainstream culture, which over the last thirty years has transmitted to those at the bottom of society anything but conventional respectability. We'll turn to consider this singular state of affairs in all its oddity in a moment. But first we must look at a troubling population that partly overlaps the underclass. I mean the homeless, the group that has made the relationship between the rich and the poor one of the most disturbing questions of our age.

CHAPTER FOUR

The Homeless

ere is a man moving his bowels on the Seventy-ninth Street sidewalk in the pouring afternoon rain. Behind him rises the Beaux Arts splendor of the Apthorp Apartments, an opulent relic of New York's vanished age of civic confidence. The squatting man, his smile sheepishly vacant, slowly tears up a newspaper and wipes himself with great deliberateness. Passing along this busy thoroughfare, embarrassed and dismayed, I can't keep at bay a discordantly uncharitable thought: what a fitting end to years—years!—of preposterously muddleheaded reporting on the problem of homelessness.

This is not kind, I know. But the shocking actuality of homelessness is so utterly different from the picture journalists have drawn that it's hard to keep patience with their almost mystifying distortion and misrepresentation of the unsettling truth. Can all of today's reporters commute from the suburbs? If you live in a city, after all, you can't help glimpsing the painful reality, as here on Seventy-ninth Street, before averting your eyes in shame. You get used to reassuring children after they've seen such sights—after they've been startled by sleeping bundles of rags at first indistinguishable from the trash by which the sleeper lies, after they've been frightened by aggressively insistent beggars or implacably angry, wild-eyed mutterers pushing refuse-laden shopping carts.

We urban dwellers have had to meditate on sights like these black plastic garbage bags, laid out last night like rotund soldiers in neat platoons of twenty or thirty beside each apartment building. This morning, like so many mornings, they are slashed open, their contents wildly strewn all over the pavement in a sickening riot of rot and disorder.

Dogs? hazarded a visitor from out-of-town.

No. The homeless have been scavenging. Once I saw magazines I had thrown away spread out in rows on a busy sidewalk, offered for sale by a homeless entrepreneur.

Of course it's especially raw in my borderline neighborhood, by turns gentrifying and degentrifying. Here—one block from a park where the homeless live, three blocks from the mostly underclass housing project into whose windows my old apartment looked, around the corner from a crack house—the poor are real, not the figment of a reporter's or advocate's imagination. Just look: you can't help seeing the true texture of life at the bottom.

The evidence of your senses shows you firsthand what scientific studies have been revealing with ever-increasing insistence: the homeless are radically different from the picture the advocates and the press painted all through the eighties and beyond. The fictitious picture is, to be sure, a dramatic attention-grabber. For starters, its scale is heroic: homelessness is a big, big problem. The advocates claim that three million Americans—over 1 percent of the total population—have no roof over their heads. Many more are allegedly so precariously housed that they might find themselves out on the street tomorrow. Already urgent, the homelessness problem can only intensify.

But like so many of the "facts" about the homeless, these numbers are pure fantasy. They were pulled out of the air by the wildest of the advocates, the late Mitch Snyder, a troubled, stubble-bearded radical activist who headed an antiquated Washington antiwar commune grandiosely styled the Community for Creative Non-Violence. The commune sheltered the homeless, and Snyder, available right down the street whenever legislators needed an "expert," was asked by a congressional committee in 1980 exactly how many Americans were homeless. He simply made up a number: exactly 2.2 million fellow citizens, one American out of every hundred, lacked homes, he pronounced. Two years later he upped his estimate to 3 million.

Snyder always declined to debate these figures; getting numbers right, he haughtily remarked, could only concern "Americans with little Western minds that have to quantify everything in sight."

Networks, newsweeklies, and most national dailies readily swallowed this fabrication. For a decade, "three million homeless" became a journalistic mantra.

But this number isn't just false: it is grotesquely, outrageously false. Responsible scientific investigators went out looking for Snyder's huddled masses. Guided by experienced policemen, social workers, and local homeless people, researchers combed major cities after dark, searching out the homeless in alleys, cellars, vacant buildings, thickets, all-night movies, and parked cars, including those rented out at fifty cents a night by an enterprising Washington garage attendant. The evidence they turned up after such diligence suggests a number around *one tenth* of Snyder's—probably 300,000 to 360,000. This is a lot of people, but it is hardly the apocalyptic catastrophe requiring total national mobilization that Snyder and his fellow advocates, supported by a credulous press, have depicted.

It's not merely the size of the problem that the advocates have misrepresented. More important, they have hopelessly muddled the larger question of who the homeless are and how they landed in their deplorable plight. In particular, listening to the advocates' insistence that increasing numbers of the homeless are families rather than unattached individuals, you'd think that Ozzie and Harriet were out on the street with their frightened kids clinging to their knees. Turning on the TV news to see what congressional advocates for the homeless are up to only strengthens that impression. Says advocate Robert Hayes, an ex-Wall Street lawyer who heads the National Coalition for the Homeless: "I can't tell you how often a congressional committee has called and said, 'We need a witness for a hearing. Can you get us a homeless family: mother, father—father out of work in the past four months from an industrial plant—white?'" Though such families can be found among the homeless—and could especially be found in the very early eighties, when the first wave of America's successful industrial restructuring painfully dislocated Rust Belt, logging, and oil patch workers—they are most untypical and are never homeless for long.

The broad intention of this distortion is to make viewers sympathize by identification, even if that entails shading the truth. But within that general intention is a sharply focused political point. Here are mainstream citizens doing everything right but nevertheless struck down by the homelessness plague— as you could be. The advocates have no doubt whatever about the source of the contagion. Says Hayes: "The homeless are indeed the most egregious symbol of a cruel economy, an unresponsive government, a festering value system." They are the victims of a ferocious, unjust economic Darwinism that has made the rich opulently richer at the calamitous expense of the poor, that has swept away jobs through "deindustrialization," that has gentri- fied affordable housing off the face of the earth for the benefit of self-cherishing yuppies. Indeed, the homeless are a moral ther- mometer, registering in their numbers and degradation the ris- ing heartlessness and inequality of the American social order.

By now even the homeless themselves have incorporated these sentiments into their begging jingles. One drug-wasted regular on my downtown subway wove it into a craftily up-to- the-minute fabric of rock music and "concerned" politics as he lurched through the train jingling his cup each morning.

> We got a problem, [he rather woozily sang]
> We gotta address it,
> It needs a so-lu-tion—
> It could happen to you or meeee....

Throughout the eighties, many turned the indictment explic- itly partisan. A Case Western Reserve professor "of family and child welfare," to take only one example, confidently predicted in *The New York Times* a rash of Hoovervilles that he dubbed Reaganvilles. As an academic expert on the homeless, sociolo- gist Peter Rossi, sums up: "The advocates want you to say, 'There but for the grace of God—and the fact that Reagan didn't look at me directly—go I.'"

And then it became George Bush's turn. As columnist Anna Quindlen pronounced. "If empty shelves became a symbol for the failure of Communism in the Soviet Union, people living in cardboard boxes are the most visible sign that America is on the skids. They are living, breathing symbols of an economy that, no matter what the Astigmatism president says, is a mess."

You don't have to live in my neighborhood to know that this whole farrago just isn't so. All you have to do is go home by train or subway and pay attention. What you see, if you stop to look, is craziness, drunkenness, dope, and danger. Far from being the index of the nation's turpitude, the homeless are an encyclopedia of social pathology and mental disorder.

And what has produced homelessness is by no means Reaganomics or yuppification or any other primarily economic dislocation. What the homeless encamped in the streets, parks, and train stations in the heart of our cities really embody is the most extreme and catastrophic failure of the cultural revolution of the Haves and the social policies that resulted from it.

Look at who the homeless really are. The various subgroups of them overlap, so that separating them into categories yields only approximations. But the overall picture is clear.

In outline, it looks like this. Homeless families account for a little over a quarter of all homeless persons. These aren't conventional or ordinary families: put aside the image of Beaver Cleaver and his folks scouring the country for work. Instead, homeless families—almost *all* of them—consist of a single mother and her children. Almost *all* such families are on welfare. Half of them, according to one authoritative study, are headed by women under twenty-five years old, many themselves the illegitimate daughters of single mothers.

Homeless families, in other words, are an extension of the underclass. For the most part, they are headed by a subgroup of welfare mothers who haven't succeeded in keeping a roof over their children's heads. They live in welfare hotels and shelters, and they are homeless not in the sense of having been living on the streets but rather in having been evicted from their own apartments or having been thrown out by friends. Or they have declared themselves homeless—no one checks to see if they really are—in order to get bumped to the head of the waiting list for permanent subsidized housing.

By contrast with homeless families, single homeless individuals are mostly men—at least three of them for each single homeless woman. Not as young as homeless welfare mothers, they are still youngish, with an average age in the mid- to late thirties. A majority of the single homeless are blacks and other minorities, with the proportion of minority persons ranging from 89 percent in New York to 23 percent in Portland, Oregon.

The single homeless are an even more pathological population than the underclass. Around one third of them are alcoholics, and the majority use drugs. In New York City shelters, 65 percent of the homeless singles tested by urinalysis showed positive results for drugs or alcohol, with 83 percent of that group testing positive for cocaine.

A startling number of them are criminals. Checking the records of several homeless beggars recently arrested for misdemeanors in New York's Pennsylvania Station, for example, police were taken aback to discover that two of the men were wanted for murder. Half of those arrested for rape in Santa Monica, California, in 1991 were homeless men. At least 40 percent of the single homeless nationwide have been in jail, for an average of two years. Somewhere between 13 and 26 percent of the incarcerated, depending on which study you pick, served their time for major crimes or felonies. While some of the criminal homeless landed in jail for crimes committed after they became homeless, the majority—63 percent—were criminals first and homeless second. So for most of this group, one can't argue that homelessness drove them to crime. Putting it mildly, all this adds up to something very different from the mainstream impression the advocates have tried to evoke.

It's a tough stretch to follow the advocates in seeing the criminal or drug-taking homeless as victims deserving compassion; but for one of the largest, most conspicuous groups of the homeless, those who are mentally ill, compassion is properly in order. These disturbing figures—the lumpish shopping-bag ladies, the muttering men in rags pushing grocery carts— did not create their deplorable fate. They are the involuntary victims not only of their disease but also of a society that mocks them with a benefit they don't need in place of one they need desperately.

Ten National Institute of Mental Health studies of different large cities consistently show that around one third of the homeless—well over 100,000 souls if the homeless total 350,000—suffer from serious mental illnesses. If anything, the number may be higher: a recent, authoritative psychiatric study of the homeless in Baltimore found that almost half the women and 42 percent of the men suffered from a major mental disorder. Add in alcohol and drug abuse, and you account for 80 percent of the homeless single women and 91 percent of the homeless men in Baltimore. A 1988 Los Angeles study showed that 44 percent of the single homeless in that city had been hospitalized for psychiatric reasons. Two thirds of the New York homeless who live on the streets, rather than in the shelters, are schizophrenic, another study found.

How legions of the mentally disordered ended up on the street, cold, sick, fearful, and in harm's way, is an object lesson in how the cultural revolution worked—how advanced ideas about personal liberation came together with advanced ideas about political enfranchisement to create a climate of opinion and a body of social policy that harmed those at the bottom of society in the name of doing them good. That's why it's especially interesting to look, as we'll do now, at the whole deinstitutionalization debacle, which, from its flawed conception to its disconcertingly unrealistic execution, was the direct expression of key ideas of the cultural revolution of the Haves. Indeed, the very process of rethinking the question of madness and its relation to society was central to the process of formulating the ideology of the cultural revolution, for madness came to stand as a metaphor for the whole instinctive, impulsive, irrational inner life which the Haves sought to liberate in themselves.

Before deinstitutionalization, the state mental hospitals, without question, cried out for reform. The issue became notorious when three thousand World War II conscientious objectors returned to peacetime life after their alternative service as attendants in the mental hospitals of twenty states. They unfolded shocking tales of degradation and inhumanity: of naked men huddled by the hundreds into rooms bare of furniture and foul with excrement, which dirtied the men themselves and the food they ate; of drunken, sometimes sadistic staff members; of substandard nutrition and medical care; of a routine of numbing regimentation and monotony. Barbarous and inhuman, the entire system, they charged, was radically, hopelessly defective.

But not until the introduction of powerful antipsychotic drugs such as Thorazine in the mid-fifties did the problem begin to be addressed. These drugs allowed psychiatrists to treat the symptoms of schizophrenia and other serious mental afflictions well enough to release some patients from the state hospitals. After 1955, the mental institutions began to empty with increasing rapidity.

Antipsychotic drugs could treat only some patients, however, and Thorazine-driven deinstitutionalization would soon enough have come to its limits. Ideology, not pharmacology, pushed deinstitutionalization far beyond those limits and created the ultimate, deplorable fate of the deinstitutionalized.

You can see the new ideas forming and hardening in four books that enormously influenced both the general reading public and the psychiatric profession. Two of the books depicted the inmates of institutions as another victimized group, innocent, powerless, outside the mainstream, oppressed by society at large. Like the Have-Nots, they cried out for liberation. The other two presented their critique of mental institutions as a critique of modern society as a whole, which they saw as spiritually oppressing those who lived in it. Inmates, like the oppressed and victimized in general, are metaphors for the rest of us. They are metaphors for the way life in society squashes all of us harshly into a mold of conformity we don't really fit, suppressing our inner impulses so thoroughly that we end up dessicated, self-estranged, and joyless.

In this metaphorical way, all four books also suggested that both aspects of the cultural revolution—the political liberation of the excluded and the personal liberation of the Haves—were the completing halves of a single, comprehensive liberation. The Haves couldn't be liberated without creating a free social order that would also liberate the Have-Nots. In a similarly metaphorical way, some readers took the next step and inferred that because the American social order requires suppression of impulse, as any society must—and because it has at its disposal means of coercion such as involuntary commitment to asylums, as all societies do—it might in its entirety be as tyrannically unjust as the unreformed state mental hospitals at their worst.

Of the quartet of writers, the most important was Thomas Szasz, a Hungarian-born psychoanalyst and professor of psychiatry. For Szasz, mental illness was nothing more than a protest against oppression. The truth is, he announced in his influential 1961 book, *The Myth of Mental Illness,* there is no such thing as mental illness. "'Mental illness' is [only] a metaphor," he declared. "Minds can be 'sick' only in the sense that jokes are 'sick' or economies are 'sick.'" Strictly speaking, only bodies can be sick.

Unlike the symptoms of real disease, he says, the symptoms of mental illness by no means spring from some physiological dysfunction. Instead, they are messages or communications. Through his symptoms, the patient is making a mute statement, as if holding out a signboard, about his own life problems. Schizophrenics express through their delusions a wish to be great or loved or admired. Hysterics, their physical symptoms lacking any physical cause, are saying: "I would be and do something great—if only I didn't have this paralysis or tremor or pain, which will require someone to take care of me, like a child or an invalid."

Since hysterics and the mentally ill in general are not visited against their will by "sickness," they don't need "treatment." We should respond to them, argues Szasz, as people making statements which we are obliged to hear with respect. Madness thus becomes just one more discourse, saying—if rightly understood—perfectly reasonable things.

But why do the mentally ill put themselves through such contortions to express what's bothering them? Why not just step forward and speak their minds? Szasz's explanation sounds a note that rang with increasing insistence in the elite wisdom that fostered the social pathology of the present.

Madness, he argues, is largely the fault of society, or at least of the powerful classes who control it. For people are compelled to communicate by signs instead of ordinary language when they are subjugated, and fear makes direct statement impossible. They resort to signs when they are afraid of the response of the more powerful superior—be he political panjandrum or plutocrat or even husband—to whom they wish to address a demand for help and support or a criticism for oppression and neglect.

That is why women are so frequently hysterics: until recently, says Szasz, women have been chattels, slaves, only uteri without rights or personhood. In this early statement of the feminist complaint, the liberation of the mad came to symbolize the liberation of the Haves in still another, highly charged way, insofar as feminism has been overwhelmingly a liberation movement of the privileged.

No less powerfully did the liberation of the mad symbolize the political liberation of the Have-Nots. Were not psychotics usually drawn from the very lowest class of society? Szasz asks. That's because, trapped at the bottom, they too fear to speak their minds. In their disease, they are protesting against deprivation, oppression, and lack of opportunity in every sphere. Rightly understood, their psychosis is a political protest, expressed in a way that is safe for them to express it.

To respond by locking them in a madhouse is the ultimate degree of oppression and injustice. Accordingly, we must not permit involuntary hospitalization for so-called mental illness, or any kind of involuntary "treatment" for what is after all an imaginary ailment.

The second book, Berkeley sociologist Erving Goffman's *Asylums,* appeared the same year as Szasz's volume and similarly concluded that treatment for mental illness is really nothing more than the oppression of the marginal and powerless. The book's key point is that mental patients seem as crazy as they do not because they truly are crazy but because the mental hospital itself causes them to look that way. In making that point, Goffman pushed two of the cultural revolution's central ideas to their furthest possible extreme: the idea that character and behavior are nothing but products of the social circumstances in which people are immersed; and the idea that the behavior that springs out of a given set of circumstances is appropriate and natural relative to those circumstances and mustn't be judged by standards of morality or reasonableness that are foreign to the circumstances.

Posing as the sports director's assistant at the Washington, D.C., mental hospital where poet Ezra Pound had once been incarcerated, Goffman plunged into his fieldwork with the devotion of an anthropologist going into the bush to live with "his" primitive tribe. Like an anthropologist, too, Goffman concluded that however strange and barbarous life in the madhouse may appear, it nevertheless adds up to a coherent culture, a "continuously meaningful social world." In the terms of that special world, what an outsider would call "crazy" behavior is in reality appropriate, reasonable, even normal. To see that, though, you need to look sympathetically from within, rather than superciliously from without, blinded by the limiting worldview of your own quite different culture. Cultural relativism, about which Chapter Ten will have more to say, can hardly get more extreme than this.

Because the social world that surrounds mental patients is so freakish, says Goffman, no wonder the behavior those institutions produce in almost all patients, regardless of their psychiatric diagnosis, is so bizarre-looking. Suppose you entered a world that strips you naked upon arrival, separates you from every possession that helps manifest your identity, clothes you in a uniform that brands you a lunatic, arbitrarily inspects your mail or your rectum, makes you spend every waking and sleeping hour in public, labels your whole previous life a failure, takes away your autonomy and freedom, makes you behave alternately like a hypocrite and a child in relation to your keepers, and at any time can decide peremptorily to lock you naked in a padded room with a window through which all can see, or give you shock therapy or even (this is 1961) a lobotomy. What would you be like?

In mental institutions even more than in most other situations, the individual self is almost nothing but the product of its external circumstances. As Goffman puts it: "The self ... is not a property of the person to whom it is attributed, but dwells rather in the pattern of social control that is exerted in connection with the person by himself and those around him. This special kind of institutional arrangement does not so much support the self as constitute it." An inmate and his behavior are what the institution, not the mental disorder, make them.

Suppose too that you were the sort of person that mental hospitals are full of—an alienated, rebellious malcontent, an insolent, uncooperative person prone to snide, under-the-breath comments or petty sabotage and vandalism. Suppose that from your point of view all the "offenses against propriety" that you committed in your preinstitutionalized life were in fact "expressions of disaffection"—"a moral rejection of the communities, establishments, and relationships that have a claim to one's attachment." You will find to your bafflement and frustration that mental hospitals insidiously turn all these acts of rejection into proof that you truly belong in the institution because you really are crazy. No wonder, says Goffman, that some patients end up at such "mad" extremes of rebellion as writing on the walls with excrement.

But short of such extremes, to stigmatize the general run of provokingly rebellious behavior with the label of insanity, as often happens, is not so much a diagnosis as a political judgment. Worse, it is often an "ethnocentric" judgment, presumptuously applying the standards of the psychiatrist's own culture to condemn acts that in terms of the patient's subculture may be perfectly unexceptionable rather than troublesome or inappropriate. When we institutionalize such people, are we not administering nothing but punishment instead of the medical treatment we claim to be giving? Though Goffman differed from Szasz in that he proffered no solution, he stood shoulder to shoulder with Szasz in leaving readers with the sense that here was a large, oppressive political wrong against those outside the mainstream—a wrong sorely needing to be set right.

Moreover, the implication of what Goffman had to say went far beyond the mad to embrace the marginal and disaffected in general, especially among those Have-Nots who felt themselves to be outside the mainstream and who were falling into the newly emerging underclass. Surely their pathological behavior was nothing but the product of the unfavorable circumstances to which the Haves had unjustly consigned them. Surely the Haves are wrong to judge or punish that behavior; they ought to set about changing the extreme and degrading social circumstances that produced the extreme behavior as swiftly as possible.

The mass audience that missed getting such notions direct from Szasz and Goffman got an unforgettable version of them one year later from Ken Kesey's best-selling novel, *One Flew Over the Cuckoo's Nest.* Like Goffman, Kesey had done fieldwork, as a psychiatric aide in the Menlo Park, California, V.A. hospital. The claustral, totalitarian world Goffman described took on even more vivid actuality in Kesey's sometimes overwrought pages, which depict psychiatric treatment as simply a program of manipulation, control, humiliation, and torture.

Set in an Oregon mental hospital, Kesey's book follows the career of his almost preternaturally sane hero, a game, laid-back, optimistic Paul Bunyan figure. An idealized embodiment of the personal liberation the Haves were groping toward in their cultural revolution, Kesey's hero can find pleasure anywhere. He likes cards, drink, freedom, people, a good joke, and a good laugh. He has a vast, ingenuous, attractive tolerance for others and a comfortable, unembarrassed acceptance of his own impulsive inner life. He is brave without malice. Most important for Kesey is his matter-of-factly uninhibited sexual life; with its frank, unkinky liking for women and its easygoing mutuality and decency, it is wholly life-enhancing. He's in the advance guard of the sexual revolution that loomed so large in the Haves' quest for personal liberation.

Kesey's hero is above all an emblem of what happens to the freedom of impulse in a society yet to be liberated. Having feigned madness not to escape the Vietnam draft but to get transferred from jail to what he thought would be easier time in the nuthouse, Kesey's hero finds himself in a nightmare allegory of social institutions in general. As Kesey sees it, and as his audience readily understood it, the asylum is a metaphor for the social order itself—a vast, implacable engine dedicated to regimenting and tyrannizing over people, forcing them to fear, to conform, to be hypocritical, to suppress their impulses and hate themselves, robbing them of freedom, pleasure, and individuality.

The malevolent authorities in this fictional madhouse dote only on the smoothly purring operation of their totalitarian system. Mechanical, inhuman, as inscrutable, arbitrary, and pigheaded as the corporate, bureaucratic order itself, the system, like a juggernaut, must roll over each messy human need or expression of individuality or reluctance to conform that gets in its way and that would slow down anything less inexorable. Any manifestation of health, quirky and self-assertive in the natural human way, is antithetical to the system and inevitably gets stamped out in this least salubrious of all environments.

The people Kesey's hero meets in the mental hospital have already been squashed in their previous lives by social or parental oppression. They are people in whom the life-affirming impulses—spontaneity, optimism, openness, humor, playfulness, sexual potency, and that self-respecting masculine authority that Kesey would cheerfully call "balls"—have been crushed. Instead of trying to help regenerate those energies, whose proper function is all that being healthy really means for Kesey, mental institutions, being only an intensification of life outside the walls, just deepen the victimization.

Instinctively, Kesey's life-loving hero tries to make the patients into men again, stirring them up to laughter and rebellion, even smuggling in an ideally cuddly tart to give them what Kesey, in his briskly simplistic way, thinks they really need. The institutional authorities find it provocative enough that Kesey's hero asserts his own healthy humanity and tries to restore his fellow inmates to theirs. Worse, he succeeds in showing the authorities—who have retained their own vital energies in the only way one can in the modern world, by channeling them into life-denying rigidity—that they too are compounded of common human flesh, vulnerable to mortality and desire. For these fundamental challenges, the sadistic institutional brass inevitably resolve to destroy him. Their threats and intimidation don't faze Kesey's almost invulnerable superhero, nor do multiple shock treatments; it ultimately takes lobotomy.

The condemnation of the entire social order that lurked, implicitly for the most part, within Szasz's, Goffman's, and Kesey's books became thunderingly explicit in the last of the works that clinched the case for deinstitutionalization. An instant classic of elite culture when it appeared in 1967, *The Politics of Experience*, by Glasgow-born British psychoanalyst R. D. Laing, didn't just bring these ideas sharply into focus but took them about as far as they could go. In the process, Laing depicted with unprecedented urgency the kind of inner liberation that the Haves were seeking.

Profoundly disturbed, in Laing's judgment, modern man has been twisted out of shape by a social order given over entirely to materialism and mechanical rationality. A process of education and acculturation that amounts to soul-murder has alienated him from the intuitive, ecstatic, sacred elements that are essential components of the human spirit. He has been stamped with an artificial sense of a separate, distinct ego that cuts him off from all other men. Little wonder that today his normal condition is an unassuageable sense of forlorn estrangement; he has lost a part, perhaps the truest part, of his innermost self.

Surely, a social order that blinds and disfigures all who participate in it is, in the most literal sense, insane. We who are well adjusted to it can hardly be called sane.

Man needs to recover his inner self and his wholeness. Madmen often are trying to do just that: they are engaged in a journey toward that valuable realm the rest of us have lost. Their "unreason" is in truth a higher reason: they know that the rational, mechanical modern order can't be ultimate reality. But as they strive through their madness to reach wholeness, they frequently grow confused, unable to reach the goal they but dimly perceive: hence their symptoms of mental disorder.

Who are we to say that their madness is worse than ours? In our mad society, how can we—insanely believing our disfigured selves to be normal—put the most sane in madhouses?

With his prophetic tone and belief in a lost world of unseen immensities more real than the mechanistic, unhallowed world we inhabit, Laing harks back to his fellow Scot, the Victorian sage Thomas Carlyle, and beyond that to the Romantic poets Wordsworth and William Blake. From that venerable tradition, for instance, comes his assertion that education casts shades of the prisonhouse upon childhood, effacing our intimations of immortality. Ringing equally with Calvinism and cannabis, Laing's extravagant discourse is made up of the shreds and patches of powerfully moving old truths, sadly debased in their Laingian incarnation.

But in the sixties, elite opinion found it very exciting. Psychiatrists, policymakers, intellectuals, even college kids embraced

Laing and his fellow debunkers of mental illness. The young found Laing especially thrilling for his implicit endorsement of the drug-altered consciousness with which the most advanced seekers of personal liberation were then experimenting. Opinion makers gladly acquiesced in smudging the sometimes fine but always discernible line between madness and sanity, reason and unreason. They readily mistrusted the competence and good faith with which social authorities make such fundamental discriminations, sometimes impugning reason itself as a fiction used to injure the already oppressed.

They accepted without resistance the view that reason is relative, defined by nothing but culture and politics. They entertained the idea that the utterances of the mad, cutting through the evasions and hypocrisies of cultural life like the boy who said that the emperor had no clothes, might be a kind of truth. They toyed with the conceit that mental patients are political prisoners, that liberating the asylums might be analogous to liberating the Bastille—and symbolic of freeing all the vital, natural impulses locked within every sane, civilized, repressed mind. They seriously considered that madness might be merely an "alternative life-style," a liberated, iconoclastic approach to living no less reasonable and valid than the various countercultural experiments in living that were at the cutting edge of the inner liberation of the Haves. They suspected that psychiatry—like other established institutions—might be a form of thought control, forcing people to have acceptable, all-American sentiments rather than the then-emergent countercultural views.

As such ideas gathered strength, they went a long way toward delegitimizing involuntary institutionalization—or any involuntary treatment—of the mentally ill. But at the end of the day they were real lunatics who were actually released, often into cruel homelessness.

Fueled by ideas like these, freighted with symbolism, deinstitutionalization got under way in earnest in the early sixties. The National Institute of Mental Health, created in 1946 to solve the crisis in the asylums but slow to devise a plan, finally issued its first major pronouncement, pointing the way to making these ideas reality. Though NIMH's statement had been ready in 1960, the commissioners—overwhelmingly liberal

Democrats, as surveys show psychiatrists as a group to be—
withheld it until 1961 to see if John Kennedy would win the
presidency. They rightly judged that he'd give their proposal a
sympathetic ear, according to psychiatrist E. Fuller Torrey, a special assistant to NIMH's director from 1970 to 1975 and author
of *Nowhere to Go,* an absorbing account of the deinstitutionalization saga.

NIMH, Torrey recounts, recommended that no new state
hospitals should be built, and no patients should be added to
those already crowded. Instead of letting such institutions anchor
the nation's mental health care system, a new network of some
3,600 community mental health clinics should arise. Tacked
on to general or state hospitals, they would treat acute mental
illness and look after released asylum patients. Quickly diagnosed, patients could avoid hospitalization, which according
to the Goffman-inspired new orthodoxy makes people sicker.
They would benefit from the social stimulation of living in the
community—though it was unclear why the patient would benefit from being in the environment that, psychiatric orthodoxy
held, had helped cause his problem in the first place.

But it all made sense to Kennedy. In 1963, he persuaded
Congress to establish community mental health centers for the
seriously mentally ill, hoping to halve the number of patients
confined to grim custodial institutions within a decade or two.

Anointed official policy, hailed by elite opinion as a liberation for the mentally ill and for society as a whole, deinstitutionalization swelled the flow of patients out of the mental hospitals that Thorazine had begun. The number of state hospital
inmates fell by almost 200,000 in the sixties and another 205,000
in the seventies. From 1955 to 1984, the nation's state hospitals mothballed 80 percent of their half-million beds. As state
hospitals shrank or closed, New York State alone axed 71,000
beds.

The first patients put blinking and bewildered outside the
walls did alright. Either they really were well enough to scrape
by, or they had families to look after them. But by the late sixties, the hard-core sick began to get pushed out of the back
wards where they'd vegetated for years. Some moved into board-
inghouses catering to released mental patients, where conditions

often matched the cruelty and squalor of Dotheboys Hall, Dickens's hellish school for unwanted children. In 1979, police rescued twenty-one ex-patients from four such houses in Queens, New York, where they had been kept as virtual prisoners in gulag-style filth, cold, and misery. Deinstitutionalized patients in a fifth house were found sharing quarters with the decomposing corpse of one of their fellows.

Others of the deinstitutionalized ended up in single-room-occupancy hotels, or SROs—seedy urban rooming houses with private rooms but shared toilets. At first, the SROs yawned wide with vacancies, and by the mid-seventies a quarter of the 100,000 residents of New York City's SROs were severely mentally dysfunctional persons. But then urban revival and gentrification began to sweep away SROs, putting many of the already fragile deinstitutionalized, too dysfunctional to earn the rent of slightly more expensive housing, out on the street. Atlanta has now torn down eleven of its twelve SROs for new office construction; since 1978, urban renewal has swallowed about a third of San Diego's SRO units.

Downtown Los Angeles's skid row is a microcosm of the process. Now-booming wholesale fish dealers and toy importers who have always been there are expanding from within. From the north, Little Tokyo is encroaching, and a new state office building has bitten a chunk out of the northwest. From the southwest, a gentrified residential neighborhood is pushing in, while a huge regional wholesale produce and flower center has opened to the southeast. Down by the river to the east, artists have brightened up a dingy warehouse area and moved in. What's left of once-cheap housing is cheap no more. An SRO room, $100 a month in 1980, now costs $200, with the result that some residents live there for two or three weeks and then move into a homeless shelter for the remainder of the month when their money runs out.

Shrinkage in low-cost housing was hardly the primary problem that the deinstitutionalized faced. The very foundation stone of the theory on which deinstitutionalization was based was that the severely mentally ill could live in the community *if* they received adequate outpatient psychiatric care and supervision in taking the medication that kept them out of the wilder abysses of craziness. This care they never got—thanks to yet another wrinkle in the newly emergent ideology of the Haves.

True, community mental health centers were built. True, they had been intended to provide just such services to just these patients. But the centers, once established, neither served those clients nor provided those services, as NIMH officials knew from early on. A third of the centers had no emergency services at all; another third had laughably inadequate ones. Only 6 percent had day hospitals, essential for seriously ill patients needing partial hospitalization. Half had no inpatient beds whatever, making a mockery of the original theory that long commitment to state hospitals would give way to short, stabilizing stays in the community centers. Between 1968 and 1978, an almost negligible fraction of that paltry provision of beds—never more than 6.5 percent—was filled by persons who had been released from public mental hospitals. And in writing regulations for the community mental health centers, NIMH brass forgot to require a working relationship between the centers and the state mental asylums whose ex-patients the centers were to supervise.

What went wrong? Above all, the community mental health centers, even before the first one opened its doors in 1967, had been hijacked by Great Society, pie-in-the-sky, cultural revolution thinking. In an era when everything was believed possible if only Government set its heart on doing it, psychiatrists decided that government-supported mental health centers, instead of accomplishing so mundane a goal as keeping the seriously mad from being overwhelmed by their disease, on the public streets, would provide American society with mental health.

Psychiatry doesn't know how to do that, and the plan the centers dreamed up smacked less of psychiatry than of social work, even social activism, of the standard-issue sixties variety. Bad social conditions cause mental illness, as up-to-the-minute, Goffman-inspired NIMH panjandrums saw it, and poverty is the most pathogenic social condition of them all, with inequality a close second. Mental illness in some fundamental sense isn't really an individual matter: an individual's mental state (as Goffman would say) largely reflects the social and economic circumstances that surround him, just as culture and ideas are said to be no more than the passive reflections of economic reality. It's vain to expect individual mental health where you don't have community mental health. As NIMH's planning chief put it in 1968: "The individual's mental health is formed by the total society in which he exists." Here again the two liberations sought by the Haves—the outer and the inner—are seen as inseparable.

Mental illness is rife today because society is itself sick, as the Kesey-Laing-Szasz refrain would have it. "The city ... is in pain," NIMH's planner explained: "It has symptoms that cry out for relief. They are ... anger, violence, poverty, and hopelessness.... The totality of urban life is the only rational focus for concern with mental illness ... our problem now embraces all of society...."

The mental health profession, this NIMH official declared, should be a "change agent in society," helping to "construct a social system that produces mentally healthy individuals." Accordingly, stated the director of NIMH, community mental health centers would "share with other community leaders in environmental manipulation to eliminate known producers of stress," an unproblematic undertaking now that modern enlightenment has removed from such ideas "the overtones of quackery which have in the past been attributed to them."

And sure enough, community mental health centers began to busy themselves hectoring landlords of slum housing, setting up remedial education courses, registering the poor to vote so they could cast their ballots for social hygiene, and counseling the worried but mentally sound on how to preserve their mental health. A Los Angeles mental health center, its director crowed, helped make the community safe for mental health by circulating a petition and successfully lobbying city officials to get a traffic light installed at a busy crossing near a school. Presumably freed from anxiety that Junior would be flattened by a truck, parents could enjoy a brief moment of tranquillity before learning to worry about whether he'd be blown away at McDonald's by an untreated paranoid schizophrenic with an assault rifle.

It's often said that deinstitutionalization failed because not enough community mental health centers were built, and indeed only 789 centers, fewer than half the scaled-down goal of 2,000, ever went into operation. But as psychiatrist E. Fuller Torrey says in *Nowhere to Go,* if those that were built don't do the job, more of them wouldn't do it better but would only fail to do it on a grander, costlier scale—like so many of the social policy efforts of the last thirty years. More centers would only mean more half-baked social activism and more taxpayer-supported marriage counseling and crisis counseling of what Torrey labels the worried well, rather than treatment of the deep-dyed crazy, whom the mental health profession came to despise for their unsightly, incorrigible affront to mental hygiene. Promising a Great Society, as Torrey mordantly concludes, the whole community mental health center movement delivered a grate one.

Powerfully swept along by the seemingly irresistible intellectual current rushing toward deinstitutionalization, state mental hospital directors found additional incentive to empty their institutions among the myriad unintended consequences of Great Society programs. Such programs as Medicare, Medicaid, Supplemental Security Income, and Social Security Disability Insurance made federal benefits available to the mentally ill living in nursing homes, group residences, even in general hospitals—but not in state mental institutions. States pounced gleefully on the opportunity to transfer the cost of treating mental illness from their own coffers to those of the federal government. State hospital administrators found themselves evaluated for raises on how well they succeeded in dumping their patients into federal hands and how skillfully they constructed Kafkaesque barriers to readmission. If patients ended up worse off—like the lice- and maggot-infested homeless psychotic discharged from a Pennsylvania state asylum who couldn't get readmitted and who was found dead behind a Philadelphia crisis center, his feet eaten by rats—that was too bad.

But ultimately, and most ironically, the states saved almost nothing by these machinations. While closing wings, buildings, even some whole institutions and cutting the patient population 66 percent between 1969 and 1981, most state hospitals balked at firing staff, whose salaries eat up three quarters of the budgets of those institutions. In some states, such as New York, the number of employees perversely rose even as the number of patients precipitously declined. As a result, in constant dollars, aggregate state mental hospital expenditures fell an almost negligible 3 percent during the period. Meanwhile, federal expenditure on the seriously mentally ill skyrocketed, so that the total government tab—including federal, state, and local spending—zoomed from $1 billion in 1963 to just over $17 billion in 1985. Adjusted both for inflation and for the number of patients, that's a fourfold increase. However mind-boggling, it did the truly crazy not a scintilla of good, for it bought them generally worse accommodations and much less psychiatric treatment than they had received from the asylums.

CHAPTER FIVE

Homelessness and Liberty

The destruction the psychiatrists began, the civil liberties lawyers completed, sacrificing the mentally ill homeless on the altar of an idea of liberty and liberation exaggerated to the point of fanaticism and caricature. In all their efforts on behalf of the homeless, the sane as well as the crazy, the lawyers illustrated how radically the ideal of liberation at the heart of the cultural revolution could, taken to excess, harm both the oppressed who were to be liberated and the Haves who proposed to liberate them. But this was the typical stance of the civil liberties bar: of all the elites spearheading the cultural revolution, none more consistently pressed the new ideology to its logical extreme, however absurd or fatal.

Certainly the lawyers snuffed out any lingering possibility that the state hospitals and the community mental health centers might treat the vast majority of the seriously mentally ill. Bruce J. Ennis, head of the New York Civil Liberties Union's campaign for deinstitutionalization, had read Thomas Szasz and was fired with righteous enthusiasm. Here was a cause to fight for! Determined to make Szasz's vision a reality, he exhorted his troops that their "goal should be nothing less than the abolition of involuntary hospitalization." Coupling the doctrine of Goffman and Kesey to the dogma of Szasz, another civil liberties crusader averred that patients "are better off outside a hospital.... The hospitals are what really do damage to people."

It took the lawyers less than a decade to win total victory. In 1971, a judge ruled, in effect, that patients can't be hospitalized against their will unless they receive adequate psychiatric treatment, which requires a minimum ratio of staff to patients. To achieve those ratios, some states chose to dump patients into the street rather than increase staff. In 1972, another judge established the now-standard criterion that people can be forcibly hospitalized only if dangerous to themselves or others. A third judge ruled in 1975 that patients must be treated in the "least restrictive setting," meaning that, if even minimally possible, they must be treated outside state hospital walls. Finally, yet another court held in 1979 that a psychiatric patient can refuse treatment, period.

The mentally ill, and society at large, paid dearly for these victories. With civil liberties lawyers pressuring them constantly, judges and psychiatrists have generally required someone to come within a whisker of killing himself or his neighbor before invoking the danger-to-himself-or-others standard. In the interval, the untreated mad have endured and inflicted a multitude of suffering.

For instance, a schizophrenic in Wisconsin, mute and refusing food, ate excrement instead. But he was seen eating it *only once*, his public defender protested; could the doctor on the witness stand swear that *one time* would inevitably harm someone? No? Case for committal dismissed. In Washington, D.C., police brought an attractive young woman panhandler, incoherent and hallucinating, to the hospital, where the examining psychiatrist judged her no danger to herself and released her. She was raped and murdered in an alley a few days later.

Such extreme examples aside, are not the mentally ill suffering harm simply by being left to wander uncared for, as madmen haven't in civilized countries since before the Enlightenment? Isn't it harm for them to be routinely abandoned to the condition of homelessness in which we find them on every urban thoroughfare: the paranoid bag ladies with their swollen legs and rag-wrapped feet, the gauntly wasted schizophrenic men on their pilgrimage from one garbage can to another in search of cans and bottles?

Incompetent to care for their health, they are riddled with disease: in one study, doctors found the homeless afflicted on average with eight or nine different physical ailments, and doctors at a clinic in a New York homeless shelter discovered that 43 percent of their patients tested positive for tuberculosis between 1982 and 1988. More recently, the difficult-to-treat strain of TB that has become epidemic among the homeless has made their ill health a sharp concern of everyone.

The community at large inflicts much of this harm by withholding treatment: with medication for their psychoses, many of the homeless mentally ill don't *have* to suffer so. For proof, look at St. Francis House, a Manhattan residence for such people run as an SRO by Franciscans, helped by a part-time nurse and social worker and some part-time volunteer psychiatrists. Meet Stan, a round-faced, alert resident, thirtyish and infectiously cheerful, who earnestly tells you that all that people like him need are some good job-training programs. You might be inclined to believe him if you met him somewhere else; here, the restless look in his eyes gives you pause, and when he explains that midwesterners like him think that the voices he hears are divine, not disease, you know it's not training that he needs.

A year and a half before I met him, a psychiatric outreach program had found Stan living under a bridge in New York's Riverside Park, by no means cheerful or engaging, bolstered up and armored against the world's hostility with multitudinous layers of coats and hats. Six months of slow wooing coaxed him out of his burrow into an office; more months of coaxing persuaded him to see the psychiatrist. Then he improved steadily on antipsychotic drugs. Says his psychiatrist: "He shed those layers of clothing like he was shedding his psychosis." Treatment for him as for the mentally ill in general isn't torture, but rather much-needed help.

True, he still isn't all there. True, like most St. Francis House residents, he spends lots of time lounging around his shabby neighborhood; he forages for empty cans: his isn't a life you'd choose. But it is at least a human existence, far better than the almost animal state from which he was rescued.

Before his deliverance, imprisoned in his coats and hats, Stan embodied the homelessness problem at its most visible and pitiable. Afflicted, frightened, and needy, the mentally ill like Stan are the people most of us have in mind, consciously or not, when we talk about helping the homeless. Many of this group are the deinstitutionalized, most discharged between 1975 and 1987, when the mental asylum population fell by 86,000 and homelessness became a national problem. But perhaps even greater in number are the younger of the seriously mentally ill, who—thanks to the successes of the civil liberties lawyers—have never been diagnosed or medicated, much less institutionalized, and who often make themselves sicker by dosing themselves with the readily available street dope or alcohol that temporarily quiets the voices they hear.

The mentally ill homeless—all 100,000 to 150,000 of them—can be helped, as Stan's case shows, but clearly the public housing programs touted by the homeless advocates as the number one solution to homelessness won't do them an iota of good. Faced with a mental health care system in shambles after a quarter century of liberal "innovation"—despite an annual government mental health expenditure of $17 billion that never reaches them—they need mental health care that works.

Voluntary institutions like St. Francis House, offering treatment and supervised living, provide an exemplary model, at a cheap fourteen or fifteen dollars a day per resident, plus five dollars a week for medicine. The nation's 789 community mental health centers, redirected toward their original purpose and backed by vigorous outreach programs, could care for most of the mentally ill homeless who can take their medicine and live uninstitutionalized. The state hospitals that still function can treat those who need institutionalization, either permanently or periodically.

State hospitals are essential institutions. If they were often inhumane before deinstitutionalization, they should have been reformed, not abolished. Today, they should be diversified by having supervised living facilities and outpatient mental health clinics added to them, taking advantage of an already existing plant and staff. And all public mental health agencies, instead of allowing patients to drop into the cracks between them, need to work closely together in a network.

But none of this can be accomplished without the difficult distinctions a civilized society must make between nonconformity and madness, and without forcibly caring for those for whom liberty means the freedom to suffer outdoors in rags, covered with sores and railing incoherently at torments both imaginary and real. At an absolute minimum, the harm-to-oneself-or-others formula needs to be applied with realism rather than with today's airy faith that somehow the degradation rampant on the street is a constitutionally protected "alternative life-style." The homeless mentally ill are not sixties street people, insisting on the freedom to march to the beat of a different drummer, in defiance of the middle-class conventionality of their upbringing. They are not bravely living out the Beatles' battle cry of sixties liberation, "Why don't we do it in the road?"

If anything, realism needs to be even more clear-sighted with the harm-to-others part of the formula than with the harm-to-oneself part. Neglect is not just inhumane but sometimes dangerous, for the untreated mentally ill commit crime much more often than their sane fellow citizens, and much of it is violent. The criminal mentally ill and the homeless mentally ill are frequently the same people, as can be inferred from the fact that 40 percent of the homeless have done jail time—for offenses other than vagrancy, since the vagrancy laws are virtually unenforced today. And if you are troubled that more Americans with serious mental illnesses are homeless than institutionalized, you will also be troubled to find as many of them in jail as in public mental asylums.

Instead of shuttling between the prison and the streets, would it not be better for this group of the homeless mentally ill to be receiving treatment in a mental hospital? Unquestionably it would be better for the rest of us if we didn't have to wait for them not merely to do wrong but actually to spill blood before they are treated, as the lawyer-created criterion for involuntary committal seems to require.

I have in mind people like the "overtly psychotic woman who was walking the streets carrying an axe," whom psychiatrist E. Fuller Torrey, based on a long experience of treating schizophrenia, asked the Washington police to commit. "They refused," Torrey writes in *Nowhere to Go,* "saying that she had not done anything with her axe."

I have in mind the man Debra Sanchez saw one spring day in 1986 when she was sitting with her children in a park in upper Manhattan. He was screaming. Striding to her bench, he screamed at her and her children, screamed about killing. Her children terrified, Sanchez asked a policeman who happened by whether the man could be taken away. "No," the policeman replied, "these guys from the homeless shelter are harmless. Don't worry about the yelling."

A month later Sanchez saw the harmless screamer on the front pages of the New York papers: he had killed two and wounded nine with a sword on the Staten Island ferry. Psychiatrists had evaluated him a few days earlier as a psychotic paranoid, after he'd been raving that he was going to kill, as God and Jesus had commanded him. Instead of committing him, the doctors released him, two days before he obeyed his delusional orders.

I have in mind the immensely tall, bean pole–skinny man who screamed night after night for months across the street from my bedroom window. Carrying his limbs and torso more like mechanical parts bolted together than like flesh and blood, jerkily bending from the waist like a jackknife to roll and scoop up a pair of dice with a compulsive fervor, he would begin screaming around midnight, in such a powerfully stentorian voice and with so unmistakable a charge of hatred and aggression that despite the indecipherable gibberish of his words his screaming curdled the blood. If you were asleep, he woke you up. He woke up your children, and made them quail with fright. He screamed at passersby while following beside them for half a block or so, his anger-contorted face pressing toward them.

Then he began pushing passersby, almost punching them. One day I saw him reach toward a youth just rounding the corner hand in hand with his girlfriend and grab him by the private parts. The police, called often, would move him around the corner or down the block for ten minutes; occasionally they'd take him to the hospital psychiatrists, who'd release him in an hour or two.

One night I went down when I saw policemen bundling him into a squad car for a visit to the hospital. Perhaps they might describe the pushing and grabbing to the doctors, I suggested, and tell them that he seemed to be a decompensating schizophrenic? Perhaps they might even mention that the hospital that had released the Staten Island ferry murderer had been reprimanded and fined by a disciplinary body the day before? I never saw—or (thank God) heard—him again. But this was after six months of nightly visitation. I never found out what happened to him; the hospital would release information only to immediate family members.

I have in mind, too, the farcical case of Joyce Brown, who called herself Billie Boggs, after a local TV talk-show host with whom she fancied herself in love. In late 1986, Brown, then thirty-nine, took up residence on a heating grate on Manhattan's Second Avenue. For almost a year, she screamed an avalanche of obscenity at passersby, particularly at men who, like herself, were black. "Kiss my black ass, you motherfucking nigger," she would scream, lifting her skirt and shaking her bare buttocks at them. "Kiss my black ass! Come suck my big black dick!"

As if braving the bulls at Pamplona, she ran out into Second Avenue and dodged the traffic. She stank enough to make you gag. She urinated against the wall of the Chemical Bank; spreading out a paper napkin, wrapping a sheet around her with the remnants of modesty, she moved her bowels onto the sidewalk for the bank's janitor to clean up at the start of his day's work. She panhandled for quarters, enragedly shredding or burning any bank note the charitable might give her with misguided munificence. Once she reportedly attacked an old man who offered her a dollar, raining punches upon his head. Another time, taking a swing at one of the black men she was cursing, she got the worst of a slugfest.

Raised in a hardworking New Jersey family, she'd been badly troubled since high school. At eighteen, she was addicted to heroin and cocaine. Convicted of heroin possession and jailed on another occasion for assault, she compiled a police record that notes charges of larceny, property damage, and disturbing the peace. Though she was hearing voices, talking to herself, and screaming at people by the time she was thirty, she still worked full-time as a city hall secretary in New Jersey until her bizarre behavior got her fired in 1984. Her paychecks—and, later, her disability checks—went mostly for drugs, not rent. Evicted in 1983, she sponged off her long-suffering sisters until they gave up and threw her out, as did both the homeless shelters she turned to thereafter.

Once she landed on Second Avenue, she caught the eye of New York's then-mayor, Edward Koch. City of stupefying extremes, New York didn't require that someone be merely a danger-to-himself-or-others before he could be committed; he must be an "imminent" danger. Koch, seeking to loosen the standard to "danger in the foreseeable future," remembered seeing Joyce Brown and thought of her as a prime test case for his new standard. A city agency in due course brought her to Bellevue Hospital; a psychiatrist admitted her.

With such rationality as she still possessed, she lost no time in calling in the New York Civil Liberties Union.

At her commitment hearing, the city, backed by expert testimony that Brown was severely insane, argued that she was a danger to herself, slowly dying from self-neglect. The NYCLU saw her predicament with different eyes. In its view, she was the victim of a city drive to hide evidence of its failed housing policy. Her only lapse: affronting the aesthetic sensibilities of New York's Haves, to whom the mayor was obsequiously pandering.

Abnormal? the NYCLU's expert witness demanded. Not Joyce Brown. Do not cabdrivers also pee on the street? Does not every modern movie use bad language? Hadn't protesters burned draft cards, just as Brown—presumably in a similar protest against materialist America's oppressiveness—symbolically burned dollar bills? Brown, taking the stand with the cool lucidity she was able to muster when her attention was focused on something other than her inner voices, declared herself a "professional" street person, exquisitely competent to ensure her own welfare.

The judge, an ex-Legal Aid lawyer who'd spent a career as an advocate for the poor, found that, while the psychiatric experts canceled out each other's testimony, Brown's own poised behavior moved him to release her as no risk to others or herself and as "not unable to care for her essential needs." Her problems and those of others like her, he observed, must be laid at the door of the city's immoral housing policies. "The blame and shame," he piously concluded, "must attach to us, not to them."

The day Brown was finally released into the arms of her NYCLU lawyers, she kept repeating, as if she'd studied Szasz and company, "I was not insane; I was homeless. I was a political prisoner." A month later, having made the rounds of the TV talk shows, she was the guest speaker at a Harvard Law School forum on "The Homeless Crisis: A Street View." "We need housing, housing, and more housing," she declared. "My only problem was that I didn't have a place to live, and that's the city's fault." Scarcely two weeks later, she was back on the street, screaming and panhandling again. Lack of affordable housing, it is clear, played no part whatever in landing her there, this time or any other.

Slowly dying from self-neglect? "Not unable to care for her essential needs"? Wait a minute! Surely this is not the point. The fact is, this lady was a public menace. All day long, her screaming disturbed the peace, a crime. She regularly exposed herself lewdly, a crime. She physically harassed passersby, a crime. She turned the street into a toilet, a violation of the city's administrative code. Killing your fellow citizens with a sword isn't the only way of being a danger to others. You can also fling down and dance upon the whole fabric of commonplace laws and regulations that make our life in common possible. Yet it's not hard to understand why the police left Joyce Brown or the screamer under my window alone, instead of hauling them off to jail. These aren't criminals but madmen, and the police were properly reluctant to criminalize insanity, which calls for treatment, not punishment.

"Freedom is slavery" was *Nineteen Eighty-Four's* totalitarian cry; but listening to the civil libertarian activists attacking the institutionalization and treatment of the insane homeless in the name of liberty, you hear the message that "slavery is freedom." Is it not a despicable notion that it is freedom to be left enslaved to madness, to the absence of rationality that is the basis for human freedom—that it is freedom to rave and defecate on the street, to be left untreated and afraid? Is it not a cruel satire of civil liberty to assert that those incapable of rational choice must be left free to choose?

It is painful that so much of what the civil libertarian advocates have said about homelessness and freedom—not just as regards the insane homeless but the homeless in general—has been so dismayingly, almost perversely, obtuse about what makes freedom possible that it has ended up chipping away at the very foundations of freedom. Take, for instance, the civil libertarians' campaign to establish the freedom of the homeless to sleep and beg and carry on their lives in such public spaces as parks and train and subway stations. Could Aristotle or John Stuart Mill walk through the menacing knots of homeless in the Manhattan subway stations, could Madison and Hamilton survey the debased squalor of the Grand Central waiting room, what incredulous horror would they not express at the distorted version of democratic liberty grotesquely on display there. Freedom, they understood, grows out of the social order; for without laws, policemen, and civility to protect it against brute force, freedom is valueless.

These public places—the grand, columned train stations, the metropolitan parks—are powerful embodiments of the democratic social order: splendid constructions made by communal effort not for the pleasure of kings and aristocrats but for dignifying the ordinary lives of ordinary people. That for a decade train riders have had to hurry through the stench of waste and atmosphere of threat with averted eyes, that park users have had to steer clear of the tents of the mad and keep their children out of the tall grass for fear of AIDS-contaminated needles discarded by homeless drug users—these are scandals that starkly symbolize how far an extreme, specious "liberation" has succeeded in eroding the boundaries of the social order that guarantees true liberty.

In the end, what but this erosion have the successes of the advocates for the homeless really accomplished? It is a gloomy question to consider. Who has profited by allowing the homeless to occupy and debase public places? Indeed, who has benefited by public shelter systems, established in response to litigation by advocates for the homeless and open to all comers?

Not the homeless mentally ill, as we've seen. Advocates have won them the right to deinstitutionalization and the right to public shelter. And now? Behold the homeless insane in one unit of Manhattan State Hospital, closed as an asylum and reopened as a homeless shelter. Some of the same people who were patients here in the old days are in residence today—but now they get no treatment. A big advance. But many of the homeless mentally ill don't even like to use the shelters, fearing them as dangerous.

Take away the mentally ill, who did not benefit, and who is left? The biggest contingent is that miscellaneous collection of alcoholics, drug users, petty criminals, and dropouts who used to be called bums. Some of these are the predaceous people who make the shelters dangerous for the mentally ill. Yet because they have been lumped together with the mentally ill into the catchall category of "homeless," they have received some of the sympathy that the obvious distress and helplessness of the homeless mentally ill have aroused for homeless people in general. Were the insane homeless to receive proper care—which would deliver them from homelessness—public sympathy for the remaining homeless would chill precipitously and appropriately.

Besides, is it really a favor to alcoholics or drug users to give them the run of the train stations and to provide them a shelter system at a staggering public cost—a third of a billion dollars a year in New York City alone? To tell sometimes surly, even threatening, drunks or druggies that they are embodiments of First Amendment freedom as they overrun public spaces is to encourage them in wrongdoing and self-destruction.

When large numbers of shelter users turn out to be addicts—as were three quarters of the residents of a South Bronx shelter studied by a Columbia University anthropologist—isn't the shelter system a massive subsidy that makes it easier to persist in alcoholism and drug abuse? When people with jobs turn up in homeless shelters, it's often not because they can't find affordable housing, despite the claims of the advocates, but rather because they prefer to spend their wages on drugs and let the public house them.

In Philadelphia shelters, before recent reforms, drug-using parents not only took free housing but also commonly traded thirty dollars' worth of food stamps for ten dollars worth of crack. Why not, since the shelter would feed their children? As a matter of policy, the state ought not to abet people in self-destructive courses, as it now does in shelter systems that in big cities have become the subbasement of underclass life, ministering much more often to vice than to victimization.

Worse, a society that defines people ruining their lives through drink or drugs primarily as bearers of the inalienable right to turn the public realm into a realm of pathology is declaring that it doesn't fully believe in the importance or legitimacy of the public realm and is not unconditionally prepared to defend it. In the same way that social scientists James Q. Wilson and George L. Kelling showed how one broken window left unrepaired can lead to a rash of vandalized windows, a sense of insecurity, and eventual neighborhood decline, toleration of such disorder encourages social disintegration and crime. It also drives people to turn their backs on the public realm and insulate themselves within private life, impoverishing the common life that guarantees freedom and civilization.

You can get a sense of the reckless disregard with which the public realm is customarily devalued today by listening to one of the clergymen of the Broadway Presbyterian Church in New York. This church, across the street from Columbia University, runs a soup kitchen that feeds the homeless. Most of its clients are exuberantly able-bodied young men, who regularly turn the neighborhood into a gamut of aggressive panhandling. Late one summer night in 1989, a young computer engineer who lived near the church was stabbed to death in the lobby of his apartment building. Suspicion fell on one of the soup kitchen's homeless clients, who had vanished.

In the aftermath, when neighborhood residents complained bitterly to the church about the atmosphere of daily threat and intimidation that the soup kitchen had created, one of the church's ministers gave them this pastoral advice about ensuring their safety: "You just have to curfew yourself." Clearly the reverend gentleman lacks understanding of what a community is for. In the name of justice, he requires the law-abiding to lock themselves in their homes if they don't want to live by the law of the jungle.

It is a confused society that turns values on their head like this—that expects rightdoers who uphold the civic virtues to make way for wrongdoers and thinks of the social order as an infringement upon freedom rather than freedom's foundation. Since values confidently held and confidently shared are the bonds that knit communities together, and since the democratic social order rests on something so intangible as consent and belief, so fundamental a confusion of values necessarily entails social unraveling, in which each individual's sense of the meaningfulness and coherence of his or her own life grows confused too. Of all the signs of social disintegration that have been plain enough around us for some time, the plainest is homelessness: it is social disintegration that has driven so many of the homeless to their deplorable plight.

Almost every form of social decomposition and overturning of values leaves dazed victims washed up on the street, like debris after a shipwreck. Homelessness is ruin, and many of the homeless set off down the familiar, well-worn roads to it because the social and familial strictures and structures that once barred the way have so extensively crumbled. Says Donald Johnson, executive director of the Star of Hope Mission shelter, Houston's largest: "A lot of this is the fruits of the sexual revolution, the drug revolution, the freedom to be yourself, the self-gratification revolution, the Me Generation. 'I'm not responsible. I'm not accountable.' Most people survive it, but some don't."

The blighted insubstantiality of family structure that produces so many of the homeless has an almost surreal intensity, like the buckled remains of a bombed-out building. One group of the alcoholic and drug-using homeless, for example, are underclass men, raised in flimsy families and communities that make an inadequate crucible for character. The homeless in general are three times more likely than the nonhomeless to have grown up in a one-parent family, and five times more likely to have been brought up without either real parent.

For a more exotic version of disintegration, here are a mother and her beautiful blond daughter of fourteen or fifteen, both dressed like leftovers from the Summer of Love and both having breakfast at a church-run shelter in Manhattan. The other residents don't like them: they feed the communal milk to their cat, the others charge, and the mother pimps for her daughter at the McDonald's down the street—a sad twist on sexual liberation. They slept on the street last night, having missed the shelter curfew; they had attended a performance at Lincoln Center, they say. And what degree of social breakdown is revealed by three young couples received at the Salvation Army shelter in Phoenix at different times within a single month in the late eighties? Each couple had a defective baby. And each couple, living as lovers, turned out to be brother and sister.

At the chaotic extreme of social disintegration is a group of the homeless called "throwaway kids." The callous cruelty of that name captures the cruelty of their lot. They are teens and subteens abandoned or abused by parents too drunk, drugged, or crazed to care for them. Or they are youngsters who have run away from foster homes, to which some were consigned by parents themselves homeless.

Often these kids live in abandoned buildings; *sixty* of them once scrambled out of one that caught fire in Los Angeles. They live by thievery, dope peddling, and "subsistence prostitution," as one social scientist calls it. They suffer from poor health. They don't go to school. Older men—meaning twenty-eight- or thirty-year-olds—keep some of the girls, often throwing them out when they reach nineteen or so. Of the many throwaway kids seen by the Children's Hospital of Los Angeles over several years, one half were drug abusers, one third had injected intravenous drugs in the past year, one quarter said they were involved in prostitution, 40 percent had been sexually or physically abused before age ten, 80 percent were clinically depressed, and one in five had tried suicide.

Inevitably, some of the girls get pregnant, and some decide to have the baby, starting yet a second generation of homeless children. "They have literally no way to care adequately for this child," says Kay Young McChesney, a social scientist who has studied this group. But, she adds, all these emotionally starved young mothers talked to her with painful earnestness about how good their babies were, how they never fussed at being hungry as other babies would. Of course, as McChesney saw, they were malnourished and too listless to cry.

As has happened with other social ills, the homelessness problem has grown to such proportions and become so resistant as a result of the new ideology of liberation. The large-scale efforts to relieve homelessness based on that ideology—in particular the efforts sponsored by the civil liberties bar—have ended up making the problem more entrenched, partly because they unintentionally further the social disintegration that causes it. Homelessness is the clearest case of a social pathology whose cure requires first of all that we stop doing most of the things currently seen as solutions to the problem. If you are doing something that is making a problem worse, stop; redoubling your efforts won't make an improvement.

This seems an almost self-evident proposition in the case of the mentally ill homeless: surely they need to stop being "liberated" from the very thing that could help them. But the other two reversals I have in mind are less self-evident, and to anyone who believes what civil libertarian advocates have made the prevailing wisdom on helping the homeless, they will sound like heartless enmity toward the afflicted. But since the advocates have been so wrong about the mentally ill homeless—becoming their worst enemies, in fact, however unintentionally—it wouldn't be astonishing to find the rest of their program equally faulty, notwithstanding their sincere protestations of goodwill and the willingness of congressmen and movie personalities to endorse their views by sleeping on heating grates for publicity. Sincerity and good intentions, even when widely shared, are no guarantee of correctness.

The first essential reversal is to reclaim public spaces from the homeless by prohibiting begging, bedding down, and distributing food to homeless people in train and bus stations, parks, and subways. On streets that have become a gamut of homeless panhandlers, this reclamation requires enforcement of the regulations banning loitering to beg that most municipalities still have on their books. This doesn't require locking the homeless up in prison but only "moving them along" or, if need be, jailing resisters for a day or two.

The second necessary reversal requires sharply curtailing public shelter systems. The big public shelters have become a subsidy to drunks and drug users, scaring away many of the mad who really need help. When even the advocates who insisted shelters be established in the first place now condemn them as violence-filled jungles and demand that safer alternative lodging be provided, you know something is hopelessly amiss.

It shouldn't be possible to be so protected from the natural consequences of your own self-destructive actions as to have a taxpayer-provided roof over your head with no questions asked and no conditions imposed. Take your meals at the soup kitchen, panhandle unmolested at the railroad station for crack or wine money—you can usually make at least a tax-free twelve dollars in a few hours, not much worse than the minimum wage—and you have achieved the life of a significant fraction of the homeless. This life is squalid, to be sure, but it insulates those who live it from the most immediate bad consequences of their behavior and removes an extremely effective deterrent to such behavior.

Public shelters, open to all comers, may cause at least as much homelessness as they cure. They draw more people out of housing than off the street. It's not just that they give people the option of not paying rent; they also allow people who've been doubled up with family or friends to move out—or to be shoved out with less guilt. That's one reason why cities and counties with liberal shelter admissions policies have larger homeless populations than jurisdictions with less "generous" policies, and why homeless populations suddenly grow as provision for the homeless is liberalized. A scant two years after Washington voters passed Initiative 17, guaranteeing shelter to all District of Columbia residents, for instance, homeless families in D.C. shelters increased by 500 percent. One woman phoned from Hong Kong as soon as she heard of the guarantee to say that she had just enough money for plane fare, so would the authorities please reserve space for her and her children.

Right-to-shelter policies promote dependency. Take the case of Lowell, a twenty-seven-year-old I met in New York's Catherine Street family shelter. With winning smile and ingratiating manner, he formerly made $350 a week as a manager of a Burger King; his wife, who lived in the shelter with him, was earning $160 at one of the chain's other branches. He landed in the shelter when an aunt evicted him from his little apartment in her house. Within several weeks, after getting back from work late enough to be locked out of the shelter several times, he quit his job. Too much hassle.

He told me he could easily find another job, but the idea left him cold. "If you get a job, you're going to be abused financially," he said. "No one has ever paid me what I'm worth." So he was spending his time lettering signs for the shelter and feasting on grandiose fantasies of becoming a famous graphic artist. Alas, his signs plastered on every wall showed no trace of the requisite talent. Meanwhile, he had no complaints. "You know what we had for dinner last night?" he asked. "Steak! We have a TV, a video room. I see more movies here than I ever saw outside. You really can't ask for more." If he had less, he would bestir himself quickly and soon be neither homeless nor a dropout from the labor force.

I don't at all mean to say that you won't find genuine distress being relieved in shelters. Of course some of those taking refuge there have been driven from their homes by fire, job loss, domestic violence. People do suffer misfortunes that overwhelm them, or they lose their way, grow confused, lose heart, and temporarily stop struggling. I have talked to them in shelters, seen the fear and humiliation that breaks through the armor of rigid reserve and haughty impassivity. But such people are seldom homeless long, and they are a very small minority of the public shelter population.

Public shelters don't distinguish among the unfortunate, the malingerers like Lowell, and the truly asocial. At Catherine Street, for instance, you look in one large, messy, fourteen-bed room housing four or five families and discover a malevolent-looking young man and his sixteen- or seventeen-year-old wife lying in adjoining beds at noon. A few doors down the hall you come upon four beds drawn close together to mark out one family's turf, each bed made up with military precision, each pillow surmounted by a handmade stuffed animal, a goldfish swimming in a bowl on the nightstand—all this betokening a far different mode of life, far higher aspirations. But to the shelter, all are equally homeless, all equally deserving of being housed at the taxpayers' cost.

At the very least, it would make sense for public shelter systems to institute much more discriminating admissions policies and house far fewer people. They would create less dependency if they also offered only temporary, not open-ended, shelter.

Even so, privately supported and privately run shelters are vastly preferable to public ones. Private shelters resist turning into huge, ravenously expensive, permanent bureaucracies with specious "entitlements" that continually expand the clientele and sink clients into permanent dependency. What's more, private shelters have a purposefulness that public ones lack. They have standards and values. They aim to change lives and save souls, to rescue the sinner and redeem the irredeemable. Laudable and necessary in a humane community, these goals nevertheless move beyond the scope of the state.

Suppose the following reversals occurred: what would happen? Picture for a moment the public shelters of the great cities shrunk or closed, the mentally ill in appropriate treatment, private shelters relieving temporary distress and trying to rehabilitate such drunks, drug takers, and dropouts as they deem salvageable, public places swept of beggars and sleepers, and a sense of public order restored. Would the sum total of distress be greater? Would thousands upon thousands of the homeless who formerly slept in the public shelters or in the subways now be freezing under bridges and starving on skid rows?

I think not. Were it to stop being so easy to drop out into a truly dead-end life—were compassionate citizens to stop sympathetically viewing the alcoholic, the drug-addicted, and the idle as poor, downtrodden victims to whom giving handouts is a public necessity—this variety of homelessness would become far less attractive. And in an intact social order, where petty lawlessness and self-destructive irresponsibility are not suffered to flourish in the heart of the city, many fewer would feel tempted to fall into such a fate.

We have misconceived every part of the homelessness problem—who the homeless are, how they got that way, what our own responsibility for their plight really is, what help to give them. We have abandoned the mad to the streets in the name of a liberty that mocks them. We take the sympathy we owe them and lavish it indiscriminately upon those who happen to look like them and be standing near them. If our public spaces are hijacked and despoiled, that somehow helps assuage the vague guilt we feel but can't quite bring into focus. If that erodes our social order, who are we—the guilty—to call others to account?

Enough. It's time to stop kidding ourselves and clean up the mess that a specious liberation has made.

CHAPTER SIX

Victimizing the Poor

The sexual revolution, the counterculture—all the parts of the cultural revolution that forwarded the liberation of the Haves were such spectacular transformations of our values and beliefs as well as our behavior that even as they were taking place no one could miss that something lasting was happening in American cultural history, changing the inner landscape of the American soul. By contrast, we tend to think of the other part of the cultural revolution, the part aimed at the liberation of the Have-Nots, as a purely political phenomenon, a matter of passing the Civil Rights Act, registering voters, integrating schools, redrawing electoral districts, and so on. But all the vast political changes grew out of earlier changes in beliefs and ideals.

Even before the advent of the counterculture, the prevailing American beliefs about the causes of poverty, about the relation of the poor to the rest of society, began to change radically. And our revolutionized way of seeing and understanding the poorest poor has gone far to build a prison around them and lock them within their fate. Despite their presumably benevolent, humanitarian objectives, the things we tell the worst-off about themselves are bonds and fetters.

In particular, one belief central to the new culture of the Haves has wreaked incalculable mischief: the idea that the poor are victims, that poverty is in itself evidence of victimization. For by persuading the worst-off that they are the casualties of

121

social injustice—or even the mere unfortunate playthings of vast economic and historical forces that grind them irresistibly to the bottom—we make them passive, hopeless, and resentful. Out of charitable eagerness to absolve them of blame for their condition, we rob them of the sense of personal responsibility, control, and freedom without which no one can summon the energy and initiative to change his fate.

Ever since Marx described capitalism as systematic exploitation, the idea of the victimized poor has cast its dispiriting shadow over the intellectual landscape of modern times. Before Marx, poverty had a much more personal, moral dimension. The poor were either "deserving"—widows, cripples, sober workmen looking for a job, all proper objects of compassion and charity—or "undeserving" drunkards, vagabonds, and others able but unwilling to work and therefore worthy only of ostracism and contempt. Such people were poor by choice and moral failure, their poverty an appropriate judgment upon them.

But Marx's doctrine made poverty impersonal, systemic, independent of individual choice or morality. Not only does a capitalist economy exploit workers, Marx asserted, but also it always creates a class of unfortunates even below the level of ordinary exploited wage earners. Capitalism summons into existence a surplus population, an "industrial reserve army," for whom jobs in normal times simply don't exist. These would-be workers are forced to stand by in unhappy idleness and poverty until drafted into the labor force by boom times, only to be demobilized back into unemployed misery when the boom fizzles. Such an army further serves capitalists by imposing a discipline on regularly employed workers, who must rein in their just demands when so many stand eager to replace them.

If poor people don't work, then, don't blame them. It's not their fault. Blame instead the economic order that subjugates them. And if you want to end poverty, you are wasting your time tinkering at the individual level. The only real cure is revolutionary reconstruction of the entire system.

Though intellectuals began to entertain such thinking seriously when the Depression made them fear that something systemic might indeed be wrong with capitalism, these ideas didn't start spreading into the general culture until the 1960s.

It's easy to trace the process by which the culture redefined the poor as victims, because three enormously influential texts, which this chapter will consider, clearly mark the separate steps in that development. The first and by far the most important is *The Other America* by Michael Harrington, cohead of the Democratic Socialists of America at his death in 1989. Since the book's appearance in 1962, right at the outset of the cultural revolution, its main ideas have remained the heart of the prevailing orthodoxy about the poor. Today, a generation later, you still find paperback piles of *The Other America* in campus bookstores from Cambridge to Berkeley, and you still find it cited regularly in newspapers and magazines. And *The Other America* has directly shaped events: it helped persuade President Kennedy to make an antipoverty crusade central to his agenda; and, when Lyndon Johnson seized the assassinated Kennedy's antipoverty campaign as his own, the book's eminence made Harrington an inevitable choice for the task force that dreamed up the War on Poverty.

Throughout Harrington's book, you can see what extraordinary distortion went into the redefinition of the poor as victims, notwithstanding Harrington's sincere concern for the poor and his real insight and originality. Today we habitually, usually unconsciously, make the falsification he taught us, and it is part of the reason the Harringtonian conception of poverty has done such damage to the poor: it's hard to correct something you can't see clearly.

Central to Harrington's argument is the contention that what you see of poverty isn't the truth about it. Where poverty is concerned, you must distrust the evidence of your senses, since poverty's real truth is not only hidden but almost diametrically the opposite of its misleading manifestations. Harrington taught the culture of the Haves how to look directly at the reality of the underclass—and then to look straight through it, without really seeing it at all. With this lesson digested, it became possible for participants in the poverty debate to argue— as they now do all the time—as if what they saw in front of them somehow really did not exist.

The whole tendency of modern thought, of course, has encouraged people to distrust their own perceptions. We moderns learned deep, skeptical distrust from Freud, who taught that *real* reality was hidden, buried deep in the psyche below the prettified surface that we see. We learned it from Marx, who spoke of mighty economic forces that determine human relations and beliefs in ways very different from what might appear to the naked eye.

In the same vein, Harrington also claimed to rip the mask off the surface appearance of things. He began by charging that beneath the seeming affluence of postwar America, a staggering forty to fifty million people lived in a grim poverty invisible to their well-off fellows—and a standing reproach to them. Worse, contrary to another widespread belief that Harrington was especially anxious to debunk, the trend of rising national affluence would not improve their lot (though we can see in hindsight it was doing exactly that for all but the emerging underclass). For the process that was enriching the Haves, Harrington insisted, was precisely what was impoverishing the Have-Nots.

"The other Americans," he wrote, "are the victims of the very inventions and machines that have provided a higher living standard for the rest of the society.... As the society becomes more technological, more skilled, those who learn to work the machines, who get the expanding education, move up. Those who miss out at the very start find themselves at a new disadvantage," condemned to an "economic underworld." "They might say: Progress is misery." From Harrington to William Julius Wilson and Kevin Phillips, this key idea of the victimization of the poor by the increasing technological sophistication of the economy remains the conventional wisdom of our time. As political strategist Kevin Phillips recently put this Harringtonian theme, the unequal eighties, era of the billionaires and the homeless, produced "new wealth in profusion for the bright, the bold, the educated and the politically favored; economic carnage among the less fortunate."

Occasionally government has conspired in speeding this program along, Harrington argued, victimizing the Have-Nots even more keenly. Federal farm subsidies, for instance, gave billions to rich farmers to let land lie idle and boost productivity through mechanization. Progress, yes; but as a direct result, millions of newly redundant agricultural workers were forced off the land into bewildering cities, where their rudimentary education and backwoods simplicity doomed most of them to failure.

The point of all this is to press the community as a whole, and government as its instrument, to take tangible responsibility for the plight into which, Harrington claimed, the system has forced the poor. The poor pay the price for the advancement of the well-off, and as innocent victims of society they are entitled to reparations. Concluded Harrington, making yet another key contribution to the redefinition of poverty: "Most of the people on welfare rolls are victims of government action and technological progress. They receive only a fraction of the compensation they deserve, not in charity but in justice."

If you ascribe poverty to the workings of the economic system, this conclusion is virtually inescapable. Automatically, the category of the undeserving poor ceases to exist. Every poor person becomes deserving of compassion and aid, because his nonwork results from no personal failing but from forces much mightier than his individual will.

Even if he is unfit for work from drink or drugs, that is the result not of vice but of despair at his powerlessness to advance. For poverty, Harrington argued in the most original part of his book, gets inside people. It transforms their inner lives, stamping them with a distinctive personality. The organization of that personality, and the behavior that flows out of it, might be spectacularly pathological, but the pathology springs from the poverty, not vice versa.

Just as Harrington didn't deny that the economy was expanding, creating real opportunity, so too he didn't deny that the behavior of the poor was flagrantly self-destructive. But just as he dismissed economic expansion as unhelpful, even hurtful, to the poorest poor, he also found a persuasive strategy for waving aside the emergent pathology of the poor as virtually irrelevant, a mere reflection of their economic circumstances.

This act of legerdemain is all the more extraordinary because Harrington in many respects is so insightful about the reality that he energetically explained away. And the reality was brand new; for what gives *The Other America* a further dimension of historical interest is that Harrington, without knowing it, was describing the underclass at the very moment that it was first emerging into existence, as yet on a very small scale. His was a new kind of urban poor, living in new public housing projects, supported by AFDC, and already just beginning to be disturbed in its behavior.

Harrington glimpsed accurately, and then veiled with mystification, that the poverty of the emergent underclass *was* a cultural matter, a matter of beliefs, feelings, values, and pathological habits that were conspiring to turn underclass misery permanent and intergenerational. His argument would have been far less influential had he simply denied the reality of the disorder that all could see. His power flows from his success in describing the reality and simultaneously making it a matter of no importance.

How he did that is an object lesson in the modern reconstitution of reality: he interposed a theory between the observer and the reality, a theory that thereafter clung like a halo around the raw reality, transforming its meaning for literate observers. The result: today, for many people, the magic of ideology converts the drug users they see with their eyes into The Homeless that they see in their minds, trailing clouds of explanation about how economic injustice has forged their fate.

Jean-Jacques Rousseau once said that the rich, with feelings in every part of their possessions, would cease to feel happy if the poor ceased to feel miserable. Only the comparison allowed them to measure the magnitude of their own good fortune. For his part, Harrington might say that the poor would suffer less misery if the rich enjoyed less happiness. It matters crucially, Harrington argued, how the poor feel when they contemplate the gulf between themselves and the rest of society. It matters because those feelings of isolation, failure, impotence, and resentment, more than anything else, lock them into their last-place position in the economic order, preventing them from taking their empty plates to the table of opportunity.

That gulf between rich and poor, the feelings such inequality engenders—that's what made Harrington so uneasy about the progress that he blamed for victimizing the poor. The truth is, he was in other respects no enemy of progress. He was no

Victorian Carlyle or Ruskin, fulminating against industrialization and urbanization in the name of a venerable communal life, more humanly valuable, if less rich in material comforts, than the impersonal modern order sweeping it away. He didn't even view the forcing of agricultural laborers off the land with acute indignation. When displaced black farmhands migrated to the cities, as *The Other America* acknowledges, they improved their lot. No one, after all, could wax nostalgic about the traditional life of the southern sharecropper.

But what stirred him up about progress was this comparative aspect: despite their rise in absolute incomes and living standards, the ex-sharecroppers and their children, and other such "victims" of progress, remained at the very bottom of a *lengthening* economic ladder and seemed likely to remain there. In an era of mushrooming affluence, Harrington argued, those at the bottom don't care that compared to the poor of the last generation or the peasants of Asia they are much better off. What counts is that when they look above their own circumscribed horizon to the rising prosperity of the vast majority of their fellow citizens, they feel all the poorer—unlike the poor of the Depression, who saw companionable poverty all around them. "At that moment the affluent society ceases to be a reality or even a hope," says Harrington, "it becomes a taunt."

It is this comparison that drives poverty deep into the soul, making it part of a person's inner identity. "Poverty twists and deforms the spirit," Harrington wrote. "There is . . . a personality of poverty, a type of human being produced by the grinding, wearing life of the slums. The other Americans feel differently than the rest of the nation. They tend to be hopeless and passive, yet prone to bursts of violence. . . . To be poor is not simply to be deprived of the material things of this world. It is to enter a fatal, futile universe. . . ."

Far from being defined by the mere scarcity of money, says Harrington, "poverty in America forms a culture, a way of life and feeling, that makes it a whole." The culture of poverty— poverty's worldview and way of behaving—is characterized by an ingrained lack of aspiration and a sense of futility that grips not just individuals but also whole communities, a depression that is economic and spiritual at the same time. People grow up fatalistic, solitary, a prey to mental illness, their lives marred by broken marriages, drunkenness, and crime. They don't defer gratification or save for the future: why would they, in a barren environment where pleasure deferred is probably pleasure lost?

To people like this, the expanding economy that Harrington clearly saw proliferating new jobs and new opportunities means little. "Their entire environment, their life, their values, do not prepare them to take advantage of the new opportunity," he argues. "It takes a certain level of aspiration before one can take advantage of opportunities that are clearly offered."

That's why education has proved so frustratingly powerless in the face of today's poverty, even though in the past schooling fueled the rise of so many of America's poor. "A person has to feel that education will do something for him if he is to gain from it," Harrington concluded. The culture of poverty explains too why expensive new housing projects almost always turn into gang-ridden slums, not a redemptive channel to the mainstream but rather "the creator of people who are lost to themselves and to society."

The artfulness of this argument is that it frankly acknowledges the behavioral and cultural disturbance of the underclass while attributing that disturbance to the structure of the economy and to feelings that allegedly grow out of a perception of economic inequality. Such a tactic has since become almost a reflex of our culture, as when, for example, John Cardinal O'Connor of New York responded to the rape of the Central Park jogger by declaring in a sermon that the city must share the blame for conditions that breed crime. So once again what matters is the economic reality; meaningful change can take place only at that level. Economic realities are "root causes," to use today's jargon for this kind of thinking; underclass behavior or values are mere outgrowths—the natural, one might almost say the appropriate, consequences of an unjust economic structure.

Harrington had a complicated and honest mind, though, and he came close to confronting the fatal flaw in his own argument. If lack of money and economic inequality give rise to the culture of poverty, why don't all poor groups living in the very same slums develop such a culture? Why do similar economic circumstances produce that culture, with all its self-defeating resentment, only in some slum groups but not in others living in the same squalid tenements at a different time? The inhabitants of those slums, from the mid-nineteenth-century Irish immigrants onward, have in many ways been more similar than different—newcomers to the cities, marginal and despised peoples, not just impoverished but often victims of oppression and violence in their original homes. They generally have met with discrimination from other Americans too, and they found an economically unequal America. Yet most have not developed a culture of poverty.

Far from it. The poor ethnic neighborhoods of prewar America, like the Chinatowns of today, were rich in leadership, values, and the spirit of community, Harrington concedes. Vibrating with ambition, they were "a goad to talent." "The people found themselves in slums," Harrington says, "but they were not slum dwellers." In the same dilapidated tenements, in an America arguably more equal economically, today's slum denizens lack precisely that transforming cultural dimension. They remain of the slums, slummy.

The truth is, as Harrington half knows but can't accept, that culture isn't a mere emanation of economics. Culture is a no less fundamental human reality than economics, and it can determine what happens in the economic realm no less powerfully than economics can influence culture. In implying the primacy of economics, the very phrase "culture of poverty" is misleading.

The underclass subculture doesn't grow out of the structure of the economy. Though Harrington correctly described many of the feelings that lie at the root of that subculture, he erred in attributing them to the sting of economic inequality. Underclass culture is a much larger, deeper reality. It is formed in the total historical experience of the groups that compose the underclass—and especially in their close and complicated interrelationship with the totality of the larger culture.

And what was the larger culture telling the nascent underclass in the years just before Harrington wrote—when the underclass was coming into existence and its worldview was beginning to crystallize? The destructive message that became so pervasive in the sixties, thanks in part to Harrington's popularization of it, had already begun to be sounded. The crucial message the big-city poor heard all through the fifties, with increasing insistence, was that poor people weren't responsible for their pathological behavior, which in those days consisted primarily of juvenile delinquency and nonwork. Living on welfare in housing projects, as they already did, this as-yet small group received the message at the point where the culture of the Haves most directly touched them: they received it from the social workers they constantly dealt with.

Social workers tend to be cosmopolitan, "progressive" people, and the mainstream culture they brought to their charges was mainstream culture almost at its most up-to-date. They had read writers like Allen Ginsberg, Jack Kerouac, Norman Mailer, and Robert Lindner (author of *Rebel Without a Cause*). From them they heard that American society was an engine of arid, oppressive conformism that could suffocate talented people and drive them mad. They had heard from economist John Kenneth Galbraith's *The Affluent Society* that for all its material success, American capitalism—mainstream American life, with its work ethic and anxious pursuit of happiness—was a deplorable spiritual failure, leaving a sad wreckage of ulcers and wayward youth in its wake.

The big-city social workers, led to their careers by abhorrence of social injustice, were finely attuned to such a critical, even adversarial stance toward the existing social order. In this as in other respects, they were, in their modest way, among the first sparks of the cultural revolution that began to smolder in the fifties before bursting into flame in the sixties, and they carried the torch of the cultural revolution of the Haves to the poorest poor at a critical moment in their history. Often enough, social workers were conveying to their clients something quite different from the mainstream values the poor needed to hear articulated with persuasive confidence.

Social workers in the fifties increasingly were schooled by two academic orthodoxies to encourage the poor to see themselves as victims. The most up-to-date theory, propounded by Lloyd Ohlin and Richard Cloward of Columbia University's School of Social Work, held that young poor people, imbued by society with the same urge to get ahead as everyone else, find themselves obstructed by lack of opportunity and so turn in frustration to delinquency. In a similar vein, sociologist Harold Wilensky and social work professor Charles Lebeaux, commissioned by the International Conference of Social Work in 1955, produced an influential report and later a book arguing that delinquency was a response to the status anxiety that lower-class youngsters inevitably feel as a result of the relative deprivation that industrial capitalist society inflicts upon them. The social system, not delinquents, causes delinquency.

The earlier orthodoxy, still very much in vogue in the social work profession—which had been even quicker than the medical profession to embrace psychoanalysis in the wake of Freud's 1908 visit to America—held that delinquency springs from individual psychopathology, the responsibility not of the delinquent but of his disordered upbringing. According to both reigning social work theories, antisocial behavior should excite pity, not censure.

These advanced ideas were firmly enough rooted in the general culture to flower on the Broadway stage by 1957. Leonard Bernstein and lyricist Stephen Sondheim could depend on matinee-goers to smile knowingly at the hit musical *West Side Story,* when gang hoods sing to the cop on the beat:

> Dear, kindly Sergeant Krupke,
> Ya gotta understand,
> It's just our bringing-up-ke
> That gets us outta hand.
> Our mothers all are junkies;
> Our fathers all are drunks;
> Golly, Moses! naturally we're punks.

One hood is held out as the personification of the psychological theory of delinquency:

> This boy don't need a judge,
> He needs an analyst's care.
> It's just his neurosis
> That oughtta be curbed—
> He's psychologically disturbed.

Pleased to be given his excuse, he crows:

I'm depraved on account of I'm deprived!

A fellow gang member embodies the more up-to-date "lack of opportunity" theory:

This boy don't need a doctor,
Just a good honest job.
Society's played him
A terrible trick—
Sociologically, he's sick.

He too is pleased to parrot a formula that lets him off:

Juvenile delinquency is purely a social disease.

But even in 1957, the sophisticated lyricist smelled the bad faith in the lack-of-opportunity argument. As another delinquent sings:

They say go earn some dough,
Like be a soda-jerker,
Which means, like, be a schmo.
It's not I'm anti-social;
I'm only anti-work—
Gloriowski! that's why I'm a jerk.

They didn't call it "chump change" in 1957, but flipping hamburgers already called forth little enthusiasm.

In the fifties, such ideas were still at the margin of the culture. Harrington brought them firmly to the center, where their influence multiplied prodigiously. Thereafter the poor no longer heard about their victimization and their entitlement to reparations only from social workers but from everyone—with ruinous consequences.

To his credit, Harrington saw that the culture of poverty—even though he insisted that it grew out of the economy—had taken on an almost autonomous life of its own. Solider than a mere shadow of the economic reality, it would not dissipate instantaneously in the wake of changed circumstances. There would be a lag, with more lives wrecked. But since Harrington nevertheless was certain that the cultural problem was an emanation of the economic circumstances, the only solution he could offer was economic: a massive federal "war on poverty" designed to offer rather vaguely imagined "real opportunities" to the poor, differing somehow from the opportunities the growing economy already offered and "changing the social reality that gives rise to their sense of hopelessness." The closest he could come to tackling the cultural problem—the values problem—head-on, instead of attacking the alleged economic "root causes," was to say that the war on poverty could be won only if waged with a generosity of spirit that sincerely invited the poor to seize the opportunities genuinely offered them.

So deeply ingrained did Harrington believe the cultural problem to be, however, that he thought it would take a total, systemic, social and economic transformation to cure it. Probably the only definitive solution, he remarked in an aside, would be "the abolition of the neighborhood and the culture it contained." Then society could turn to the task of "establishing new communities, of substituting a human environment for the inhuman one that now exists." Instead of calling for a full-scale Marxist revolution to achieve this goal, Harrington only called for the creaky central planning of a kind that has produced a New York City school bureaucracy of 5,500 administrators, for example, and that has recently been discredited throughout Eastern Europe as an engine of enslavement and impoverishment, not of equality or social justice or liberation. But his radical, and radically mistaken, point was that we can't solve our poverty problem without changing our system, the system that inevitably victimizes the poor.

At the deepest level, however, *The Other America* asked the wrong question by asking why pockets of individuals remain poor in a rich society. Poverty is no mystery, it has been said. The real wonder is how societies become rich in the first place. History doesn't teach that it takes prosperity to call forth the will and ingenuity lacking in Harrington's "culture of poverty"; it teaches, instead, that energy and inventiveness have with centuries of toil cleared the ground and nurtured the growth of prosperity. What kindles the spirit that conjures up prosperity? The answer is culture—values and beliefs—not economics.

After *The Other America,* the new orthodoxy of the victimized poor got two finishing touches as it hardened into dogma. Though Harrington had ultimately conjured away the cultural problem at the base of poverty, he had unintentionally suggested troubling questions about the responsibility of the poor for their own condition by analyzing so insightfully the feelings and beliefs that lie at poverty's heart. To stamp out any doubts before they could kindle a more exacting interpretation of poverty, polemicists on the political left howled down the idea of the culture of poverty with a scorn startling in its angry vehemence, notwithstanding the left-wing credentials of the idea's chief originators, Harrington and anthropologist Oscar Lewis.

Doubtless they thought they were doing the poor a favor. Seen without the idea of the culture of poverty, Harrington's "victims of progress" appear to be even more utterly victimized, their fate shaped entirely by external forces and not even in the slightest by their own outlook and behavior. This way, they seem still more deserving of help.

Of the howlers, the most vehement and influential was William Ryan, a Boston College psychology professor and self-described social activist. His *Blaming the Victim,* begun in 1966 and published in 1971, is one of the two books that completed the evolution of the idea of the victimized poor. *Blaming the Victim* doesn't so much persuade as hector; but with its wild, exhilarating, cartoonlike energy, its outrageous, melodramatic exaggeration, its hammy indignation, and its overbearing, sarcastic humor that constantly careens from the funny to the bullying, it is often an entertaining, if noisy, read.

The nonsensical idea of the culture of poverty or of cultural disadvantage, Ryan fulminates, attributes social problems like poverty or crime or school-leaving to alleged defects within the pauper, the criminal, or the dropout. At first glance, this theory at least isn't as bad as out-and-out racism or social Darwinism, Ryan allows; it doesn't odiously claim that people are failures or deviants because they are born inferior. Instead it blames past injustices—racism or "the cycle of poverty," say—

for producing current defects in present-day people. Nevertheless, these individuals end up labeled just as defective as any social Darwinist would label them.

But the relevant defect isn't in individuals, Ryan counters. "Social problems are a function of the social arrangements of the community or the society," he asserts, and in the present, not the past. So if slum children fail in school, it isn't because of their "limited background" or "parental lack of values," but rather because the schools—geared to middle-class children and expecting lower-class pupils to fail—make them fail. If lower-class girls have illegitimate babies, it isn't because they are more promiscuous than their middle-class counterparts but because they can't afford birth control pills or abortions. And poverty is the fault of society, not of poor people.

Wishing to think themselves people of humanitarian goodwill, the Haves entertain a cockeyed notion like the culture of poverty to get themselves out of a dilemma. "They cannot bring themselves to attack the system that has been so good to them," says Ryan, "but they want so badly to be helpful to the victims of racism and economic injustice." So they simply "blame the victim" by focusing on his or her defects and deviance. "They are, most crucially, rejecting the policy of blaming, not the victims, but themselves," Ryan says. "If one comes to believe that the culture of poverty produces persons *fated* to be poor, who can find any fault with our corporation-dominated economy?" If black families turn out young men "incapable of equality," then there's no need to question the pervasive racism of our institutions.

It gives the Haves a clear conscience to blather on about the culture of poverty and about redeeming the Have-Nots by repairing their cultural deficits. But such an effort is of course "nonsense," Ryan sneers. Who ever heard of a group bettering its position by changing its culture, which Ryan refers to as mere "life-style"? You can't raise your salary by improving your table manners, he harrumphs, or acquire IBM stock through "more elegant taste in clothes," or gain power through "an expanded vocabulary." Without pausing to let you object that what's really important are the internal habits of mind and feeling that make up culture and that lie beneath such external manifestations as table manners, Ryan concludes: "The solution seems rather obvious—raise their incomes and let their 'culture,' whatever it might be, take care of itself."

For the truth is, he concludes (as Harrington had concluded before him), that the whole institutional structure that supports so comfortable a life for the humanitarian Haves—the corporations, the schools, the police, the government at every level—*is* to blame. That structure keeps the poor in poverty; poverty is the cause of social pathology; and powerlessness is what perpetuates poverty. The only cure for the social pathology that ails the Have-Nots is a radical, fundamental social transformation, a significant redistribution of wealth and power.

Today Ryan's phrase has entered the language: you can scarcely pick up a newspaper article about a social problem without hearing some expert or advocate piously caution that we mustn't "blame the victim." The phrase was used 495 times in the several hundred newspapers and magazines included in the widely used Nexis computerized data base in 1991, up steadily each year from 155 mentions in 1987. Who is to blame, then? The system, the system. The system "victimizes" the Have-Not. He is insulted, injured, and innocent.

One last element completed the modern view that poverty is caused by the total social system that so liberally benefits the Haves. That element arrived, unexpectedly, from the ivory-tower world of academic philosophy at the start of the seventies, contributed by Harvard philosopher John Rawls's *A Theory of Justice.* The idea's timely urgency made Rawls's otherwise indigestible tome the only book from that discipline in years to attract a wide general audience.

So large did the idea that "the system" causes poverty loom in *A Theory of Justice,* so freighted was it with anxiety and guilt, that Rawls took the logical next step of making the condition of the Have-Nots the moral touchstone of any society. As Rawls saw it, inequalities of wealth and power can be morally justified only if in some way they can be shown to benefit not society in the aggregate but, in particular, the poorest poor, the "least advantaged." To the extent that such inequalities are not so justified, precisely to that extent are the Have-Nots victimized by the structure of society. And, in Rawls's uncompromising view, to that extent is the entire social order unjust and illegitimate.

To Rawls, as in the moral imagination of the culture as a whole, the poor had moved in from the fringes and become central. They had become a measure of value, a point of reference, against which social policies and arrangements were to be scrutinized. This was an extraordinary development, making the condition of the poor, rather than the overall national wealth or freedom or virtue or artistic achievement or true democracy, the justification of the whole society. Thereafter the Have-Nots, no longer responsible for their own poverty and laden with a weighty but invisible burden of meaning more real than the reality you can see, came to stand as a mute, unanswerable judgment upon the Haves and the social system they uphold.

That development would have amounted to an almost complete cultural revolution by itself. But it was only one transformation of the moral vision of the Haves among many.

CHAPTER SEVEN

Race and Reparations

Poverty and race are inseparable issues in America. To talk about the poor is often to talk in code, with poor blacks on one's mind if not on one's lips. Concern about the "victimized" poor, especially, repeatedly turns out to be a proxy for anxiety, and guilt, over racial injustice.

The numbers partly explain why. Nearly one out of every three poor Americans is black; nearly one black in three is poor. Of the long-term American poor, blacks account for a disproportionate 65 to 90 percent, depending on age. The poorer and younger the long-term poor, the higher the percentage of blacks.

Behind the numbers lies a yet more telling history. If uneasiness about the poor is implicitly concern about the black poor, then the Haves' worry that the poor are victims is not baseless. Two centuries of slavery and another of discrimination and segregation did indeed produce victims on a world-historical scale. Today's black poverty is the most visible reminder of a history filled with equal measures of pain and shame on the subject of race.

Little wonder if, in the aftermath, the issues of poverty, racism, and victimization have become inextricably jumbled together. And the civil rights movement collapsed them together even further. It brought to many of the Haves their starkest glance into poverty, disclosing to them that the black poor were the heart of America's poverty problem. At least since 1963, when a quarter of a million blacks marched on Washington to

139

protest poverty along with racial discrimination, poverty has explicitly been a civil rights issue rather than a purely economic one.

But the confusion of racial and economic matters in the idea of the victimized poor has created a tangle of further confusions. Yes, injustice and victimization long kept blacks poor, but the injustice was racism, not some recondite economic inequity such as Michael Harrington or Kevin Phillips describe. Blacks are not Marx's "industrial reserve army," barred from regular employment by the very structure of capitalism, as white radicals and (more recently) black civil rights leaders have imagined. To escape victimization, poor blacks didn't need a vast remaking of the economic order. They needed something large but more specific: an end to the pervasive racial discrimination that limited economic opportunity, along with so many other opportunities to share in the full resources of American society.

The crucial barriers have fallen. They fell years ago, giving way before the force of the civil rights movement and the 1964 Civil Rights Act, as thinkers as politically disparate as Thomas Sowell, Shelby Steele, and William Julius Wilson have argued. Not by any means has racism been expunged from the fabric of American life—and possibly the increasingly rancorous tone of racial politics has pushed that goal further off into the future. But institutionalized racism has dramatically abated.

Only think that in the forties, two thirds of whites told pollsters that they believed in school segregation, and the majority of whites thought blacks inferior. By contrast, by the start of the eighties, four out of five whites believed blacks to be fully their equals, and by 1990, 95 percent of whites backed school desegregation. White attitudes on social mixing had grown, and were continuing to grow, correspondingly more accepting, and white acceptance of intermarriage, 4 percent in 1958, had risen to 40 percent by the mid-eighties. In 1958, 38 percent of Americans told pollsters they'd vote for a black for president; 84 percent said they would in 1990.

Attitudes about economic equality improved most dramatically of all. It's a huge shift from the majority white view in the forties that whites should get job preference to the 1972 poll data showing that almost all whites support equality of economic opportunity for blacks. All this has meant that for years blacks have not been barred from the economic mainstream. What other conclusion can be drawn from the proliferation of the black middle class in the last quarter century? Though doors still remain to be unlocked, as a general principle opportunity is open for whoever wishes to seek it.

But the idea of the victimized poor didn't allow the Haves to rest content with overturning the barriers of institutionalized discrimination. In the grip of that notion, many Haves tacitly assumed that oppression and exclusion had damaged blacks enough so that some were defective, like Harrington's sharecroppers adrift in the bewildering city. Mere equality wasn't justice enough for such victims; it wasn't adequate to solve their problem.

For such violation they deserved reparations, a view still powerfully held. In 1989, for example, Representative John Conyers moved to have a congressional committee decide whether blacks should get financial reparations for their ancestors' sufferings under slavery. The following year, columnist Charles Krauthammer suggested in *Time* magazine paying $100,000 cash reparations to each black family. A sign waved by black demonstrators during New York's 1991 Crown Heights disturbances demanded "Reparations Now."

For the Haves, the idea of reparations often went hand in hand with the idea that blacks needed to be insulated from a reality whose demands some were not quite competent to meet, having been damaged by racism's long history. White assumptions about victimization and reparations, in other words, contained a measure of unacknowledged, guilt-inducing contempt.

And these ideas produced much more harm than good. They subverted in three key ways the liberation offered by the Civil Rights Act by holding poor blacks back from seizing the opportunities newly opened to them.

The first subversion was accomplished by the reparations that were duly paid. For they were paid—most notably, in the form of welfare. As Michael Harrington had asserted in the early sixties, the poor got welfare as appropriate compensation for their victimization, as a matter of justice, not charity. Since the structure of the economy and the legacy of oppression have kept them from earning an adequate living, the government must provide it instead.

Persuaded by this line of argument, and impelled by a sincere intention to do good, the Haves hugely expanded the welfare system in the sixties, so that today the whole welfare package provides a living often equal in economic terms to a $20,000-a-year job, payable, if not quite on demand, then very nearly so. For three decades the Haves have proudly asserted the justice of this arrangement, with an increasingly breathtaking denial of its nightmarish results for the Have-Nots and for society as a whole. Indeed, it is hardly news that welfare corrupts. Lao-tzu knew it in 500 B.C., two and a half millennia before Charles Murray: "The more subsidies you have, the less self-reliant people will be." Some truths are universal.

Certainly welfare shields its recipients from the demands and obligations of the ordinary world, as the Haves thought reparations should do. Even with the recent, largely cosmetic workfare reforms, the obligations imposed by AFDC are minimal and easily evaded, especially since mothers with very young children—by definition welfare's core clientele—are exempt. As we wait for workfare to perform its wished-for therapeutic mission of gradually, supportively leading these women into the work force and mainstream life, it looks as if we will be waiting for generations yet to come.

But the very name "welfare" is a cruel satire. It's hard to say whose welfare it has promoted or which of its long-term recipients has been made better by it. Veteran welfare mothers are right to speak of it as a trap. Available, ease-inducing, will-dissolving, insinuatingly easy to get hooked on, welfare is the social policy equivalent of hard drugs, capable of taking over one's entire life and blighting it. To change the image, it has turned out to be the thalidomide of social policy, humanely therapeutic in design but engendering monstrous deformity instead.

A Gulliver, transported to the Robert Taylor Homes or the Castle Hill Houses to see the fruits of the welfare system in all their exotic strangeness, would reel in stunned amazement at a central, vast, fundamental irrationality, no less glaringly obvious than it is destructive. Here is a society lamenting its plague

of intergenerational poverty, crime, and the whole host of attendant social pathologies that define the underclass. And yet in
welfare it has created a machine for perpetuating that very
underclass, by encouraging the least competent women—with
the least initiative, the worst values, and the most blighted family structures—to become the mothers of the next generation
and pass along their legacy of failure.

A naïve Gulliver might expect that something called Aid to
Families with Dependent Children wouldn't go out of its way
to multiply the weak families that produce children doomed
to remain in the underclass. But not only does AFDC increase
the number of *poor* families by offering an income to impoverished women if only they will have a child, it also increases
the number of poor, *weak* families by giving that income to
unmarried mothers. To be sure, strong-minded single women
who try hard certainly can raise children successfully, but the
overwhelming conclusion of study after study is that two-parent
families do the job more dependably.

Even putting aside the cockeyed notion of the Haves that
welfare is reparations or an "entitlement"—a notion without
which the welfare culture couldn't exist—the idea that society
ought to give an income to the single mothers of illegitimate
children and set them up in apartments, without a hint of
stigma, is curious enough from a historical perspective to require
comment. It gained acceptance just when the Haves were too
enthralled by their own sexual revolution to condemn the sexual license of others, however irresponsible—when, in the service of their own "liberation" and "self-realization," the Haves
suspended judgment on sexual and family matters, lest they be
judged.

At that moment, as the divorce rate more than doubled
from 10.3 per thousand in 1950 to 22.6 in 1980, the epidemic
of divorce and remarriage and open marriage and redivorce
among the Haves signaled the fraying of the ideal that people
should work at marriage with tolerance and forbearance because,
among other benefits, stable two-parent families are good for
kids. At that time, of course, the prevailing wisdom was that
children resiliently recover from the loss and pain of divorce in
no time. But that was before Judith Wallerstein and Sandra

Blakeslee's research, reported in *Second Chances: Men, Women, and Children a Decade After Divorce,* demonstrated to their dismay and contrary to their preconceptions that for children the wound of divorce never heals.

In other words, the welfare mess became as bad as it has become partly because America's sexual revolution so devalued the traditional family that public opinion was willing to treat unmarried single-mother families as in essence no less functional than real families. I worry as I write this that such talk about the value of the traditional family might sound extremist: that anxiety is a gauge of how much the status of this primary social institution has sagged. In the cultural devaluation of the family, the two great liberations of our generation—the personal liberation of the Haves and the social liberation of the Have-Nots—came together to produce failure.

For the Haves, the idea of what a family *is* has grown remarkably fuzzy in the last decade or more. For instance, under the headline "Family Redefines Itself, And Now the Law Follows," *The New York Times* reports a New York court ruling that a homosexual couple is legally a family, so the survivor can't be evicted from the pair's shared apartment. Citing that ruling, a New York teacher went to court claiming that his homosexual lover, like any family member, should be entitled to coverage under his health insurance policy. In Los Angeles, reports *The New York Times* as another example of the family "redefining itself," city employees who officially register their "domestic partnerships" are entitled to paid bereavement leave and unpaid leave to tend their ill partner.

By recognizing such households as families, these authorities weaken the authority and status of traditional families related by blood and marriage, demoting them to one alternative out of several. Indeed, the *Times* slightly dismisses the traditional family as a "stereotype"—something hackneyed, conventional, simpleminded, and not quite in tune with today's enlightened reality.

The social policy goal ought to be to encourage and strengthen traditional, two-parent families in every way as the essential socializing institution. No other institution has proved so successful at equipping people with the values and habits necessary for productive, meaningful lives as this one, itself based on the willingness of individuals to turn their most basic impulses and energies to accomplishing some larger social purpose beyond their individual imperatives. At a time when most public institutions, especially the schools, fail to articulate and convey values, the weakening of this primary value-transmitting institution is doubly a disaster.

Behind *The New York Times*'s headline lies the assumption that social institutions evolve in some organic way, just as a language evolves, slowly changing as individuals randomly, experimentally modify existing practices. The law, like the dictionary, simply registers what has already occurred. In this view, it is as if social and cultural changes of such magnitude had nothing to do with will and choice and intense struggle among competing values—as if judges and great newspapers and other key spokesmen for the official, institutional culture did not make changes by endorsing certain developments, treating them as natural and inevitable, while rejecting others.

Such a view allows one to endorse change without responsibly discussing what its consequences might be or, more fundamentally, whether it is right or wrong. Such questions are bound to seem beside the point anyway if you believe that the family in some mysterious way is "remaking *itself*," rather than being remade by human agents according to their own values and interests.

For the poor, the consequences of the steady unfocusing of the norm of what a family is have been far-reaching. Since the Haves could no longer make a ringing defense of the traditional, two-parent family, they could see no grounds for objection when the government gave increasing amounts of taxpayers' money to expanding numbers of unmarried mothers with illegitimate children. They had nothing to reply when black advocates for the poor and their white radical supporters began to assert, as they now formulaically do, that there is nothing wrong with the single-parent family, that children thrive in it, that it is a time-tested, historically sanctioned form of the black family that functions admirably because it is suspended in a richly nurturing web of kinship relationships beyond the nuclear family.

No matter that the historian Herbert Gutman has shown conclusively in *The Black Family in Slavery and Freedom, 1750–1925* that such an account of the black family is utterly mythical, that until very recent times blacks clung with upright tenacity to the ideal of the stable, two-parent family, even under slavery's hardship. If all families are alike, if the differences between single-parent families and traditional families are mere matters of taste and style, then the question of what works best for children and for society at large is dismissed even before it is asked.

Yet considering the overwhelming reality of the families whose proliferation the welfare system abets and fosters—the poor health of the children resulting from parental incompetence, the school failure rooted in parental neglect, the destructive behavior, the emotional deformity and intellectual stunting, the failure of the children as adults—what response can there be but condemnation of that system?

Or consider the underworld of foster care, which reveals from another vantage point the damage welfare entails. Here are legions of hurt children summoned into existence by the welfare culture only to be neglected or abused, so that now they are motherless as well as fatherless. In New York, 87.5 percent of the 45,000 children in foster care have been plucked out of welfare families. Is this evidence of a system that protects the welfare of the child, or rather of one that encourages unfit women to be mothers?

With examples of welfare's blighted harvest of failure in mind, one remembers with horrified incredulity the movement for welfare rights in the mid-sixties—as if breeding illegitimate children at the expense of one's working neighbors were a proud right of the citizens of a free democracy rather than a matter for shame and censure. One recalls too that the angry sit-ins under the aegis of the National Welfare Rights Organization, coupled with the ugly mau-mauing of welfare offices to demand expanded welfare benefits, succeeded all too well in tripling New York City's welfare caseload and, in only one year, almost quadrupling the amount the city paid out in supplemental welfare benefits.

Even today, assertions are made that all is as it should be in welfare's unwholesome world, where young women grow

middle-aged as wards of the state. In the brutal housing projects that are our soviet socialist republics, welfare mothers live
under a grim socialism, a comprehensive system that gives them
a meager, dreary living if they accept the most shrunken scope
for choice and free will, the lowest horizon of hope for the
future, the narrowest possibilities for self-realization. But in a
recent *New York Times* op-ed article that could have been written by Lewis Carroll, political scientist Frances Fox Piven, a
founder of the National Welfare Rights Organization, and Barbara Ehrenreich, cochair of the Democratic Socialists, argue
against adding any workfare requirements to the existing welfare system: "Welfare recipients are already making a contribution to society: they are rearing children, and they are doing
so under the adverse conditions of extreme poverty and single
parenthood. Why is a job flipping hamburgers or working in a
Kmart a greater contribution than caring for the next generation of citizens?"

If only they *were* rearing citizens, in the full meaning of that
word, rather than another underclass generation, incapable of
real participation in the civic life. And don't most nonwelfare
mothers work, rearing much better citizens than welfare mothers, without support from the state?

Unhappily the welfare system, malignant at the core, will
work its mischief for time to come: from the evidence so far,
workfare seems most unlikely to come to grips with AFDC's real
defects.

True, researchers have found that if welfare clients are
required to seek jobs, some will try and succeed, and total welfare costs will decline. The same researchers report that more
ambitious workfare programs—those that try to regenerate the
worst-off of the Have-Nots with training programs and restore
them to the world of citizenship and work—also show positive
results. But very lukewarmly positive—a mere $271 gain in
annual earnings for the average single mother who participated
in the program's first year. These results are as tepidly positive
as the Job Corps, which after all the shouting increased the average trainee's earnings less than $200 a year; or as trivially pos-
itive as the job training programs of the Manpower Development and Training Act, which raised participants' earnings a

scanty $150 to $600 a year, with the increase dwindling to half that meager figure within five years.

Champions of workfare and training programs will argue, reasonably, that any positive result, however paltry, is not to be sneezed at. Yet even with workfare, the system will still make it easy for poor single women not to worry about the consequences of getting pregnant.

Such a huge problem cries for more basic reform. In an ideal world, there doubtless would be no welfare; and if the policymakers who brought AFDC into the world and those who expanded it in the sixties could have foreseen what it would bring forth, they would have hesitated, appalled. But in the world that we have, welfare is an obdurate fact. Charles Murray may be right that it ultimately would be a gain in human happiness to scrap the entire system of welfare, Medicaid, food stamps, and so on, leaving no recourse but the job market; but even those who suspect he *is* right have little inclination to conduct the experiment and find out, since they fear the casualties would be too great. For most other Americans, so strong is the cultural revolution's belief in the justice and necessity of welfare that the political likelihood of abolishing it is zero.

The practical question for now, then, is how to change the existing bad system so that it does the least possible mischief. To begin with, it has been a mistake to concentrate on the mothers. Unfortunately, not much can be done to regenerate the great mass of underclass mothers, to release them from the shrunken and self-defeating version of humanity in which they are imprisoned. Work requirements—if inflexible enough to be unavoidable—will spark a transformation for a few, but most will go through the motions with all the sullenness of Moscow street sweepers. It will be just another "program" to be shirked and outwitted.

But though most long-term welfare mothers won't be saved by work requirements, workfare—as long as it is *work* rather than endless preparatory courses in how to work—has the advantage of eliminating the corrupting option of an indolent life on welfare, with an income equal to what a low-paid worker makes. The salutary, culture-altering message for all would be that work is valued, that everyone is responsible for his or her fate, and that everyone is part of the community, because, among other things, everyone works.

The real focus belongs on the children, though, not the mothers. That means, first, changing the welfare incentives so that women who are unmarried, too young to begin families, and too poor or unskilled to support them are not encouraged to have them. I'm sure I will be accused of all sorts of things for suggesting that people likely to be incompetent parents shouldn't be abetted in having babies to be supported by the state. But looking out at the mournful prospect of the underclass, I find it cruelty to induce the bringing into the world of children who will be so badly nurtured as most of these, and who will grow up with so many of their human excellences unawakened.

New Jersey's proposal not to raise welfare payments to mothers who have a second welfare child is a step in the right direction: a high proportion of families with more than one welfare child are likely to be dysfunctional underclass families, and this provision discourages the production of new underclass recruits. I would suggest three further reforms of this kind.

First, *unmarried* mothers should not be set up in their own apartments, an attraction of the current welfare system to teenage girls unhappy at home. Instead, they would have to live in group shelters with rules of behavior. Coupled with a work requirement, this provision would make getting pregnant and having a baby a much less attractive option for poor young unmarried women.

Moreover, it would make a wholesome distinction between the widowed and divorced mothers of dependent children— women who have made a public, legal commitment to the ideal of a stable family but who have lost their husbands—and those women, generally very young, who have embarked on motherhood with no such sense of responsibility or commitment. If the state is to promote the strong families that are best for children, it must once again distinguish between these two kinds of families when dispensing benefits.

The purpose of these shelters would be to try to strengthen the families and, most particularly, the children who live in them. Accordingly, my second proposal is to require resident single mothers to attend daily workshops on child care and child rearing. These would begin with child development truisms, unknown to many welfare mothers: babies cry because they need something, not because they are being "bad," for instance; or children need to be talked to and responded to, not ignored, not threatened, not hit.

Finally—and this is the most important point—preschool children would be cared for during working hours in day care centers in the shelters, where, from the beginning, a Head Start–style program would ensure that they felt valued, and that they learned cause and effect, big and little, before and after, similar and dissimilar, good and naughty, friendly and unfriendly, the names of colors and feelings and animals, and the whole array of cognitive and moral categories that underclass children don't adequately acquire and without which it is hard to learn and think.

From such seemingly modest efforts dramatic results can flow, as the High/Scope Educational Foundation proved with the celebrated early education project it began for underclass three- and four-year-olds in Ypsilanti, Michigan, in 1962. After dividing children randomly into one group that went through its two-year program and a control group that didn't, researchers then followed all but four children in both groups from the time the project ended until 1990. As of 1984, the latest year for which the data have been analyzed, two thirds of the program kids finished high school, compared to half the control group. Thereafter, nearly twice as many program kids went on to college or job training, and by the time they were out of their teens they were dramatically more law-abiding and self-supporting than the control group kids, who were twice as likely to have illegitimate children and be on welfare.

If you can make such a difference in averting the underclass fate starting with three- and four-year-olds, it's certain you can make a more profound difference if you start much earlier, at an even more crucial developmental stage, and if in addition you teach and motivate the mothers to further the child's early learning. It isn't just intelligence that is at issue in this development; it is the qualities that come under the rubric of character—patience, perseverance, pride in a job well done, respect for others, determination, loyalty, and so on.

What will happen to the children if welfare mothers don't choose to participate in this new scheme? If mothers decide instead that they are willing and able to support themselves and their children, even by flipping hamburgers, so much the better for the children to live in families that take part in the mainstream world of work instead of being enmeshed in welfare's marginal existence. But if mothers refuse to enter the group homes and fail to support the children, then the state will intervene to take the children away, as it does now.

Welfare was the first subversion of the liberation promised by the Civil Rights Act. The second major way that liberation was subverted was that the culture of the Haves withdrew respect from the humble but decent working life in the process of embracing the idea that the poor were victims of an unfair society. Seen through the distorting lens of this idea, a poor person who doesn't work deserves sympathy and compassion, not harsh judgment; his idleness is imposed upon him by the structure of the economy, by the lack of opportunity, not by irresponsibility and moral failure. If he takes welfare, he should not be stigmatized: welfare is no more than his right.

At that moment, the very thing that gives a hardworking poor person his decisive moral superiority over the nonworking poor person starts to dissolve, as Charles Murray has movingly written. Whether a poor person works or not grows morally neutral. If it is not blameworthy *not* to work, no definitive praise attaches to someone who works and supports his family. A growing disdain for the working class at large as benighted "hard hats" and Archie Bunkers, all beer and bigotry, hastened that withdrawal of respect.

A breadwinner's income itself becomes less meaningful, since it no longer greatly distinguishes him economically from the nonworking poor person to whom a beefed-up welfare system provides an equivalent income. The low-income worker is shunted to the side, out of view of the larger culture, while the culture's official spokesmen overwhelm his or her nonworking neighbor with compassion and understanding.

He is shunted aside in a more important way, too. According to the ideology of victimization, by working in his low-wage job, he is not a fellow participant in the community but a victim of an unjust, unequal economy that makes the Haves richer while keeping him on a lower plane at an ever greater disadvantage. Seen in this way, he is no longer part of the same universe as the Haves: a fellow wage earner, a family man, a citizen. In one perverse sense, he is even less worthy of respect than the nonworkers. They at least are smart enough to know that the available low-wage work is exploitation and victimization. Too canny to be hoodwinked, they have enough dignity to refuse to participate in their own victimization. They resist; they hold themselves inviolate.

Most families don't rise from poverty to neurosurgery or mergers and acquisitions in one generation. It goes by stages, it takes time, and it often starts humbly. But if cleaning houses, making up hotel rooms, cutting meat, or cooking french fries is being a sap—if it makes the person doing it feel himself in a demeaning, false position, earning "chump change" in a "dead-end job," rather than being decent and honest—then it is that much harder to put a foot on the bottom of the ladder. Perhaps that's why getting started is easier for immigrants: they are detached enough from the larger society not to hear its messages clearly, and they come with values and goals strong enough to turn their menial jobs into a liberation rather than a servitude.

The new taint of indignity upon low-wage work undermined blacks especially. Even though closed opportunities had kept many blacks in menial low-wage work for generations, within those unjust limits blacks had made lives of dignity and rectitude and had preached the mainstream values by which they lived to their children. But right at the moment when the Civil Rights Act genuinely opened opportunity, when those values of work and self-respecting propriety could have fueled real economic advancement, they came under assault.

Prompted by the culture of the Haves, children of upright black workers were quick to see their parents' admirable attitudes as a badge of servility and inferiority. Didn't their parents know that they were trapped in jobs that led nowhere, that merely exploited and oppressed them, as the majority culture was insisting? Didn't they know that the right attitude wasn't dutiful effort and hopeful patience? When Black Power demagogues charged that such a life was Uncle Tomism, unworthy of respect, they were only intensifying a message that the culture of the Haves had already voiced.

It wasn't just white teenagers who rejected their parents' values all through the sixties. When black adolescents of that era spurned the "straight" values of their parents as passive and politically naïve, the consequences were especially harsh. Before they even gave themselves a chance, legions from an entire generation smothered within themselves the outlook on life that could have brought them success, adopting instead a defiant resentment that locked them out and helped form the underclass.

Finally, the idea of victimization paralyzed the black poor in the face of opportunity precisely by encouraging them to think of themselves as the helpless victims. This vigorous fanning of already smoldering feelings caused the conviction of victimization to blaze up to a higher pitch of self-destructiveness just when those feelings most needed damping down.

For paradoxically the success of the civil rights movement often intensified the sense of victimization instead of assuaging it. The civil rights movement's enflaming of white guilt with a stark display of the wrongs done to blacks made victimhood a means of extracting benefits, as essayist Shelby Steele has pointed out, and thus it wedded blacks more firmly to the victim's identity. But while giving blacks a sense of strength as a group, victimhood simultaneously made them feel all the more helpless as individuals, unable to advance by personal effort but only by collective protest.

More important, the Civil Rights Act's opening of opportunity flooded blacks with anxiety and self-doubt. They were free to succeed—but also to fail, as Steele remarks. To deny the very existence of such unwanted feelings, many blacks clung all the more fiercely to their sense of victimization. If blacks fail, they vociferated, white racism is to blame, not individual blacks. Blacks can't be held responsible when the whole society is stacked against them. Hence while racism was dramatically abating, charges of racism grew more shrill.

Out of fear that the newly open mainstream society might reject them *personally,* based on their individual merits or demerits, reject them more deeply and woundingly than when whites simply rejected all blacks because of the color of their skin, blacks often tended preemptively to reject white society. The more they feared failure, the angrier they became, for anger is easier to bear than fear and vulnerability.

Fear transmuted into anger led some blacks to see oppression that wasn't there, and the imaginary oppression grew to monstrous, truly delusional proportions. At the more modest end of the scale is poet and playwright Amiri Baraka, formerly LeRoi Jones, who publicly likened the Rutgers University English professors who voted not to give him tenure to Nazis and Klansmen. At the extreme, a dismaying number of blacks today are ready to believe that the government itself is conspiring to kill them.

Look at a recent poll of blacks of all classes in New York. Was it true, could it possibly be true, that the government purposely strives to discredit black officials like Marion Barry, the crack-smoking ex-mayor of Washington, D.C.? Over three quarters of those interviewed said yes. Washington blacks believe it so firmly that they call the imagined conspiracy "the Plan."

Was it true, could it possibly be true, that the government deliberately makes drugs easy to get in the ghetto, in order to harm blacks? Yes indeed, said three out of every five respondents to the poll. Even more ominous in the wildness of paranoia it suggests, 29 percent said it was true or possibly true that the AIDS virus was created in a laboratory expressly to infect and destroy blacks.

When you believe that the government or the whole white race is waging genocidal biological warfare against you, how can you possibly see that opportunity is open before you? If you believe the government is *forcing* blacks into such self-destructive acts as taking drugs and sharing dirty needles, how can you possibly think that you have either the power or the responsibility to forge your own fate?

So strongly did fear of freedom lead many blacks to assert their victimhood, so much store did they put in victimhood as a source of collective power, that increasingly they came to define black identity in terms of victimization, as Shelby Steele argues. To be black is to be a victim—to be poor, ghettoized, marginal. "The purest black was the poor black," in Steele's formulation. Blacks who wanted to retain their sense of racial solidarity had only that downtrodden stereotype with which to identify.

For purposes of upward mobility, it is a hopeless model. It takes for granted, as Steele once explained to me in an interview, that any attempt to enter the mainstream, to declare yourself a full-fledged American, to rise into the middle class, is a racial betrayal—what blacks mean when they accuse each other of "acting white." It's why one mostly black high school had to have its academic awards ceremony at night, semiclandestinely, since jeering at the winners had become all but universal among the rest of the students.

Nor is it a helpful model for maintaining a viable community. A schoolteacher friend told me how her mostly black class sneered at her as being not authentically black for telling them to throw their candy wrappers in the trash cans, not on the street.

Such a limiting ideal confronts middle-class and solid working-class blacks with a painful conflict. What does it mean for them to be true to themselves? True to what? To the mainstream ideals and values that made them what they are, or to the poor, downtrodden, passive, resentful identity that they hope might make them feel whole as blacks but that is antithetical to their entire life's achievement?

What should they tell their children? "If you're raising your children encouraging them to be black and to identify with the mass of black people—and you make this a crucial element of their lives—then in effect you're conditioning them, almost, to be poor, to not subscribe to the same values that you yourself are living by," Steele told me.

So basic a conflict helps explain such painful happenings as the well-known self-destruction of Edmund Perry, a promising Harlem teenager, the pride of his neighborhood, who won a scholarship to Exeter, the elite New England prep school. After graduation, with a coveted acceptance to Stanford in his pocket, he came home for the summer before starting college.

Yes, his years at Exeter had been full of strain; he never really fit in; he was left with a sense of bitterness. Yes, he mirrored the divisions that raged inside his high-strung mother—a woman both angry and ambitious, wanting mainstream success for him yet seething with resentment at the insults and injuries that she believed the oppressive mainstream world had inflicted upon her. Yes, he often spouted what his Exeter classmates took as militant politics steeped in black rage, but which an older black friend of his rightly recognized as a badly needed "psychological defense mechanism" against the strains and rejections of life in the high white world. But despite the sharp and painful conflicts, the world really did lie all before him.

At the heart of the conflicts raging within him lay his sense that the journey to the world of Exeter had estranged him from the world—and the identity—with which he'd grown up, a world he appeared implicitly to reject and betray by leaving it, by his effort to meet the different standards of his new community. You can't simultaneously belong to the mainstream and to a world that defines itself by its rebellious, often nihilistic, rejection of mainstream values.

A young woman who knew Perry, and who also had made the dislocating odyssey from a New York ghetto to a New England prep school, spoke about the resulting sense of alienation to journalist Robert Anson, who wrote about the Perry case. "What's even harder than going to one of those schools ... is coming home from one," she said. "You really aren't a part of th[e] neighborhood any more." Your horizons have widened; your perspective has shifted. But you feel acutely the need to show that you still belong, that you haven't inwardly rejected your community, thereby betraying your race and falsifying your identity.

How? "You gotta snort more coke, smoke more reefer, shoot more baskets, and give up more poontang," she explained. "You've got a week to prove you are black, before you're on that bus Monday morning, heading back for class."

Perry evidently felt the need to give that proof, most likely to himself above all. One June night in 1985, wanting movie money, he and his older brother tried to mug a young man near the Columbia University campus. The man, it happened, was a plainsclothes cop. In the struggle, he killed Edmund Perry with a shot in the belly, resolving with terrible finality the youth's inner clash between the mainstream world in which he felt so misplaced and the ghetto world he had left behind but died trying to show he still belonged to.

Whether or not this story fulfills Aristotle's criteria, to my mind it counts as a modern tragedy, painful beyond expression. And it has such power to appall because both the tragic fate and the inner flaw that sparked it have a social significance beyond the merely personal.

The identification with victimhood has ever-expanding evil consequences. It engenders rage and resentment that seem amply justified and worth acting upon; it rejects responsibility; it falsifies reality. At its outer reaches, it can explode catastrophically; within its more ordinary bounds, it can sap and sabotage, causing those who believe it to become their own victimizers, fulfilling their own prophecy, which comes true only because they believe in it.

The poet William Blake spoke of "mind-forg'd manacles"— the ideas engendered from within one's own imagination that one invests with power enough to enslave oneself. Victimization is one such idea. Because it has such malign power over the black poor, the Haves must not endow this idea with even more power, as they have so relentlessly been doing. They should not give the black poor the message that they are damaged souls who require reparations. In acknowledging and deploring the injustice that blacks have suffered, the Haves must add that the injustice must now be transcended. One mustn't forget it; one must acknowledge how one's history has made one who one is; but to remain obsessed with past injustice is to remain forever in its thrall.

I know this is easy to say, and one can dismissively reply that only those who have been at the receiving end of racism should pronounce on it. I know that blacks still chronically suffer racial slights and insults, and so one doesn't need highfalutin psychological explanations to account for black anger. But how different are the insults of today from the injuries of yesterday, when opportunity for blacks was radically more limited. Even though millennial perfection hasn't arrived, opportunity is now open, and the great question is how many of the once-excluded will seize it, despite their scars. The culture of the Haves needs to tell them that they *can* do it—not that, because of past victimization, they cannot.

CHAPTER EIGHT

Rebels with a Cause

It had all the makings of one of those heartwarming Hollywood movies where the tough but loving schoolteacher, sporting a red-and-black-checked lumberman's shirt, charms and bullies his delinquent pupils into changing their ways and becoming model citizens, teenage-style. Here, in real life, was George Cadwalader, a central casting dream: an ex-Marine captain wounded in Vietnam, he was big, rugged, and handsome, with smiling crinkly eyes, bushy brows, limitless courage and self-confidence—and a plan irresistible in its mixture of idealism, toughness, and adventure. He would gather up a crew of hardened delinquent boys from the toughest urban neighborhoods of Massachusetts and transport them to a wild, deserted island, with all its associations of sagas from *Robinson Crusoe* to *Treasure Island*. There they would build their own house, grow and cook their own food, cut the firewood that would both warm them and heat their dinner. By coming to grips with the basic realities of life, they would learn self-reliance, responsibility, and teamwork, discover their own inner strength and confidence, and be converted.

But it was Cadwalader who got converted.

He woke up one morning to discover all the chickens his little community was raising for food fluttering helplessly on the ground, dazed with pain. In a paroxysm of sadism, each chicken's two legs had been savagely twisted and smashed, wrenched out of their joints and hanging useless. All that could be done for the broken creatures was to put them out of their misery. Which boy had done such a deed in the dead of night Cadwalader never knew for certain, nor did he ever know the motive.

But he knew beyond a doubt that the certainties with which he'd started his experiment in rehabilitation had crumbled within him. He and his associates had begun by holding "without question the assumption that bad kids were simply the products of bad environments," he recalls in *Castaways,* his striking account of the experiment. "We believed changing the environment could change the kid." Yet the vast majority of his charges didn't change, despite transplantation to the radically different, militantly salubrious environment Cadwalader had designed for them.

Far from it. When he followed up the first 106 boys who had gone through his program, he discovered that in seven years they'd been charged with 3,391 crimes, 309 of them violent. For the most part, he came to feel that the boys "appear incapable of love, driven by unfocused anger, and prone to impulsive behavior without regard to consequences.... [W]hen I look objectively at the trail of destruction left by our own graduates, I cannot avoid the conclusion that the world would have been a better place if most of the kids I grew to like at Penikese [Island] had never been born." And so he is led to ask, "How many chances does an individual deserve before we are justified in giving up on him? What do we do with those we have given up on?"

Cadwalader accurately calls his island enterprise an experiment: as a scientist would, he subjected his hypothesis about the causes of crime to empirical testing, controlling as many variables as possible. The theory proved false. In removing his boys from modern society and stripping life to its bare essentials on his unpeopled island, Cadwalader found that violence and crime are *not* generated by an individual's social environment. Violence and aggression are not impulses that the environment puts into the human heart; they have their own intractable, independent existence and can flourish regardless of an individual's social circumstances.

The theory that Cadwalader felt he had disproved, much as he would rather have confirmed it, is central to the new worldview of the Haves. And because it tends to excuse criminals from personal responsibility for crime, pinning it on social circumstances instead, the theory has given potential wrongdoers exactly the wrong message. Moreover, it has produced a criminal justice system, administered by a generation of judges steeped in the new culture of the Haves, that confronts actual criminals with a leniency offering little deterrence to crime.

Theories of crime have to make an assumption about whether men are predisposed by nature to force and violence or whether violence gets into their hearts from some outside source. Cadwalader's original assumption about man's inborn character—a key assumption of the new culture of the Haves—is that men are intrinsically peaceful creatures, inclined not to disturb their fellows and, when necessary, to cooperate harmoniously with them. As nature formed them, they don't attack and invade each other. Crime is an artificial growth, grafted onto human life by the development of societies and governments.

This theory, which goes back to the ancients, fascinated the eighteenth-century political philosophers. Rousseau, for instance, had imagined that men in primitive times were constitutionally peaceful. It took the later, unfortunate invention of private property to incite them to attack and dominate each other in a struggle for goods. The horrifying result, Rousseau argued, was a state of universal war whose violence caused mankind to establish societies based on a social contract. All would give up their freedom of aggression in order to reestablish peace.

But, Rousseau added with a wry twist in one of his early works, the contract itself ingrained crime into the very fabric of social life. For it was a swindling, lopsided contract, into which the rich lured the poor for the real purpose of protecting the possessions which they alone needed to protect. So even as men regained a measure of security from the criminal impulses that had arisen among them, the unjust inequality of wealth that had given birth to crime in the first place was institutionalized in society at the very moment of its foundation.

Theories like this are deeply rooted in the American imagination, planted there by Thomas Paine, among others. Since in the youth of the world men were peaceful, solitary tenders of flocks and herds, Paine demands in his two-fisted prose, how did crime and cruelty enter human affairs? Only because in each part of the world the peaceful inhabitants were set upon by "a banditti of ruffians," who forcibly made themselves their masters and exacted heavy tribute from them. By such brute violence, herding men together for the greater ease of oppressing them, were all existing political societies founded, and the robber chieftains who so roughly established them were the first kings.

Over the course of the ages, plunder gradually softened into taxation, and usurpation into inheritance, Paine says; but the animating principle of all societies remains nothing but the oppression of the poor and weak by the rich and powerful. No wonder, then, that men today seethe with ugly passions and commit criminal deeds; they have been deformed for long ages by the pressure of injustice and the rule of terror, their true, peaceful nature corrupted and degraded by the great criminal conspiracy against them that is political society.

To a nation founded upon the overthrow of an oppressive government and the faith that democratic liberty would nurture citizens with souls undeformed by tyranny, such ideas can't fail to be at least plausible. Americans take kindly to the notion that individuals left to themselves will naturally do right, that their rational self-interest will yield social harmony, and that crime, otherwise inexplicable, might well be the ill-starred product of governmental excess and tyranny.

Americans don't have to go back to Revolutionary times for firsthand knowledge of government-sanctioned oppression. They can think of Southern slavery; they can recall, firsthand, the outrages of institutionalized racial discrimination. With respect to their black fellow citizens in particular, many Americans are readily inclined to believe that crime is the fault of society, not of the criminal. Crime may be either the product of unwholesome social conditions or a rebellion—perhaps even a justified rebellion—against injustice and oppression.

These ideas were always alive in American culture, but they became dominant only at the start of the sixties. Michael Harrington gave voice to this interpretation of crime just as it was becoming widespread. Speaking of black delinquents and then of all delinquents, he concluded in *The Other America*: "[T]heir sickness is often a means of relating to a diseased environment." Ramsey Clark, Lyndon Johnson's attorney general and assistant attorney general in the Kennedy administration, is a luminous example of how quick were the Haves at their most established to embrace such an understanding of crime as part of the new era's revolutionized worldview. Clark takes an utterly uncompromising tack. "[C]rime among poor blacks ... flows clearly and directly from the brutalization and dehumanization of racism, poverty, and injustice," he wrote in 1970, summing up his experience as the nation's top law enforcement officer. "[T]he slow destruction of human dignity caused by white racism is responsible."

Just look at the unwholesome environment racism has produced, Clark demands. "The utter wretchedness of central city slums ... slowly drains compassion from the human spirit and breeds crime." For this the Haves are most emphatically to blame. "To permit conditions that breed antisocial conduct to continue is our greatest crime," Clark concludes.

Far worse than the crimes poor blacks commit, the crime of whites takes many insidious guises. For example, says Clark, "Nothing so vindicates the unlawful conduct of a poor man, by his light, as the belief that the rich are stealing from him through overpricing and sales of defective goods.... Society cannot hope to control violent and irrational antisocial conduct while cunning predatory crime by people in power continues unabated." Today that rationalization has become a smug cliché: you can't end crime in the streets, we often hear, until you attack crime in the suites.

In Clark's eyes, society is engaged in a vast, malevolent, criminal conspiracy against the poor and the black. It comprises such disparate outrages as "not insur[ing] equal protection of the laws ... condoning faulty wiring and other fire hazards, permitting overcrowding in unsanitary tenements infested with rats, all in violation of ordinances with criminal penalties ... the willful violation of basic constitutional rights." Inevitably, ghettos will breed violent crime and even rioting. "You cannot cram so much misery together," says Clark, "and not expect violence."

This whole structure of thought, most of it still completely orthodox today, rests on theoretical foundations that George Cadwalader found false. But it is a further sign of the times that once Cadwalader had grappled with the discovery that aggression and violence come from some source deep within individuals, not from the social environment, he was stumped. With his old theory in pieces, he had no new one to put in its place.

The intellectual framework he was so perplexedly groping toward isn't obscure, though: it is the other great tradition of political philosophy, springing from Plato and strengthened by such architects of the Western imagination as St. Augustine, Hobbes, Burke, even Freud. Yet it is a tradition with which modern thinking has largely lost touch, so much do we take for granted, without examination, the assumptions about human nature and the nature of social pathology with which Cadwalader began. We often aren't even aware that beneath all of our discussions about social policy lies a deeper stratum of issues, which have been debated for two millennia, and which make up the bedrock of first principles whereon all social policy thinking rests, whether the thinker is conscious of it or not.

This other tradition, for most of history the dominant stream in Western political philosophy, best explains the origin of crime. This tradition takes as its starting point the irreducible reality of human aggression. It holds that as men come from the hand of nature—or as they have been transformed by original sin, according to the Church Fathers' version of the theory—they are instinctively aggressive, with an inbuilt inclination to violence. "Men are not gentle creatures who want to be loved," as Sigmund Freud expressed this aspect of the tradition; "their neighbor is for them not only a potential helper or sexual object, but also someone who tempts them to satisfy their aggressiveness on him, to exploit his capacity for work without compensation, to use him sexually without his consent, to seize his possessions, to humiliate him, to cause him pain, to torture and to kill him. *Homo homini lupus*"—man is a wolf to man. "Who, in the face of all his experience of life and of history, will have the courage to dispute this assertion?"

The fundamental purpose of the social order, of the civilized condition itself, is to restrain man's instinctual aggressiveness, so that human life can be something higher than a war of all against all. The great seventeenth- and eighteenth-century political theorists, most notably Thomas Hobbes, imagined that that restraint was accomplished by a social contract: driven to desperation by the universal warfare that made their lives "solitary, poore, nasty, brutish, and short," in Hobbes's famous phrase, men in the early ages of the world entered into an agreement, by which each man renounced his unlimited freedom of aggression in order to promote the security of all. And because it could only be effective if some authority existed to enforce it, the contract also established a governmental apparatus armed with the power to punish infractions, further prompting everyone to keep his word. As James Madison expressed this thought in Number 10 of *The Federalist*: "[W]hat is government itself but the greatest of all reflections on human nature?"

In more modern fashion, Edmund Burke tacitly acknowledged that governments historically often have begun in violence and conquest, not peaceful contract; but he goes on to argue that, whatever their origin, they have accomplished the all-important task of taming unruly man and ordering his world. By their immense success in curbing man's lawless aggression and replacing anarchy with peace, governments rooted in ancient conquest are today maintained by the consent of the governed.

Sigmund Freud offers a still more up-to-date version of this line of thought. The taming of aggression and the replacement of the rule of force by the rule of law isn't something that happened only in the history of the race, Freud argues. It takes place in each individual's history, too.

In early childhood, under the continual pressure of parental demands, each person is made to renounce the unlimited aggressiveness with which he was born. During this protracted process, central to early childhood, one's innermost being is transformed. As one internalizes the civilizing demands of one's parents and the community that speaks through them, one acquires an entirely new mental faculty, a part of one's inner self given one not by nature but by society. This, in Freud's rather unlovely term, is the superego, analogous to the conscience; and like conscience, it punishes one with feelings of shame and guilt, while speaking with the voice not of divinity but of society.

This new inner faculty is what crucially differentiates men from the beasts. For central to Freud's thought, as to the whole tradition in political philosophy roughly sketched here, is a belief uncongenial to our revolutionized culture: the belief that man's full humanity and highest, most characteristically human achievements can unfold only in society. Only in their social relations do men achieve the rational, moral, cooperative, historical existence that defines our humanity; only as a social creature, his aggressiveness held in check by the inner transformation that immersion in the social medium works on him, does man become fully man, able to build cities, create art and science and commerce, and attain virtue.

Looked at through assumptions like these, crime takes on an entirely different appearance from the one it has in Ramsey Clark's eyes and in the culture of the Haves today. Not only does the social order not *cause* crime, it is the very thing that *restrains* crime to the remarkable extent that it is restrained. The social order is precisely what makes man's life something other than a scene of constant mutual invasion, in which all live in continual fear and danger of violence.

Seen in this light, crime takes on the closest links to culture. For though the whole governmental structure of force and threat—police, judges, and prisons—is a key means by which society restrains aggression and crime, it isn't the principal means, according to this tradition. The most powerful curb isn't force at all: it is the *internal* inhibition that society builds into each person's character, the inner voice (call it reason, conscience, superego, what you will) that makes the social contract an integral part of our deepest selves.

So while to prevent crime we should worry about whether judges are too lenient or legal procedures too cumbersome, it is still more crucial to ensure that the inner barriers to violence and aggression are strongly in place. This is a cultural matter, a matter of how people bring up their children, a matter of the messages that get passed from the community to the parents and thence to the children. The object is both to transmit the necessary prohibitions against aggression to each individual and to win each individual's inner, positive assent to the social endeavor.

Paradoxically, the hardest of hard realities—whether people commit crimes or not—comes down to a very large extent to nothing more than values and beliefs in the world within the individual. Do we deeply believe thou shalt not kill, thou shalt not steal—so deeply that these injunctions are a constituent part of our deepest selves? Do we believe in an idea of justice that embraces us and our community? Do we value such qualities as honor, duty, mercy, honesty, kindness? Do we subscribe enough to the values of our community that we would feel guilt or shame to have transgressed against them, dismay or outrage that others should have flouted them?

It's no wonder that, at the dawn of political philosophy, Plato, in constructing his ideal society in the *Republic,* should have been obsessed with the myths and fairy tales that will be told to children. He well knew that these emanations of culture are the carriers of values, the molders of worldviews and of characters, and that if they are askew, no republic can truly thrive.

When crime flourishes as it now does in our cities, especially crime of mindless malice, it isn't because society has so oppressed people as to bend them out of their true nature and twist them into moral deformity. It is because the criminals haven't been adequately socialized. Examine the contents of their minds and hearts and too much of what you find bears out this hypothesis: free-floating aggression, weak consciences, anarchic beliefs, detachment from the community and its highest values. They haven't attained the self-respect or the coherent sense of self that underlie one's ability to respect others.

This is a predictable result of unimaginably weak families, headed by immature, irresponsible girls who are at the margin of the community, pathological in their own behavior, and too often lacking the knowledge, interest, and inner resources to be successful molders of strong characters in children. Too many underclass mothers can't enforce the necessary prohibitions for children—or for themselves. And most underclass families lack a father, the parent that Freud, wearing his psychoanalyst's hat rather than his political philosopher's, sees as the absolutely vital agent in the socialization of little boys and in the formation of their superegos.

When the community tells people from such families that they are victims of social injustice, that they perhaps are not personally to blame if they commit crimes, and that it is entirely appropriate for them to nurse feelings of rage and resentment, it is asking for trouble. Worse, the new culture holds that, in a sense, such crime isn't pathological; it is something higher and healthier. It is rebellion—the manly response that Americans have shown to oppression since the Boston Tea Party, the response that Robin Hood and his outlaw band gave to injustice before America was even thought of.

A key element of the cultural shift I am tracing, the idea that criminals might be admirable rebels, was all but explicit in the sociological orthodoxy that saw juvenile delinquency as a rational challenge to a society that denied to delinquents the same opportunity to get ahead as their nonimpoverished fellow citizens. By his lawbreaking, the delinquent could win those goods that he desired as much as any other member of society. At the very least he could manifest the worth that society was denying him by demonstrating his "heart" and "guts."

But one could hardly articulate the idea of the criminal as rebel more explicitly or forcefully than Norman Mailer did in his incendiary manifesto, "The White Negro," briefly mentioned earlier. Today, the essay reads like a firework sparkler fiercely sizzling until it sputters out in a wisp of smoke. But it was as hugely influential as it was startling when it appeared in 1957, just as Mailer was becoming a national celebrity and assuming his role as an avant-garde figure at the very forefront of the cultural revolution of the Haves.

Mailer threw down the gauntlet in "The White Negro," indicting modern society as nothing but an engine of oppression, repression, and destruction. What has it produced but the Nazi concentration camps and the atom bomb? And the modern social order holds in reserve yet another form of extinction—"a slow death by conformity with every creative and rebellious instinct stifled."

In this manmade wasteland, blacks inhabit the deepest circle of oppression and victimization. They have "been living on the margin between totalitarianism and democracy for two centuries," says Mailer. In the injustice of our capitalist order, they are Marx's impoverished industrial reserve army, "a cultureless and alienated bottom of exploitable human material." Given not just the economic violence but also the visceral hatred that assaults blacks, says Mailer, "no Negro can saunter down a street with any real certainty that violence will not visit him on his walk.... The Negro has the simplest of alternatives: live a life of constant humility or ever-threatening danger." He "know[s] in the cells of his existence that life [is] war."

What is there to do but reject and oppose such deadly oppression? "The only life-giving answer," says Mailer, "is ... to divorce oneself from society, to exist without roots, to set out on that uncharted journey with the rebellious imperatives of the self.... [O]ne is a rebel or one conforms, one is a frontiersman in the Wild West of American night life, or else a Square cell, trapped in the totalitarian tissues of American society...."

"[W]hether the life is criminal or not, the decision is to encourage the psychopath in oneself." Rebel, rebel—even if lawless rebellion leads to such psychopathic extremes as murder. Even in such rebellion, according to Mailer's Americanized version of European existentialism, you will at least assert your freedom and selfhood.

To be sure, Mailer admits, all this may not look so heroically manly at first blush. Arguably "it takes little courage for two strong eighteen-year-old hoodlums ... to beat in the brains of a candy-store keeper.... Still, courage of a sort is necessary, for one murders not only a weak fifty-year-old man but an institution as well, one violates private property, one enters into a new relation with the police and introduces a dangerous element into one's life. The hoodlum is therefore daring the unknown, and so no matter how brutal the act, it is not altogether cowardly."

Monstrous, but influential. After the publication of Mailer's work, after other writers had expressed similar views, the idea that violent black crime was a kind of regenerative rebellion gained a certain currency. Not that the majority of mainstream Haves embraced Mailer's version of it wholeheartedly or uncritically: rather, they flirted with it; they were prepared to believe that in some, even many, cases it might be true. Crime *might* be rebellion—and so crime became problematical, no longer simply crime, no longer compelling unqualified condemnation.

That's partly because central events of the sixties and early seventies seemed to bear out aspects of such theorizing. The Vietnam War, of course: to the many who opposed it, the war lent credence to the charge that American society was an engine of unjust violence. The Nixonian political scandals further blemished the Establishment. Even before that, the civil disobedience of the civil rights movement had established that society and its laws could be oppressive and could appropriately, even heroically, be opposed by lawbreaking, in Thoreauvian fashion. The ghetto rioting of the mid-sixties enforced for many the false lesson that intolerable racial injustice was beginning to drive people to justified, destructive rebellion (an error repeated in the aftermath of the 1992 Los Angeles riots, though with less confidence).

Years after the publication of "The White Negro," Mailer used the same rationale to champion the mindless vandalism of graffiti writing. It was, as he saw it, a healthily rebellious expression of inner creativity uncrushed by the oppressive social order. How much more pleasing, Mailer thought, was the exuberant individuality of those scrawls than the impersonal regularity of the stony facades they defaced.

For a while, people believed him. The New York subway trains ended up caked with graffiti because—since graffiti supposedly wasn't really bad—for years no one lifted a finger to stop it. Yet graffiti is a symptom of social decay, a sign, as sociologist Nathan Glazer has observed, that no one is in control and the forces of lawlessness are sliding out from restraint. Consequently, the harm of graffiti goes beyond its ugliness; by insinuating that you can get away with it, it is an invitation to worse lawlessness.

Mailer's message further captivated the Haves because he yoked together both of the cultural revolution's liberations. Society oppresses all of us, rich and poor alike, he asserts—in one sense correctly. However privileged we may be, the process of socialization forces us to renounce inborn aggressiveness, to keep it locked within, in a lifelong self-suppression. Moreover, any society, not just our own, puts restrictions on sexuality. Various theories attempt to explain why this must be so, but all agree that here too is a chafing unfreedom imposed upon us by the social condition.

Long before Mailer, Freud had fretted over the oppression that civilization imposes on everyone. The superego, he complained, enforces its curbs tyrannically. Restraining yourself from wrongdoing doesn't leave you with feelings of calm satisfaction, as you would think it should, because your superego rakes you with feelings of guilt for forbidden *desires,* which you can't help having, no less than for forbidden actions. As a result, the superego's demands for civilized restraint feel excessive in their implacability.

Moreover, as French philosophers had been saying since the eighteenth century, out of the mutual dependence which is our lot in society, out of the court we must pay to others to win the advancement, admiration, and love that we want, each of us must sometimes play a role, must feign concern or respect or humility, must conform to standards that aren't our own, all of which leaves us with a further sense of self-suppression. Beyond that, a particular society's standards of conformity and propriety can be excessive; and arguably in the fifties, while Mailer was writing "The White Negro" and the social revolution was beginning to gather steam, there was room for loosening.

But the final degree of inner liberation for which everyone feels a pang of longing—deliverance from the sense of inner division and estrangement, of thwarted desire, of confinement in a selfhood that feels limiting, inflexible, or inauthentic—is unattainable, given the inescapable conditions of man's life in society. Yet such is the liberation that Mailer's essay holds out in prospect—the same liberation for which R. D. Laing and Ken Kesey longed, in company with all the self-declared rebels of the counterculture.

For there is in the cultural revolution a strain of utopianism or millennialism, a longing for a perfect world without human evil, an Edenic world in which we can be whole and good, with every impulse pure and permitted and satisfied, especially sexual impulses.

Longings like these are, in the strictest sense, antipolitical, reaching to transcend law and government and to enter a world without strife or injustice to curb. Nevertheless, the person who feels such longings often takes them to be a political viewpoint, as happened on a mass scale in the sixties. And since, measured against this standard, the freest and most just society is heavily oppressive, the politics (or pseudopolitics) that issues from such longings can only be liberation, liberation, liberation. Politics, the art of the possible, turns into its opposite, the dream of the impossible.

Shortly after Norman Mailer had helped propagate the idea of the criminal as rebel throughout the general culture, well-known black writers embraced it with an extremism all the more disturbing for being presented so matter-of-factly. Black Panther party member Eldridge Cleaver, for example, declared that the most heinous crime could be an expression of political activism. This declaration went only one step beyond the ideology of Cleaver's Black Power group, which had already wedded politics and violence by espousing the idea of armed black rebellion against oppressive American society. In *Soul On Ice,* a best-seller in the sixties and still taught in some college courses, Cleaver argued that for a black man to rape a white woman was a political act, protesting against his oppression and striking out against his oppressor.

Insidiously, such a politicized view of criminals saturated the inner cities during the sixties. In his memoir *Brothers and Keepers,* for instance, author John Edgar Wideman paraphrases his brother Robby's ruminations on what led him to the criminal career that ended with a prison sentence for murder. In the ghetto, says Robby, "all the glamor, all the praise and attention is given to the slick guy, the gangster especially. . . . And it's because we can't help but feel some satisfaction seeing a brother, a black man, get over on these people, on their system without playing by their rules." After all, those rules "were forced on us by people who did not have our best interests at heart." So it's not surprising that black people look upon black gangsters "with some sense of pride and admiration. . . . We know they represent rebellion—what little is left in us."

The rebelliousness that breeds crime, Robby says, is ingrained deep in ghetto life. In his own adolescence, "it was unacceptable to be 'good,' it was square to be smart in school, it was jive to show respect to people outside the street world, it was cool to be cold to your woman and the people that loved you. The things we liked we called 'bad.' ... The thing was to make your own rules, do your own thing, but make sure it's contrary to what society says or is." You keep your dignity and integrity by your rejection of right and wrong as defined by the society that oppresses you. With all values turned upside down, it doesn't take much to turn crime into heroic, or at least honest, defiance. "Robbing white people didn't cause me to lose no sleep back then," Wideman quotes Robby as saying. "How you gon feel sorry when society's so corrupt?"

A similar vision accounts for some of the disturbing lyrics of today's rap music. In a much more domesticated version, it is the animating vision of such blockbuster films as *Superfly* of 1972 or *Harlem Nights* of 1989, movies in which black filmmakers at the center of the larger culture celebrate black heroes who are smarter, quicker, and tougher criminals than the white criminals who are their adversaries. Why are the heroes lawbreakers? "I know it's a rotten game," explains the sidekick of *Superfly*'s dope dealer hero, "but it's the only one the Man left us to play." The alternative is "workin' some jive job for chump change day after day." In this rotten world, even the police turn out to be drug and crime kingpins, as corrupt as the social order they uphold.

When the hero-crooks celebrated by these movies end up with satchels of money after outsmarting the crooked white cops, it's a different moral universe from thirties gangster movies like *Scarface* or *Little Caesar*, where the criminal protagonist falls as quickly and sordidly as he has risen. It's different too from the world of a forties movie like *The Asphalt Jungle*, which sees its gangster protagonist with sympathy but still affirms the need for police to oppose such criminals and maintain the social order.

Such a view of the admirably defiant criminal still holds the underclass in thrall. "They want us to settle for a little piece of nothing, like the Indians on the reservation," as one inner-city resident who grew up in a Harlem housing project said recently, summing up his vision of the larger society. "They got us fighting and killing each other for crumbs. In a way, the ones in jail are like political prisoners, because they refused to settle for less."

How deep the glorification of the criminal runs today can be seen in the "near folk-hero status," as *The New York Times* calls it, that murderer Larry Davis won in Harlem and the Bronx in 1986. Charged with killing and robbing six drug dealers in cold blood, Davis dodged from hideout to hideout as police closed in on him during a seventeen-day manhunt, which ended in a pyrotechnic, TV-style shootout at a Bronx housing project. Davis wounded six policemen before being captured and led out in handcuffs, cool and uninjured, to the acclaim of a cheering crowd of project residents. All through the manhunt, and after its bloody end, ghetto residents told tales of his larger-than-life outwitting and resisting the police, speaking of him with thrilled, emphatic admiration as "the dude who elude." This Scarlet Pimpernel of the projects later was acquitted of five of the murders, convicted of one, and also jailed in connection with the shootout.

The cultural revolution left none of the barriers to crime undisturbed. Not only did it undermine the inner inhibitions, but it also weakened the external deterrent, the threat of official punishment. Guided by the idea that society systematically oppresses the poor and the black, the Haves increasingly hampered the governmental apparatus that upholds the law by force.

Government, according to this view, tends almost reflexively to be an instrument of injustice against the Have-Nots, above all in its law enforcement capacity. As William Ryan put it in *Blaming the Victim,* all experts know that "the administration of justice is grossly biased against the Negro and the lower class defendant; that arrest and imprisonment is a process reserved almost exclusively for the black and the poor; and that the major function of the police is the preservation not only of the public order, but of the social order—that is, of inequality between man and man." However overwrought, Ryan's statement contains this element of somber truth: racial discrimination did taint police treatment of blacks when Ryan was writing, and in the South police did act as oppressors of blacks, as the nation learned indelibly when Freedom Riders were arrested in Jackson and elsewhere in Mississippi in 1961 or when Chief Bull Connor viciously attacked civil rights demonstrators with police dogs, clubs, cattle prods, and fire hoses in Birmingham, Alabama, in 1963.

Properly indignant at such viciousness, the majority culture responded by throwing a cordon around the government's police functions, aiming to confine the police within the narrowest channel so they couldn't surge out of control. In this effort, federal judges took the lead. With their ideas continually renewed by a flow of talented clerks newly minted from the nation's top law schools, the judges were part of the advance guard of the resulting cultural changes. They had the moral authority and political power to take new ideas and transform them into the concrete reality of law almost overnight, anointing them in the process as normal and right. Accordingly, out of the impulse to curb the police functions of the state came the well-known string of 1960s court decisions that succeeded in tying down criminal law enforcement with as many strands as Gulliver in Lilliput.

Still, it was a big step from the shameful doings of Bull Connor to the conclusion that the entire governmental apparatus for controlling crime across the nation was an engine of injustice. And it was an even bigger step to the conclusion that the proper remedy for such instances of police lawlessness as did occur was to free proven criminals—as distinct from Freedom Riders or civil rights demonstrators—rather than to dismiss and punish the responsible officials.

As with so many elements of the cultural revolution, these key court decisions of the sixties produced long-term unintended consequences. Anxious to protect citizens from a tyrannical abuse of police power, the judges erected safeguards that turned out to hinder ordinary, untyrannical policemen from bringing common criminals to justice. From *Mapp* v. *Ohio* in 1961 through *Miranda* v. *Arizona* in 1966, the Supreme Court decisions that proceeded from fears of police tyranny aimed to prevent juries from hearing evidence obtained in ways that the Court, ever more punctiliously, deemed unconstitutional. *Mapp* ruled that jurors in state courts, which try most criminal cases, can't see physical evidence obtained by search warrants in any way flawed—even, as is often the case, if the evidence proves the bloodiest guilt and would imprison a criminal whose liberty threatens the entire society. Henceforward, police might find a smoking gun, but a smart defense lawyer might well find an angle to keep it out of evidence.

Miranda, as is well known, barred using the criminal's own confession, or any statement of his, if obtained without a battery of procedural safeguards that would discourage most sane people from uttering a single word. Why even bother to invent a lie, since it might catch you out? This was a far cry from the previous rule, which had excluded only coerced confessions obtained by threat or brutality.

The inevitable result was that criminals became harder to convict, and punishment for crime became rarer. As the judges issued their rulings on suppressing evidence in the sixties, the prison population declined. By the mid-seventies, the average Chicago youthful offender got arrested over thirteen times before being sent to reform school. In big cities, more than nine felony convictions in ten result not from trials but from plea bargains, in which penalties are lighter and criminals are left with at least some sense of having beaten the system. Today, thanks partly to plea bargaining, your chance of *not* going to jail if you're *convicted* of a serious crime is two to one.

As it became possible to suppress key evidence and literally to get away with murder, crime took off. In the sixties, the overall crime rate doubled. And between 1961 and now, the murder rate has doubled, the rape rate has quadrupled, and both the robbery and assault rates have quintupled.

Related changes in juvenile justice contributed to these swollen figures. Since the beginning of this century, the law understandably has treated juveniles more leniently than adults, holding them less responsible for their actions "by reason of infancy." If they committed crimes—until recently mostly thievery or pickpocketing—perhaps they hadn't yet finished the work of childhood and fully learned to differentiate right from wrong. Were they guided and taught instead of punished, perhaps they would develop the moral sense as yet unawakened within them.

So the law, in a quasi-parental way, humanely aimed to rescue them from their faulty upbringing. By keeping its hearings secret so the offender wouldn't be stigmatized after he had been reformed, by sending him to a reformatory and not a jail, the juvenile justice system tried to treat him not as a criminal but as a "child in need of the care and protection of the state."

But during the sixties the image of the state as a kind parent crumbled before the new idea of the state as oppressive and adversarial. Once the behavior of juvenile offenders became prima facie evidence of the unjust conditions in which they lived, it followed that it was only one further degree of oppression for the state to deprive them of their liberty without even a show of due process, as routinely used to happen in juvenile court hearings.

It happened because such hearings are civil rather than criminal proceedings: they are supposed to determine what best fills the therapeutic needs of the offender, not merely what meets the needs of the community. But in Justice Abe Fortas's words, for all the insistence that "guidance and rehabilitation" are at issue, not "criminal responsibility, guilt, and punishment," still the kid gets put away against his will. Therefore, he ought to have all the protections to which an adult would be entitled.

Chief of these protections, the Supreme Court ruled in *In re Gault* in 1967, is a lawyer. And once a court-appointed lawyer became mandatory in the juvenile courts, the whole array of *Miranda*-type procedural safeguards became routine there too. However humanely intended this reform, the result is that now juvenile offenders who are caught red-handed can also get away with murder scot-free, without even the few months in a rehabilitation facility that is the juvenile justice system's severest penalty.

In a sense, the Court had the right instinct in favoring the criminal, legalistic model over the therapeutic. Sadly, today's juvenile reformatory rehabilitates few, if any, since many youthful offenders aren't pickpockets and petty thieves salvageable by rehabilitation efforts. At fifteen, even at twelve or thirteen, many youthful rapists or murderers are hardened, brutal criminals, past the point of salvation, however much that reality might confute our sense of the possible or baffle our most generous impulses.

At the extreme of underclass pathology, too many of these young criminals have grown up in anarchic family situations, with mothers too defective to socialize them. A quarter century ago, when such young people began to inundate the family courts, eminent child psychiatrist Selma Fraiberg chillingly, and accurately, assessed their inner lives: "These are the people who are unable to fulfill the most ordinary human obligations in work, in friendship, in marriage, and in child-rearing," she wrote. "The condition of non-attachment leaves a void in the personality where conscience should be. Where there are no human attachments, there can be no conscience."

The new layer of legalism the Supreme Court added to juvenile proceedings didn't mean that youthful criminals would be exposed to the sanctions of the adult criminal justice system, however (at least not until very recently, when some jurisdictions have allowed the adult courts to try some fifteen- and sixteen-year-olds accused of rape and murder). It didn't mean that their records would be unsealed, so that future courts could know their criminal histories and better protect society against them. It only meant that it would be much harder to put them in the reformatories intended to do them good.

That has been an unfortunate change. For even if reformatories can offer little in the way of rehabilitation, they do offer punishment. After surveying years of studies of the relationship between the rates of various kinds of crime and the probability of imprisonment, crime theorist James Q. Wilson concludes that "the evidence supports (though cannot conclusively prove) the view that deterrence and incapacitation work," while "rehabilitation has not yet been shown to be a promising method for dealing with serious offenders." Even mild punishment seems better at changing behavior than none, but none is what juvenile offenders too often get.

One final barrier against crime also fell to the growing fear of the Haves that police injustice continually threatened the Have-Nots. I've mentioned James Q. Wilson and George Kelling's argument that neighborhood disorder causes an increase in crime, an argument later research has borne out. An infestation of panhandlers, drunks, addicts, graffiti smearers, street hustlers, streetwalkers, and youths rowdily "hanging out" testifies to a lack of police oversight that makes citizens feel threatened and encourages serious crime.

But the impulse to protect the Have-Nots from oppression went far to prevent the police from curbing the disorder that

Wilson and Kelling found so dangerous. Police keep order—or used to keep order—by relying on an array of time-honored prohibitions against loitering, vagrancy, disorderly conduct, disturbing the peace, and obscenity. Under such laws, they can question suspicious characters and quiet the disorderly or move them along.

But lawyers and judges came to feel that the order-keeping function of the police was yet one more instrument by which the authority of society was used to harass the Have-Nots. When does taking the air turn into loitering? When the person doing it, judges feared, is a poor black in a white neighborhood. So too might poverty and blackness transform sitting on a park bench into vagrancy, or turn high-spiritedness into disturbing the peace.

As a result, the laws governing such offenses as loitering or disorderly conduct were struck down for being overly broad or overly vague. *Papachristo* v. *City of Jacksonville* (1972) effectively spelled the end for many vagrancy and loitering ordinances. Jacksonville police had picked up a dozen or so citizens, including some suspected burglars and drug dealers, on the strength of a vagrancy ordinance directed in archaic language at "rogues and vagabonds ... who go about begging, ... persons who use juggling or unlawful games," and the like. How can anyone know exactly what conduct such fuzzy, antique rigmarole forbids? the Supreme Court complained in finding it unconstitutional. Whimsically quoting an assortment of poets in praise of "idling," as if all vagrants were free spirits like Walt Whitman or sixties street people, Justice William O. Douglas wrote that an ordinance like Jacksonville's "results in a regime in which the poor and the unpopular are permitted to 'stand on a public sidewalk ... only at the whim of any police officer.'"

Gooding v. *Wilson* (1972), in which the Court first struck down a law for being "too broad," shows how triflingly fanciful the reasoning could be by which judges undid the order-keeping function of the police in the service of their well-intentioned agenda. At issue was a Georgia statute outlawing language "tending to cause a breach of the peace." This law belonged to a time-honored legal tradition of prohibitions against "fighting words," language so insulting that it might be expected to provoke someone to blows. But a Georgia court had once ruled that you could violate this law by yelling at someone who was across a raging river or locked in a jail cell. In other words, even though you might utter your words to someone who could not literally fight you, they were still "fighting words," as far as the Georgia judge was concerned, and therefore prohibited.

Supreme Court Justice William Brennan, citing this ruling, concluded that since the law went beyond words that could literally make someone fight, it must be struck down as too broad; it might encroach on the First Amendment right to make ugly statements unlikely to provoke blows. As constitutional scholar Richard E. Morgan remarks, lower courts in the wake of this decision have essentially done away with the concept of "fighting words"; in numerous cases, judges have upheld the right of Americans to call each other "motherfuckers"—the cultural revolution's standard-issue epithet—whether of the "white," "black," or "fascist" variety.

For all Americans, the wholesale overturning of the bars to crime and disorder has scrambled the moral order. What becomes of the sense of justice when, almost daily, people violate the fundamental principle of the social contract? What becomes of the sense of personal responsibility for actions when people are not held accountable even for the most evil deeds? With the ground on which the sense of values rests giving way beneath their feet, no wonder many reel with moral vertigo.

For all Americans, Haves and Have-Nots alike, the weakening of the protections against crime and disorder has debased urban life, overlaying it with fear and suspicion as well as real injury. The disproportionate number of crimes committed by underclass lawbreakers has heightened racial hostility, straining the social fabric. Straining it too are the menacing rowdiness and graffiti, the dope selling, and the occupation by the homeless of public spaces everywhere.

If the Haves sought to uplift and ennoble their own lives by the dual liberations they tried to accomplish, the condition of today's great cities is a sad monument to the Law of Unintended Consequences. Metropolitan life is the great hothouse of human possibility, nurturing characters of every stripe. In such an atmosphere, people can achieve as far as is possible the latent potentialities that the Haves thirsted to realize when they began their cultural revolution. How ironic that that revolution ended by driving so many of the energetic and ambitious out of the cities. The civic culture that fosters the full development of individuals—the sense of a community linked by mutual tolerance and respect for ambition, achievement, and energy—will be thinner and more constricted in the New York or Chicago or Detroit of the nineties than it was in the New York or Chicago or Detroit of the forties or fifties.

However much the erosion of the barriers to crime and disorder disrupted the lives of the Haves, that disruption pales compared to the disruption it inflicted on the lives of the Have-Nots. More than any economic change of the William Julius Wilson variety, it is the explosion of violent crime that has turned inner cities into blighted wastelands, virtual free-fire zones. Repeated holdups and street robberies of employees drove out small tradesmen and larger businesses alike. Crime made fear ever-present for hardworking, law-abiding ghetto citizens— who, though you might not think so from reading William Julius Wilson on the flight of upwardly mobile blacks from the ghetto, certainly do exist.

The almost daily reports of gunfire crackling outside the projects, of people cowering on the floor of their apartments, of innocent passersby getting caught in the crossfire, become numbing by their very familiarity. But it is true that a young black man has a greater chance of being murdered in the inner city than a soldier had of being killed in the jungles of Vietnam. It is true that you can send your kid to the grocery store and never see him again alive. It is true that an East New York high school, in a painfully ghoulish accommodation to anarchy, has recently established a "Grieving Room," where students gather to mourn slain classmates. In the last four years, seventy have been shot or stabbed, half of them fatally.

Quoted in a recent newspaper article reporting that two innocent bystanders in the New York ghettos had been killed and five more wounded in the last forty-eight hours, the mother of one of the wounded says: "I work ten hours a day. . . . In the morning, I have to leave before my kids do. All I can do is say a prayer, that's about it. Because you never know if you're going to come back alive, and you come home and they're going to be alive. You'll be in your house and people will be shooting through your damn window. You stick your head out your window, somebody blows your brains out."

The achievements of civilization rest upon the social order, which rests in turn upon a mutual agreement to forswear aggression. In the ghetto, the agreement is in tatters, the police are hamstrung, and the life of the civilized community is being stomped out by force and violence. In cities in which civilization should have reached its apogee, gang-ridden ghetto areas have regressed to some dark age when human life was organized around predatory, roving bands with continually shifting memberships. It is as if the peaceful citizens of those neighborhoods really were under the cruel yoke of the banditti of ruffians that Thomas Paine imagined as introducing violence and crime into the early ages of the world.

After a nine-year-old girl in a crime-ravaged Brooklyn ghetto had just been shot in the head by a thug's stray bullet, a neighbor—a law-abiding family man living across the street from a crack house—lamented: "Our lives have been reduced to the lowest levels of human existence." In such an anarchy, it's a wonder not when people fail to achieve the civilized excellences but when, like the family man quoted above, they succeed.

The primary function of any society is to guarantee the social contract. What but anarchy can you expect if the legitimate force of society has eroded? What can you expect when the guardians of that force cannot bring themselves to exercise it, like a New York judge who vibrated with protective sympathy for the defendant before him, a callously brutal eighteen-year-old murderer? The judge, trying to quell the prosecutor's outraged complaints about the defense lawyer's procedural pettifoggery, cried out feelingly: "This is only a murder! Only a murder!"

CHAPTER NINE

The Living Constitution

Let's take a step back at this point, to gain a wider perspective. The cultural changes considered so far—changes springing from the cultural revolution's impulse to bring the poor and excluded into the American mainstream—directly harmed the people they were supposed to benefit. By contrast, the next two chapters will consider this aspect of the cultural revolution not only as it immediately damaged the worst-off but also as it twisted and trashed American culture itself. In the end, shot through with contradiction and inconsistency, with old ideas half demolished jumbled together with new ideas half thought out, the culture no longer made complete sense. It no longer added up to a coherent and sustaining system of values for the Haves themselves, whatever their race.

In this way, the revolution in the culture wounded the Haves as well as the Have-Nots, splintering the American ideal so that it seemed a less solid foundation for belief. Minorities on the way up found themselves equally confused and ambivalent, since the cultural revolution seemed to devalue the principles that had fueled their rise.

But of course no one was harmed anywhere near as grievously as the Have-Nots. And ultimately the moral confusion that the deconstruction of the culture produced in the Haves came round to deepen the injury inflicted on the underclass and the homeless even when it seemed not to bear directly on them. For when the culture lost its coherence, when its bedrock

183

values became devalued in the eyes of the Haves of all races, it lost its efficacy as a guide for the behavior of the Have-Nots. They no longer had a clear set of standards and values that would guide them up the ladder of social and economic mobility and would democratically define as worthy any person, however poor, willing to adopt them.

Consider the set of changes that occurred under the idea of the "Living Constitution." This idea is central to the cultural revolution's original, creditable goal of resolving America's burdensome paradox: the contradiction between the nation's democratic ideals and its long mistreatment of blacks. Though American democracy came into the world as a vast step forward in human progress, a triumph of political imagination, it also came into the world badly flawed by the institution of slavery. Even after emancipation, it withheld full legal equality from blacks, leaving a stain still disfiguring democracy.

In setting out to reconcile the American paradox, to exorcise racial inequality, the cultural revolution of the Haves found in the Supreme Court a powerful and willing instrument. Like so many of the Haves, though earlier than most, the justices embraced the new culture's vision of change and liberation. With great optimism, they gladly wielded their power to embody that vision in the concrete reality of law. Unfortunately, as this chapter will argue, in the process the justices inadvertently confused the very idea of democracy to the point of bewilderment.

This aspect of the cultural revolution unfolded under the banner of the Living Constitution. No element of our remade culture is more sacrosanct than the idea behind that slogan, first popularized in the 1920s by a Columbia University law professor. Indeed, "idea" is too neutral a word; only a term like "article of faith," even "dogma," can catch the moral fervor and certitude invested in the concept, its centrality as a fixed star from which our remade culture takes its moral bearings.

The Living Constitution doctrine begins with the notion that the Constitution that defines our democracy is presciently adaptable to social change, but it quickly goes beyond that idea. The Constitution can do more than merely adapt. As Supreme Court justices and federal judges interpret it, the Constitution can effect vast social transformations that raise justice and liberty to ever higher stages of perfection.

This doctrine views the Constitution and the courts as a higher power that intervenes when democracy reaches an impasse. According to this doctrine, the democratic process keeps failing the democratic ideal: the freely elected Congress, the president, the state legislatures, all tend to shy away when required to take some hard, unpopular step to root out American democracy's imperfections.

In a recent affirmation of the Living Constitution faith, columnist Anthony Lewis asks why activist federal judges have become such an important feature of our politics over the last few decades. "The fault lies not in our judges but in ourselves—in the way American democracy now works, or rather does not work," he answers. Judges act when "[t]here is a stalemate of democracy," when "[n]othing can get decided." Lewis guesses that many elected officials, compelled to carry out federal court directives, "are secretly glad to be forced to do what they know is right—forced to override special interests and act in the general interest."

The Living Constitution idea crystallized in a single event, the *Brown* v. *Board of Education* school desegregation decision of 1954. *Brown* addressed itself to finishing American democracy's unfinished business. In the postwar opening of American society, the contradiction between our equalitarian ideal and our discriminatory reality loomed sharper than it had before we—blacks and whites together—had fought a war in Europe to stop the horrors that discrimination at its most evil can produce. Even so, given the South's political power in 1954, neither the executive nor the legislative branch was willing to risk trying to dismantle the system of legal, official segregation that disgraced not just the South but the whole nation. So the Supreme Court justices courageously undertook in *Brown* to start pushing back Jim Crow by forbidding government-supported schools from excluding students because of race.

In deciding *Brown,* they took a huge step forward. But for all its goodness, their decision also contained a time bomb, thanks to the way they reached their conclusion.

Since the only power the judges have is the power to interpret the Constitution, they had but one way to end school segregation: to find that segregated schools were unconstitutional. To reach that conclusion, though, the judges put themselves and the Constitution through contortions that had huge, negative consequences.

At first glance, you'd think that declaring school desegregation unconstitutional would be easy: just invoke the Fourteenth Amendment, guaranteeing citizens the equal protection of the laws. But on closer inspection that hook proves problematic. Adopted right after the Civil War, the amendment aimed to assure blacks the most elementary civil rights: to own property, to make contracts, to sue and be sued. But by contrast with the sweeping, noble vision of the equality of man that Lincoln had voiced at Gettysburg, the Reconstruction congressmen who framed the Fourteenth Amendment stated in their debates that they didn't mean it to bar school segregation, and accordingly they went on to appropriate money for the District of Columbia's segregated schools.

As Harvard constitutional scholar Raoul Berger concluded: "Segregation was left untouched by the Fourteenth Amendment." According to Berger, just looking at the intent of its authors—the chief interpretive method of one important tradition of constitutional scholarship—prevents one from arguing that the amendment outlaws separate education as unequal.

Beyond that, the justices faced the further problem of precedent. For, if there was any doubt about the matter, the Supreme Court's 1896 *Plessy* v. *Ferguson* decision had unequivocally declared that under the Fourteenth Amendment separate facilities for blacks and whites were constitutional, providing the facilities were equal. Even without the legislative history of the Fourteenth Amendment, this decision was a formidable obstacle, since the Supreme Court shrinks from reversing itself: it's hard to have settled law if the law's ultimate interpreter changes its mind.

Whatever means the judges chose to outlaw school segregation therefore would require a twisting of the Constitution, since history and precedent, two pillars of jurisprudence, wouldn't uphold them. They had no unequivocally constitutional way to do what they wanted to do. While it is understandable that they settled on a course that, as we'll see in a moment, at least gave the appearance (but not the reality) of following precedent, hindsight shows that it would have been less harmful if the judges had straightforwardly overruled *Plessy* v. *Ferguson* as wrong, declaring that, under the Fourteenth Amendment, properly understood, the government can't discriminate by race in any way.

But instead of admitting what they were really doing, the judges chose to try to conceal that in effect they were superseding *Plessy* and ignoring the Fourteenth Amendment's legislative history by declaring that *Plessy*'s separate-but-equal ruling doesn't apply in the particular case of education. Putting aside other forms of segregation, the Fourteenth Amendment really does forbid *school* segregation, they argued, because in the special case of education, separate facilities are inherently unequal.

Why? Primarily, wrote Chief Justice Earl Warren, because segregated education makes black children feel inferior, squelching their eagerness to learn and retarding their development. Consistent with the spirit of the dawning age, the legal gave way to the therapeutic; the distinction between right and wrong blurred into that between healthy and unhealthy, adjusted and maladjusted.

In the overwhelming acclaim that greeted *Brown*, the justices emerged as nine heroes who'd unknotted America's most tangled social problem. They had managed to do what the majority of Americans thought right but the other branches of government had not been able to accomplish. Such leaps have sometimes been necessary, and the justices did what great jurists had done before them. At least since the Elizabethan judge Sir Edward Coke, courts have made radical policy changes to advance liberty, stretching their authority beyond its proper bounds and making law rather than interpreting it. But when judges made such interventions, they did so reluctantly, as rare, single exceptions in extremity rather than as a habit of jurisprudence.

In the wake of *Brown*, however, such circumspection evaporated. Emboldened by the emerging culture's applause, the Supreme Court and other federal courts developed a taste for path-breaking social engineering. The great exception—the one-time lapse from normal jurisprudence—became the rule. Federal judicial activism became so routine that today Anthony Lewis can speak of it as part of the regular machinery of state and city government, affecting matters as local and particular as a municipality's sewage connections, at issue in the column of Lewis's quoted above.

But to the extent the judges put themselves in the business of dispensing solutions to knotty social problems and providing for the continual reform of society on lines envisioned by the cultural revolution, they were acting not like a judiciary but like a government. You can argue, along with Anthony Lewis, that for them to do so is efficient and progressive, perhaps even more so than when elected officials contentiously try to grapple with such problems. But you cannot argue that it is democratic. Courts may be wise and benevolent; their judgments may be (though in practice often are not) Solomonic; but in a self-governing democracy popularly elected officials, not unelected jurists with lifetime tenure, make laws and set social policy. As Raoul Berger put it: "Remember Justice Holmes's remark, 'The people have got a right to go to hell their own way.' If you don't believe that, you're not a democrat."

After the acclaim of *Brown,* the new jurisprudence played logical tricks, slyly evading problems to reach results that the judges viewed as morally irresistible. The spirit of judicial interpretation became a matter less of following where text and precedent led than of forcing them to get where judges wanted to go.

An entire academic industry sprang up to justify such jurisprudence and systematize it into dogma, now routinely taught in law schools. The reasoning of the most influential of the systematizers, Ronald Dworkin, professor of jurisprudence at both New York University and Oxford, gives the flavor of the whole genre, which omits constitutional interpretation almost entirely.

Dworkin asserts that judges should view the Constitution's principles only as very broad generalities. For particular applications of those principles, judges shouldn't look to what the Framers had in mind but rather to the enlightened understanding modern Americans have of those principles. We follow the Framers in wanting to be fair, for instance; but fairness might mean one thing to them, another to us. To take a more specific example, the Framers didn't view the death penalty as cruel and unusual punishment; we might.

The trouble with such loose reasoning is that it suggests that judges can say the Constitution means anything they want it to mean. Dworkin tries to head off that objection. Judges mustn't merely follow their own prejudices, he says. Instead, they must take guidance from the shared morality of our era, the spirit of our age. And what is that morality? Nothing other, says Dworkin, than the teachings of Harvard philosopher John Rawls, which we considered at the end of Chapter Six as a key element of the revolutionized culture. In this way the explicit notion that justice is defined by the condition of the Have-Nots, who are the moral touchstone of society and the oppressed victims of the Haves, made its way to the Supreme Court justices, who wove the cultural revolution and its victimology into the fabric of the Constitution.

In the aftermath of *Brown,* two further initiatives, forced busing to achieve racial balance in the schools and affirmative action, turned the nondiscriminatory principle of the initial decision upside down by legitimizing government-sponsored racial preferences.

Had these measures succeeded in achieving their social policy goals, perhaps the judges' tortuous reasoning to justify them might now seem warranted, despite the twisting of democracy entailed by policies based on group identity rather than on the individual rights the Constitution protects. But busing failed utterly, leaving schools more segregated than before, and most gains that affirmative action produced for its intended beneficiaries have been canceled out by the surprisingly large number of casualties among them, along with a sense of injustice pervading the community as a whole. In the end, these policies, by straining democratic principles, necessarily weakened the web of democratic values and beliefs upholding each individual's sense of the justice and coherence of the social world and his own doings within it.

How the Court's reasoning in *Brown* permitted the justices to work a transformation upon *Brown* itself, converting its affirmation of nondiscrimination into a warrant for discrimination, deserves analysis, for it is central to the process by which the cultural revolution turned the idea of democratic equality on its head.

Because the Justices in *Brown* slid around *Plessy* v. *Ferguson* instead of overruling it, their decision contained a fatal ambiguity. First and foremost, the *Brown* decision seemed to endorse the key argument of the plaintiffs: the NAACP had argued, quoting Justice Holmes's high-principled dissent in *Plessy,* that "the Constitution is color-blind," and that, therefore, when school boards assign children to schools, they should "not assign them on the basis of race." The Court signaled agreement with this reasoning in its decision, and a year later, in an opinion supplemental to *Brown,* the justices plainly declared that the case's "fundamental principle" was that "racial discrimination in public education is unconstitutional." For over a decade after the *Brown* ruling, that remained the understanding among jurists of the case's meaning.

Still, the judges had failed to be this explicit in *Brown* itself. And the reasoning they actually used, when closely reexamined, suggested an opposing principle. By using as the justification for their decision the argument that racial separation engenders feelings of inferiority in black children, the justices unwittingly left room for the inference that it wasn't enough for the state to stop separating children on racial grounds but that instead it must actively mix them, since only mixing could overcome their sense of inferiority. But such mixing can be achieved only if school boards *do* classify and assign children by race, thereby engaging—for however beneficent a purpose—in racial discrimination.

A decade after *Brown,* Congress addressed this question, with no ambiguity at all. The 1964 Civil Rights Act in effect ratified the antidiscrimination reading of the *Brown* decision and extended the principle of nondiscrimination to other key areas of the national life. The act explicitly decreed that " 'Desegregation' means the assignment of students to public schools and within such schools without regard to their race, color, religion, or national origin, but 'desegregation' shall not mean the assignment of students to public schools in order to overcome racial imbalance." The act also declared that it didn't empower judges to order students transported from school to school to achieve racial balance. During congressional debate, the bill's sponsors assured fellow legislators that the desegregation the bill required for schools only meant that children mustn't be prevented from going to school together because of race, not that any given school must achieve racial balance. Floor manager Hubert Humphrey promised his fellow senators that the bill would not result in the busing of children to relieve racial imbalance.

Yet judges, in key decisions on the way to busing, kicked free with almost casual recklessness from both *Brown's* animating principle and Congress's forcefully expressed will. Within two years of the Civil Rights Act, all the legislators' promises began to be broken—in the name of compliance with *Brown,* taking advantage of *Brown's* ambiguity to reverse its meaning entirely.

In 1966, an activist Department of Health, Education, and Welfare, ideologically committed to social engineering, set in motion the overturning of *Brown's* implicit principle of nondiscrimination by issuing guidelines for school desegregation plans that it would accept as complying with the Civil Rights Act. In some school systems, said HEW—in flat contradiction of Congress's stated intent—compliance might require assignment of pupils according to race.

The courts rushed in to give legitimacy to this reversal of the will of the people's elected representatives. First, Federal Appeals Judge John Minor Wisdom validated the HEW guidelines. He ruled that "desegregation" (the ending of legal separation by race) and "integration" (the mixing of the races) were interchangeable words as far as the Constitution was concerned, so that *Brown* really required racial mixing. If the races weren't mixed together—as thanks to residential patterns they largely were not in southern schools even after *Brown* removed school assignment by race—then desegregation hadn't occurred. As for the 1964 Civil Rights Act's prohibitions against assigning pupils by race, and even Senator Humphrey's solemn promise that racial assignments would never occur, these, Judge Wisdom declared, must be understood as applying only to northern schools, not the ones in the Deep South circuit under his judicial care.

The Supreme Court adopted Judge Wisdom's tactic of changing the meaning of "desegregation" to "integration." In the 1968 *Green* v. *Board of Education* decision, Justice William Brennan ruled that, though a rural Virginia school system had stopped assigning pupils by race and let them transfer to the school of their choice, desegregation hadn't taken place: schools remained either mostly white or mostly black. It wasn't enough to open the schools to all, regardless of race. School boards would have to send in the right proportion of kids of the right color, so there would no longer be black schools or white schools, but "just schools." Implicitly, though Brennan never said so directly, nondiscrimination by race would have to give way to discrimination by race.

The judges made this point explicitly in the 1971 *Swann* v. *Charlotte Mecklenberg Board of Education* case. Intentionally segregated school systems, they ruled, must now achieve a high degree of racial balance—and busing, they added, was a fine way to do that. Two years later, the Court's *Keyes* v. *School District No. 1, Denver, Colorado* ruling removed the issue of intentionality and declared that statistical imbalance of itself required busing. Thereafter, the great reform of society could move beyond the South and begin nationwide.

Many still remember the frightened children lying for safety on the floors of buses, the angry mobs, the policemen in school hallways, the spectacle of Federal Judge W. Arthur Garrity, Jr., ruling the Boston school system like a commissar for eleven years, issuing over four hundred decrees on matters as detailed as student transfers and the purchase of new basketballs. What is less familiar is that the experiment failed: busing proved as monumentally futile (and divisive) as Prohibition or the Vietnam War. Because of white flight to private schools and to the suburbs, nine of the nation's ten largest school systems were more segregated by 1984 than they were in 1970, before busing started.

For example, in Boston, during the decade of Judge Garrity's control, public school enrollment dropped from 93,000 to 57,000, and the student body went from being 65 percent white to 28 percent. Heartbreakingly, the same pattern holds even for the five systems against which the original *Brown* suits were brought. The Washington, D.C., schools, for instance, went from being 39 percent white in 1954 to 3.5 percent white by 1981. Busing and related efforts to integrate the schools resulted not only in more, but in more entrenched, segregation. Once white pupils had withdrawn to largely white suburbs, segregation became much harder to overcome.

The supporters of busing and other efforts to achieve racial balance in the schools were right to think that the schools were key in any effort to include the excluded; public education is the traditional route to American society's mainstream. One of the conundrums of urban America in the last generation is why the schools failed to accomplish this task for the underclass. Though many strains in the new national culture combined to produce this result, part of the answer is busing and racial assignment to achieve racial balance. For years, in numerous public school systems, education seemed to be of less concern than equality. What makes the history of busing so painful is that, after all the turning of communities upside down and all the hopes and righteous good intentions of its supporters, busing didn't improve educational opportunity for blacks but debased it in unintended and unforeseen ways.

White flight is the principal harmful consequence that these efforts visited upon the schools. Parents who took their children out of school systems because of busing or other affirmative integration efforts often were motivated by fear that, since black pupils' average educational achievement was lower than white pupils', their kids would suffer educationally from aggressively integrated classrooms. This was the opposite face of the NAACP's belief that black children would benefit educationally from being in classrooms with white children. So the white pupils who left tended to be the motivated kids whose mainstream values had helped preserve order and an atmosphere conducive to learning—exactly the qualities needed to foster the fullest development of any children.

Many of these pupils' parents had played a crucial role for the schools. Says University of Texas law professor Lino Graglia, whose *Disaster by Decree* recounts the history of busing: "Those are the people who noodge the principals and the teachers all the time about how things are running, who put bond proposals on the ballot and pass them. Now big city schools are just places for the poor of society. The harm that this has done to the schools is incalculable." What hitherto had been a democratic institution supported by the whole society became in many places largely lower-class and minority, losing its democratic universality and becoming more a backwater than the mainstream.

In an unexpected, indirect way, busing also impaired discipline in public schools, impeding teaching and learning. Social control in the schools weakens as parental involvement decreases, studies have shown. When parents cooperate with each other in taking part in school life, they are able to establish consistent standards of behavior for kids that reinforce school discipline and parental discipline alike. In communities where busing eliminated neighborhood schools, parents lost touch, and discipline suffered. And from an academic point of view no less than a disciplinary one, parents' involvement with the school makes all the difference as to whether kids doing badly will ultimately fail.

Integration is a crucial good—but not because blacks need whites in the classroom in order to get a good education. Studies have not borne out this proposition; and why should blacks learning together not learn perfectly well? Integration is crucial because a society without invidious distinctions, in which equal citizens associate freely, is intrinsic to the American democratic ideal.

But it isn't surprising that ferociously shaking society failed to accomplish this important good. What would have succeeded, and is succeeding now where it has been thoughtfully tried, is the idea of magnet schools, an approach that wins over concerned white parents by inviting them to send their children to integrated schools structured to provide some special educational feature not obtainable elsewhere in the school system. Some magnet schools concentrate on computer skills, for example; others on the performing arts or even on the traditional three-Rs curriculum coupled with traditional discipline. Where all have committed themselves to a distinctive educational enterprise, forming a community of shared values and aspirations, integration, even beyond the merely superficial level, is easier to achieve. As I've been suggesting, and will spell out more clearly later, the re-creation of a community of values is crucial for solving our most intransigent social problems, from underclass poverty to the inner malaise of the Haves.

Busing isn't the only way the Living Constitution weakened the schools, making them less able to bring the underclass into the mainstream. Schools were also impaired by one of the myriad new rights spawned by the Living Constitution. The last chapter examined how some of the profusion of Court-created new rights weakened the social fabric by hampering the police. Yet another class of new rights—pupils' rights—damaged the schools by subverting school discipline. Teachers lost much of their authority over pupils and, naturally enough, found it increasingly hard to keep them well enough behaved to learn.

As we saw in the last chapter, the Supreme Court began to transform the juvenile justice system in the mid-1960s, extending to juvenile suspects the procedural safeguards of the adult criminal justice system. Observing this momentous change, the American Civil Liberties Union concluded that what was true for the courts must also be true for the schools. In an influential 1968 article, the ACLU warned school officials to watch out: the Supreme Court's stance on juvenile justice, the ACLU claimed, meant that the schools, no less than the juvenile courts, would have to treat kids with due process too, getting rid of "rule by personality" in favor of "rule by law."

This warning proved prophetic. An Ohio principal probably wished he'd heeded it before he summarily suspended nine pupils in 1975 for spiking the punch at the high school hop. No matter, said the Supreme Court, that Ohio law requires no hearing for suspensions of up to ten days; the Fourteenth Amendment says no state can deprive a person of liberty without due process of law—and that means a hearing. Lucky for the principal that this didn't happen a few months later, by which time the Court had ruled that kids can sue their individual teachers and principals for damages for infringing their civil rights.

So much for the authority of the school as a community institution midway between the family and the government:

now there is only the authority of the government. For once school discipline was hedged around with the whole panoply of written codes and procedures, hearings, witnesses, cross-examinations, appeals, and the threat of lawsuits, it began to wither. It was easier for teachers and principals to avoid confrontations they might lose. This subversion of their authority occurred just at the moment when the decline of neighborhood schools was also compromising discipline. At about this time, the newspapers routinely began to carry stories of attacks on teachers and pupils in the school halls.

Along with the damage they did to underclass pupils trapped in worsening inner-city schools, busing and school assignment to achieve racial mixing harmed both the white families who fled and society at large. Schools, though publicly financed and administered, aren't mere organs of the state but are also, like families, churches, or businesses, key institutions of civil society. The state can legitimately pluck you out of civil society by drafting you into the army, but it makes you its instrument only to carry out its mandated function of protecting civil society. In busing, however, the state in effect drafts your kid to carry out a vast social engineering project that is based not on the social compact or the mandate of the electorate but on a highly questionable reading of the basic law of the land. When for such a purpose, and on such authority, the state treats your child not as an end but as a means, the realm of freedom has been constricted and the state has begun to turn against the civil society whose instrument it is supposed to be.

Moreover, in an age of urban anonymity and isolation, when churches and other communal institutions have lost so much of their vitality, the state inflicts real damage on already beleaguered communities by dismantling neighborhood schools. If its warrant to do so is illegitimate, the harm is intolerable; and to do so while failing even to accomplish the end that is supposed to justify the means only makes the harm greater.

Busing failed to integrate the schools; but if busing was intended to extend democracy, it must be judged the greater failure for injecting into the national life a corrosive stream of cynicism about the state's democratic good faith. After all, it is hard to see the democratic spirit in a government policy that makes distinctions by race in a vast social engineering project undertaken not by democratically elected legislators but by an unelected judiciary acting like a government.

The furthest extent of the government push to rearrange society under the aegis of the Living Constitution is affirmative action. Not confined to state-supported institutions, such as schools, affirmative action imposes the hand of the government on private employers and such private institutions as universities. If discrimination caused injustice, the logic runs, reverse discrimination will supply the cure. And not just for racial minorities: proffering their own claim of oppression, women demanded, and got, the same disquieting remedy.

Granted the power to make social policy by twisting a ring or rubbing a lamp as in the fairy tales, most of us would more than likely conjure up the kind of society imagined by the cultural revolution: an equal society, in which no one suffered poverty or exclusion, and people held jobs of honor and authority regardless of race or sex—the kind of society depicted in today's politically correct schoolbooks, where the cop is a woman, the doctor is black, the nursery school teacher is a white male, and all are happy and helpful. One can't help wondering if the Supreme Court justices thought they saw in the Living Constitution just such a magical talisman that could make everything different merely by command. Certainly affirmative action gives every appearance of being that command.

But what strange assumptions underlie it. The controlling belief is that you can fight fire with fire and end up with something more than scorched earth—that you can overcome one evil by using a dose of the same evil. But trafficking with such means and wielding such powers entails as high a cost as a pact with the devil, for when you are done discriminating, it is hard to reassert the principle of nondiscrimination. That's if you ever *are* done, of course: no affirmative action program in the world has ever been declared successful and ended as no longer necessary.

With affirmative action, a bureaucracy heavily staffed with committed partisans of blacks' and women's causes overturned the nondiscriminatory principles of the 1964 Civil Rights Act and won sweeping endorsement from the Supreme Court. The

1964 act, like an earlier executive order of President Kennedy's, envisioned that the government, as well as private employers engaged in interstate commerce or doing work on government contracts, would make special efforts to find qualified minority candidates and give them whatever training was needed.

Yet without any affirmative action at all, society was already bringing minorities into the mainstream, as can be seen in the strong, steady rise in the median wages of black full-time workers from 60 percent of the rapidly increasing white median in the mid-fifties to 75 percent in the mid-seventies, before affirmative action was in full swing. Even so, in its original form affirmative action was a reasonable use of government power to accomplish the praiseworthy goal of speeding up this movement. But a 1970 edict of the Labor Department, quickly adopted by the impatient HEW, changed the fundamental rules: it demanded "goals"—that is, quotas—timetables, and results.

The Supreme Court took it from there, flinging down the idea of nondiscrimination and dancing upon it with abandon. The Court's 1971 *Griggs* v. *Duke Power Co.* decision made clear that if your work force's racial composition doesn't reflect the racial composition of your area, you will be presumed to have discriminated, unless you can prove that your hiring criteria were strictly job-related. From *Bakke* and *Weber* in 1978 and 1979 to a clutch of 1987 cases, the Court successively decided that universities may consider race in admissions decisions, that reverse discrimination is allowable in private and public employment and in government contracting, that quotas are permissible whether intentional discrimination has taken place or not, and, finally, that judges can impose such quotas.

So now it is routine in America for less qualified applicants to be accepted into colleges over much more qualified competitors, like the black student admitted to Berkeley—though he was in the bottom third of his private-school class and had been expelled for serious misconduct—while his white classmate, in the top academic third, was refused admission. As a Berkeley official explains: "Merit is no longer the predominant factor in admissions."

Also routine are situations in which minority job applicants are hired to fill affirmative action quotas based on their grade on a Labor Department aptitude test whose results are rigged to make their performance look better than it is. By a practice called "race-norming," blacks and Hispanics are graded on a curve only in relation to other blacks and Hispanics. So for such applicants, scoring in the eighty-fifth percentile on the test represents a much lower absolute achievement than a white applicant's same 85 percent score—though this fact was until recently concealed from employers. In addition to preferential quotas, minority applicants thus gained a further arbitrary edge over white applicants.

At the end of the eighties, a much-altered Court began to curb the two-decades-long expansion of affirmative action, ruling in the 1989 *Ward's Cove Packing* decision that if the managers and clerks in a work force are mostly white, and the manual laborers mostly nonwhite, the statistical imbalance doesn't in itself prove discrimination.

There is little logic in the basic affirmative action assumption that, were it not for discrimination, each social slice—the medical profession, the construction industry, and so on—would be a perfect racial and sexual microcosm of the larger society. As economist Thomas Sowell has observed, different groups have different histories, interests, and skills, different age and geographical profiles, which ensures that their distribution in the larger society will not be random.

In attempting to make various institutions and professions unnaturally reflect the racial composition of the larger society, affirmative action has pushed and squeezed its beneficiaries in ways that have proved a decidedly mixed blessing to them. Take the case of college admissions, where affirmative action has left black students worse off than before by inappropriately matching them up with institutions whose more-than-usually exacting standards sharply reduce their chances of success. On the Scholastic Aptitude Test, required of applicants to many colleges and a demonstrably quite accurate predictor of future academic performance, blacks score markedly lower than whites on average—over 20 percent lower in 1990. Of some 94,000 college-bound blacks who took the test that year, only 115 scored 700 or more on the verbal section (out of a possible 800), and 274 did that well on the math part. Fewer than 2,000 scored over 600 on either part of the test.

At the very top schools, combined math and verbal SAT scores of over 1300 (out of a possible 1600) are average, and combined scores over 1200 are average at other prestigious colleges. But in 1983, the last year for which combined scores are published, fewer than 600 blacks in the entire country scored over 1200, though SAT scores for blacks have risen slightly in the years since then.

The result is that there aren't enough high-scoring black candidates to fill the quotas at the top schools: Berkeley alone, for example, accepted 831 black applicants to its 1989 freshman class. The best colleges skim off the highest-scoring black applicants, but those applicants have average test scores below the average white who gains admission. For example, though recently the average black MIT student scored in the top 10 percent nationwide on the math SAT, that fine performance put him in the bottom 10 percent of his high-powered MIT fellow students.

Black students who matriculate at the top schools, says Thomas Sowell, are well qualified to go to college, but they often are mismatched with the colleges they actually attend. With their SAT scores above the national average—even if less stellar than the average Berkeley or MIT score—these black students would have succeeded overwhelmingly at a good college a notch below MIT or Berkeley or Harvard or the handful of other elite schools that have snatched them up to fill their quotas. And the mismatch continues all across the higher education spectrum. The black candidates who are available to fill the quotas at the second-tier schools have lower test scores than the white candidates, and so with the third tier and on down the line.

With this burden of a disparity in academic preparation, it's no wonder that they fail disproportionately. A quarter of the blacks at MIT don't graduate; those who do often have below-average grades. More than 60 percent of the black students at Berkeley never graduate; nearly one third of black and Hispanic students there drop out in their freshman year. Of the total number of black students nationwide, only 26 percent succeed in graduating six years after matriculating. So colleges are succeeding very indifferently in helping minorities rise up the social and economic ladder.

Slogging along at their mismatched colleges, such students have two choices, as Sowell explains. Either they can decide that they really are inferior people—an alternative both cruel and false—or else they can reject entirely the standards by which they are judged failures. The problem isn't with them, they can assert; it is with their colleges, which treat them with knee-jerk racism and force upon them a racist curriculum that they cannot and should not engage, because that would make them complicit in their own oppression. Courses need to be transformed to describe the world from their perspective, they end up arguing; whites need to be given sensitivity seminars to purge them of their racism, and separate black dorms and dining tables need to be set up, so that black students can have a haven from racist affronts.

White students observing such poor performance, listening to such special pleading, being required to take black studies courses and sensitivity seminars they don't want, often respond with impatience and contempt. Just as students used to disparage "dumb jocks" admitted under looser standards than their fellow students, says Sowell, white students not previously racist become persuaded of black inferiority and angry at blacks for the elaborate charade enacted at many colleges to deny the plain reality of the failure that is taking place. No wonder, says Sowell, that precisely the colleges most heavily committed to affirmative action—and the concomitant, politically correct array of black dorms, black studies courses, black deans, and other measures that appear to set up an alternative institution with separate standards for blacks—have suffered from so many racist incidents recently.

The failure of so many black students is artificially induced by affirmative action, which constricts the life chances of qualified young people who otherwise would have succeeded, hampering rather than speeding the rise of blacks into the mainstream.

The magical thinking behind affirmative action in the wider realm of employment recalls Marxist incantations about ideas and feelings being merely passive reflections of concrete economic realities. To bring the excluded directly into the mainstream, goes the affirmative action logic, just put them there.

Their inner lives will soon come into alignment with their new outer circumstances, and they will be mainstream citizens through and through, raising mainstream children.

From the point of view of affirmative action's beneficiaries, however, it isn't like that. Says Shelby Steele, affirmative action—though it isn't racism—feels like racism: "it makes blacks something of a separate species for whom normal standards and values do not automatically apply." And so it breeds "demoralization" and "an enlargement of self-doubt" in blacks. "Under affirmative action the quality that earns us preferential treatment is an implied inferiority." The "midnight of self-doubt" into which the imputation of inferiority plunges affirmative action's beneficiaries "often transforms their advantage into a revolving door" of failure.

Thus, affirmative action that puts blacks into mainstream jobs doesn't bring them much closer to becoming emotionally part of the mainstream. And much lower down the social scale, below affirmative action's reach, the policy still communicates its demoralizing imputation of inferiority to blacks in the underclass, reinforcing their sense of the distance between them and the mainstream.

Beyond the harm affirmative action inflicts on its presumed beneficiaries is the harm it does the larger culture. For affirmative action overturns three constituent principles of democratic individualism. The first is the idea that all men are created equal. If this means anything as a political principle, it has to mean that everyone is the same in the eyes of the law, that the state does not make invidious distinctions such as discriminating by race. Nor must the state compel private organizations to do so.

Second, in a democracy the individual is the relevant unit, not the class or the race. Rights belong to individuals rather than to groups. But within our revolutionized culture is an antidemocratic strain that ignores the individual. So found a thoughtful undergraduate who, with misgivings, wrote a memo to her fellow members of the University of Pennsylvania's "diversity education" planning committee affirming "my deep regard for the individual and my desire to protect the freedoms of all members of society." Back came her memo from a politically correct university administrator, with this phrase circled and the word *individual* underlined. Said the administrator: "This is a 'RED FLAG' phrase today, which is considered by many to be RACIST. Arguments that champion the individual over the group ultimately privilege the 'individuals' belonging to the largest or dominant group."

Finally, affirmative action subverts the key democratic idea of the career open to talents, the idea that positions of honor and influence should be distributed on the basis of individual qualifications rather than on birth into a class. It subverts the idea that merit should be rewarded, that the best person should win, that everyone should have an equal opportunity for self-development, and the highest achievements should be celebrated.

But the new culture holds that merit and excellence are chimeras. "What is excellence?" Jesse Choper, dean of the Berkeley law school, asks rhetorically. "There is no litmus paper test for it. Excellence is often like beauty, in the mind of the beholder." And, like so many arguments put forth by the new culture, once any value becomes entirely subjective, its definition becomes merely a matter of power politics. One professor, a proponent of preferential treatment for minority college students, takes Dean Choper's thought to its extreme conclusion: "[W]hen you see the word 'qualifications' used," he asserts, "remember that this is the new code word for whites." Rewarding merit, however, is not only central to the democratic conception of justice; it also is vital to national achievement and prosperity.

The changes that spring from the Living Constitution amount, in themselves, to a sweeping cultural revolution, altering the theory and spirit of our fundamental laws, as well as such important areas of common life as education and employment. For many people, though, it's not that the ideology of the Living Constitution has supplanted the old system of democratic values. Rather, the new ideology has placed those democratic values in a limbo of doubt and confusion, blunting their authority, tainting them with the charge that they might be the very opposite of virtuous, magnanimous, and even democratic.

The Living Constitution has left us with two mutually exclusive versions of democracy. Either democracy is the affirmative action vision writ large—a society is democratic because all groups are proportionally represented in all its parts, from university faculties to death row—or it is democratic because all are equal in the eyes of the state, free to excel and succeed regardless of what group they were born into. Both cannot be true. And standing bewildered between them, we feel, quite accurately, that we have lost our bearings.

Everywhere we turn we see signs that the majority of Americans have begun to feel that this confusion isn't an appropriate state of affairs. They have begun to sense that our culture's muddled redefinition of democracy, its partial substitution of group representation for individual rights, represents a wrong turn.

Nothing could better rectify the damage done to American culture in the name of the Living Constitution than an explicit law declaring what the Constitution should have said in the first place, and what the cultural revolution began by trying to make it say: that our laws and our government are color-blind and do not permit discrimination by race. Period.

CHAPTER TEN

Trashing the Culture

Remember the shiver you got reading a work like H. G. Wells's *The Time Machine*? That shiver doesn't come merely from exploring a strange, increasingly nightmarish world but rather from the growing realization that the threatening world is our world, with present tendencies—be it class inequality in *The Time Machine* or totalitarian impulses in *Nineteen Eighty-Four*—monstrously exaggerated. If we don't watch out, such novels dramatize, we could end up with a world this bad.

You get the same shiver reading recent reports about campus political correctness in the newsweeklies and in best sellers like Dinesh D'Souza's *Illiberal Education*. The lesson to be learned isn't merely that colleges and universities have been seized by a paroxysm of multiculturalism, deconstruction, preferential treatment, and speech codes, souring the teaching of the humanities and polluting the communal atmosphere with racial suspicion and ideological closed-mindedness. The important point is that what is happening on campus has already happened to a less spectacular extent throughout the culture as a whole. What has happened in education is the cultural revolution writ large.

Political correctness and its various offshoots don't constitute a separate phenomenon but are an extension of the intellectual and institutional changes examined in earlier chapters. The movement states explicitly beliefs that have been operating for years in the larger culture. That explicitness makes it easier to see how profoundly the liberations that have been at the center of the cultural agenda for a generation have entailed the thoroughgoing trashing of the culture itself.

It is clear that the trashing has been intentional, not accidental. Western culture purposely has been stripped of some of its authority as part of the Haves' effort both to free themselves from some of its chafing restrictions and to improve the lot of the poor and excluded. In an effort to avoid "blaming the victim," the Haves have found fault with the standards of Western culture, censuring them as elitist, racist, "classist," and so on. These standards, it is claimed, are merely a means to justify keeping down the Have-Nots.

Key shapers of American thought and belief—especially since the end of World War II, when student bodies became larger and more diverse—colleges and universities traditionally transmitted a legacy of Western secular culture that had assumed a particular importance in the twentieth century. For ever since early-Victorian geologists began finding fossil evidence that the biblical story of creation in seven days wasn't true—ever since Darwin theorized an account of the origin of species and the descent of man entirely different from the scriptural account—the religious understanding of the world has inexorably crumbled, and a secular one has taken its place. In our century, religious certitude about divine authority has ceased to be the principal foundation of our beliefs, values, and morality.

Today this central core of life rests upon two and a half millennia of thought about what is Good, True, and Just; about what is human nature and the right kind of life for Man as an individual and a social being; about what constitutes duty, honor, friendship, love, virtue, and freedom. It rests on the lessons of history, telling us how men have organized their lives and their institutions in different epochs, and what kinds of lives that organization afforded them; how leaders have acted, and what consequences their actions had for all. It rests upon what science has been able to discover about our own nature and how it interacts with the nature of the world we inhabit.

What ultimately gives authority to ideas of meaning and value for twentieth-century Western lives, in other words, is the accumulated legacy of Western culture, with its mix of the

Judeo-Christian ethic, classical and Renaissance humanism, scientific rationality, and the free, liberal democratic individualism that was conceived in Europe and reached its fullest fruition in America. It is this legacy of "the best which has been thought and said" about the human condition, as the Victorian thinker Matthew Arnold described culture, that colleges and universities have served to pass on, partially but sufficiently, to several generations of American students. So it is of more than merely academic interest that faculties have turned to junking this inheritance which they, more than any other group of people, have been entrusted to safeguard.

Even before the campus uprisings of the sixties, three powerful, unsettling streams in modern thought—Marxism, Freudianism, and an intermingled cultural and moral relativism—had been flowing into the universities for over three decades. The first two of these systems were deterministic ways of looking at the world, explaining human actions and beliefs in terms of vast, hidden forces that govern individual fates. And all of these strands, in different ways, diminished the moral dimension of life, either by denying the individual free will and responsibility for his or her actions, or by denying that any universal standards exist by which one can judge the morality of one's own or other people's actions. These developments molded the Haves' understanding of the Have-Nots' plight, shaping not only the explicit and implicit messages the Have-Nots heard from the larger culture but also the institutions that formed an increasingly important part of Have-Not life.

Marxism, with its theory of dialectical materialism, painted a picture of human history as molded by economic forces as powerful and impersonal as gravity, forces that sweep individuals along like so much flotsam in a torrent rushing to the sea. The Freudian system also portrayed individuals as ineluctably impelled by powerful forces—psychological rather than economic—beyond their capacity to control or even perceive. Under the force of such determinism, the individual becomes a mere puppet jerked by hidden, abstract puppeteers and devoid of free will or personal responsibility.

These systems diminish the individual further by dismissing whatever he or she says or believes—however seemingly brave, noble, or disinterested—as a mere screen disguising the hidden underlying reality. For the Freudians, what you say means something other than what you think it means; you don't even know what you're really saying. For the Marxist, beliefs and ideals are the passive reflection of underlying economic relations, so that charity, for instance, or belief in personal responsibility are at bottom merely expressions of sordid class interest.

These systems affected teaching in a curious way. Under the influence of Marxism, the teaching of history more and more frequently became the discovery of class interest, class conflict, and class consciousness. *Aha,* the lesson went, *Marx was right!* In this spirit, the Constitution became a reflection of the economic interests of its propertied Framers rather than a blueprint for an extraordinary advance in human liberty. Revolutions moved to the center of pedagogical interest, with the English Civil War said to illustrate an awakening proletarian consciousness and the French Revolution explained in terms of the interests of the middle class. Attention focused too on how the working class came to develop its own distinctive class identity and worldview.

This way of looking at history has only been reinforced, from the sixties onward, by new ways of thinking about and teaching history that have sprung up out of Marxism's fundamental assumptions. If suprahuman, impersonal economic forces and material realities govern history, then those forces and realities should be what students study. If kings and statesmen, like all individuals, are merely the creatures of these forces, then they determine the shape of events no more than the cock's crowing causes the sun to rise; instead of bothering with their vainglorious doings, students should instead focus on the anonymous lives of the ordinary people who constitute most of humanity. If philosophers and artists simply reflect the material realities and class interests of their age—if ideas don't shape history—then the time that used to be spent on intellectual history would be better spent studying the worldview of peasants and trying to understand how it reflects the circumstances in which they lived. Not that these are unworthy topics; but they amount only to a fraction of the story.

Freudianism worked in a similar way in the teaching of literature. Professors presented great works of the imagination as demonstrations of Freudian truths. Hamlet, for instance, shrank into the young man with the Oedipus complex; and what Shakespeare's awe-inspiring play had to say about sexuality, evil, role-playing, the difficulty of righting wrongs, the complex ambivalence inherent in family relations, all paled in the light of the psychoanalyst's master-truth.

The professors began to forget what gives literature its interest and power: its exploration of how an individual exerts his free will and moral choice under a given set of circumstances. In literature, abstract psychological, moral, and social issues become concrete and personal, as they do in our own lives. As readers, guided by authorial insight, we try to understand why characters feel the way they feel and make the choices they make, and we sharpen our own moral and psychological acuity by judging their actions. This kind of engagement is a far cry from the Freudian reductiveness typified by one literature professor's well-received essay about the workings, in *Oliver Twist,* of Dickens's alleged fantasies about seeing his parents having sex.

By mixing Freud and Marx together, humanities faculties concocted a worldview that contained in microcosm both aspects of the cultural revolution of the Haves. That worldview was based in part on a misreading of Freud. Freud had highlighted the vast extent of anarchic sexuality and aggression in the depths of the psyche. He had argued that civilization's necessary restraint of those impulses entails a measure of inescapable unhappiness for every individual; and beyond that he had noted that many of his patients had come to him with neurotic disorders caused by an excess of sexual repression that didn't just restrain sexuality but twisted it or stamped it out. In his gloomier moments, he wondered if the unhappiness caused by the civilized suppression of instinctual impulses was just as bad as the unhappiness that would result if those impulses were not restrained. But hemmed round with misgivings though it might have been, his final conviction was that civilization is precious, for it permits all the distinctively human achievements.

In these ideas, oddly, the professors heard only a celebration of the repressed, the instinctive, the irrational. The lesson they took away was that, if repression made people sick, then shouldn't we liberate the repressed in order to regain health and wholeness? The professors extended their misinterpretation of Freud to misinterpretations of literature. In D. H. Lawrence, for instance, they saw the glorification of sex but often missed the author's attempt to imagine an ideal of human connectedness in which equal partners would be at once virtuoso lovers, friends, and intellectual companions.

The way the professors taught one work, Conrad's *Heart of Darkness*—still read in more literature courses than perhaps any other work except for current fads like Alice Walker's *The Color Purple*—sums up the worldview cobbled together out of Marx and Freud. Conrad's great story invokes the time-honored distinction between civilization and savagery, and through this distinction it brilliantly dramatizes an old theory of what civilization is for. But the professors stood it upon its head, making it say the opposite of what it really does.

Through his protagonist, Mr. Kurtz, an ambitious European participating in the imperialist Belgian looting of the Congo, Conrad shows how irrational and destructive are the instincts of sex and aggression when they are unbridled. Kurtz, energetic and determined, has gained ascendancy over the primitive tribal natives from whom he obtains mountains of ivory for export, making himself a quasi-god or king. Drunk with his power, he greedily leads the natives in indulgences of lust and cruelty so unspeakable that Conrad only vaguely sketches their outlines.

Although Kurtz is introduced into the tale as a shining exemplar of the reigning liberal European worldview, nothing in that liberalism provides him with the inner power to resist the obscene hungers to which he succumbs. To Conrad, such resistance as Kurtz might have is a matter of convention and of the European social arrangements in which his life was rooted. It springs neither from real self-discipline based on an accurate knowledge of his own human nature nor from a profound conviction of the value of the civilized order.

At the close of *Heart of Darkness,* gripped by some virulent tropical fever, Kurtz dies, muttering on his deathbed his wish to "kill the brutes" and crying at the end, "The horror, the horror!" How horrible, he means, that such impulses as those he has given in to are inseparable from human nature; how horrible that in the freedom he claimed by surrendering to them he became nothing more than an animal. As for killing the natives because they have the same instincts he has discovered in himself—well, he dies still without a clue about what civilization is and what he and his compatriots should have been doing to bring the civilized arts to Africa.

According to the most prevalent interpretation of the literature professors, however, this story is a celebration of the irrational, precivilized impulses in human nature. Kurtz himself becomes "a hero of the spirit," a dauntless explorer who penetrated to the depths of the psyche and found just what Freud said you'd find. He dared to liberate himself from the pathological repressions with which society shackles us.

The literature professors also argued that society is an engine of geopolitical as well as personal oppression, switching from the Freudian explanation to the Marxist one. Look, for example, at what Belgium's detestable imperialism did in the Congo, enslaving and killing its people and robbing its valuable resources. Hadn't Marx said that capitalist society creates wealth by violently expropriating the labor and goods of others? Does not Conrad's story thus call passionately for universal liberation?

In fact, it doesn't. Conrad didn't celebrate what his protagonist discovered; nor did he present the Belgian imperialist enterprise, with its appalling oppression of blacks, as the embodiment of civilized society. Belgian imperialism—unlike, he says, the Roman imperialism that brought the techniques of civilized life to barbarian Britain—was a corruption of civilization on the same continuum that leads to Kurtz's depravity. Kurtz's discovery is only the beginning of the reader's discovery of why man's highest nature requires the restraint of the impulses to which Kurtz gave way.

But college teaching, impatient with gratification deferred, dreamed of lifting repression and achieving a more "authentic" selfhood nourished by nonrational mental states—intuition, dreams, and the altered consciousness induced by drugs. And it embraced an extraordinary focus on the self and its satisfactions, without reference to one's social role or obligations. However insubstantial such an ideal ultimately proved for the

Haves—since in indulging the self it weakened the effortful, purposive individuality that is the core of true selfhood—it proved ruinous when used as a standard by which to understand and encourage the Have-Nots and to make social policy for them.

Marxism's contention that where you stand in the class structure determines your values and beliefs rounded out the professors' worldview in a way that harmed the Have-Nots further. Since the beliefs and values of a culture or a class spring from its material conditions and the economic and social relations it develops to meet them, according to this view, those values are by definition appropriate for that culture and cannot be judged according to any value system arising from different circumstances. If the practices of others seem ignoble, that is a matter of perspective, even of taste. You can't try to force another culture to live by your incompatible values.

By the start of the seventies, this cultural and moral relativism had overflowed the rarefied confines of the universities and filtered down even to the New York Police Department. A quiet, liberal-minded university functionary I knew had moved into a middle-income, designedly interracial apartment complex on the borders of Harlem. She was happy with her choice, save for one thorn in her side. From the run-down Harlem street onto which her apartment looked, blaring music throbbed hotly up to her window into the small hours of the night. When repeated complaints to the police brought no response, she berated the officer who answered the phone for the inactivity. "Lady," he explained with patient condescension, "it's their *culture.*" Who was she to be insisting on her straitlaced standards where they didn't apply?

From this perspective it's impossible to judge almost anything. The cultural adaptation of the underclass to the world as they find it is doubtless natural under the circumstances. One can judge neither their morals nor their mores, those small conventions of social behavior enforced by custom and public opinion rather than by law and police.

Inevitably, this relativist outlook corroded the professors' confidence in the value of what they had to teach. They already felt abashed in the face of the authority of science, which could offer objective evidence for its findings. Compared to DNA separations or an electron microscope image, what was humanistic knowledge, the understanding that comes from careful study of the Western tradition's great texts? When students resisted their interpretations as invention, ungrounded in demonstrable fact, humanities professors secretly feared that perhaps their teachings were merely opinions.

That anxiety is partly what made them so susceptible to Freudianism and Marxism in the first place. But these systems proved double-edged. They might have seemed authoritative and scientific frameworks for explaining the humanities, but they simultaneously shaved away the most valuable aspect of humanistic study: the idea that humanistic knowledge allows you to make meaningful statements about values. When cultural relativism was added to the mix, these values were shorn all the more completely of any claim to universality. Thus, while trying to expand their own authority, the professors inadvertently shrank the importance of their subject matter. Their anxiety about whether they had anything *real* to teach continued to grow.

The sixties thus found these professors ripe for conversion. As northern students went south for Freedom Rides and voter registration drives, as big-city ghettos exploded in rioting, as protests and teach-ins against the Vietnam War gathered strength, as women asserted their claims to liberation, many of these professors came to believe that they had found the key to their rankling lack of confidence about having anything important to say. Was it not that the values they were supposed to profess, the Western tradition they were entrusted to transmit, had lost relevance to the modern world? What had Jane Austen to say to an Alabama black thirsting for civil rights? What had Plato to say to the Vietnamese peasant whose hut had been napalmed? What could Henry James say to, or about, the soldier who did the burning?

A hunger for relevance revolutionized college curricula during the sixties. Campus after campus jettisoned traditional Western civilization great books and great ideas courses as obsolete, long before Stanford's recent, notorious restructuring of its Western civ. requirement. An alternative canon, supposed adequate to the new reality, emerged: Paul Goodman, Norman O. Brown, Herbert Marcuse, Frantz Fanon, Michel Foucault, James Baldwin, Malcolm X, later even the lyrics of Bob Dylan, shouldered aside Plato and Montaigne. The relevant message was Western society's oppressiveness, stifling the instinctual satisfactions of the privileged and tyrannically exploiting the poor and nonwhite at home and in the Third World.

The Western tradition wasn't charged with mere irrelevance. Worse, it was elitist—"elitist" having been transmogrified into a term of abuse meaning snobbish, effete, judgmental rather than "open," and (most important of all) specific to a class that lived in easy overrefinement thanks to its exploitation of the masses. Thus the Western tradition was infected to the core with injustice; its values had long allowed the rich and powerful few to put down the poor and weak many. But history was now sweeping away these values along with the class they belonged to, according to the fuzzy Marxism prevalent on campus. Indeed, if history moves mankind to ever higher states of consciousness, as Marx contended, the outworn thought of the past has increasingly little to teach the present.

To see how deeply tainted the whole of Western civilization really was, all you had to do was to look around you, observing on every side that Western—and especially American—culture sprang from a social system shot through with injustices that weren't casual but systematic and fundamental. Through the imperialist war in Vietnam, colonialist America (like Conrad's Belgium) aimed to exploit economically a nonwhite population dismissed as inferior. At home, blacks were the nonwhite victims of an internal colonialism; women were another exploited minority (though they were the majority); Watergate was proof positive that the U.S. government was conspiring against right and justice; the assassinations of the Kennedy brothers and of Martin Luther King, surrounded with elaborate conspiracy theories, provided that American society seethed with subterranean forces implacably opposed to the just order these martyrs sought.

This point of view, which took root on campus in the sixties, flourished there for the next two decades as the young professors who embraced it got tenure and grew gray and their pupils, who had been educated only in this worldview, themselves moved into the professorial ranks. Says Middlebury College English professor Jay Parini: "After the Vietnam War, a lot of us [antiwar graduate students] didn't just crawl back into our library cubicles; we stepped into academic positions. With the war over, our visibility was lost, and it seemed for a while—to the unobservant—that we had disappeared. Now we have tenure, and the work of reshaping the universities has begun in earnest."

Not that Parini's cohorts were ex-leaders of the campus protests of the sixties; some were rank-and-file, some passive observers or underage wannabes. For it wasn't the takeover of buildings and activist demonstrations that formed these academics. Rather it was the intellectual culture on campus all through the decade and beyond: the culture transmitted by the Fanon-Foucault reading list and by such must-read publications as *The New York Review of Books,* with its diagram of how to make a Molotov cocktail, its anti-U.S. diatribes by Noam Chomsky or the more suavely caustic Gore Vidal, or its article by Mary McCarthy heaping praise on the Vietcong, so much purer politically than the United States.

These ideas didn't make their way only by irresistible logic, but by fashion and snobbery, by the approval and force of character of those who first espoused them, as ideas often make their way among the young and the ivory tower rank-and-file. In daily life rather than in formal debate, how much more effective in demolishing an opposing idea than reams of reasoned argument can be the withering put-down of some figure cloaked in your eyes with glamor or authority. Nothing more successfully enforced Bloomsbury attitudes, for instance, than the acid scorn of Lytton Strachey, as he cringed into his shabby armchair, twisted one long, tweeded-and-brogued leg around the other, and cried, "Oh, *come!*"

By the time the professorial worldview flamboyantly blossomed into political correctness in the nineties, its basic tenets had hardened into a rigid orthodoxy. Its first article of faith: the oppressiveness of American (and other Western) culture, society, institutions, standards, and values, which shackle everyone who isn't a white male. As a statement of Tulane University's administration puts it: "Racism and sexism are pervasive in America and are fundamentally present in all American institutions.... It is difficult for us to see and overcome racism and sexism because ... we are all the progeny of a racist and sexist society." If you are white or—worse—a white male, you can't help being implicated in oppression. As University of Pennsylvania administrators were instructed during required "racism awareness seminars," the fundamental American reality is that "all whites are racists."

The most potent force perpetuating this reality, as the campus worldview has it, is the Western tradition itself. Thus political correctness began by tearing down established standards of every kind, especially those directly applicable to university life—grades, test scores, the values embodied by the great books, the meritocratic criteria for professorial hiring and promotion—as specious, mere social constructs designed to stigmatize and oppress the nonwhite and nonmale while glorifying their privileged oppressors.

According to Duke University English professor Stanley Fish, the very idea of merit, which standards are supposed to measure, is only a "political viewpoint claiming for itself the mantle of objectivity." As far as standards of educational performance are concerned, a black student activist at the University of Michigan drew the now-conventional conclusion from this principle: "Basically," she asserted, "what scores measure is privilege."

The war on standards wasn't just theoretical. It had far-reaching practical consequences. At the outer limit, one college even temporarily lost its accreditation for clinging to standards of excellence after they had become politically incorrect. In deferring reaccreditation of New York's Baruch College in 1990 for "social justice" shortcomings, the accrediting agency charged the school with having not only too few black professors and administrators (even though nearly a fifth of the faculty was minority) but also too low a rate of student retention. The college, complained the agency, "has emphasized traditional academic values without exhibiting equal concern for the values of social justice and equity." Concluded Baruch's then-president, Joel Segall, who resigned amid the brouhaha surrounding this incident: "What that means, I suppose, is equal outcomes: minority students must be graduated at about the same rates as non-minorities"—regardless of performance.

Even though the U.S. Department of Education temporarily suspended the accrediting agency in the wake of this action, college administrators everywhere were left wondering not whether, but how far, they ought to lower their "traditional academic values" to achieve the new, politically correct goal of keeping minority students from flunking out. One consequence, of course, is that as standards get discredited, the achievement that standards measure is devalued for blacks and whites alike.

As for the Western tradition's canon of seminal texts, what is it but the oppressor's ideology? As Robert Scholes, a trendy Brown University literary theorist, explains, enforcing the connection between oppression and the Western tradition: "[W]here the Empire went, the cannon and the Canon went too."

All the great texts and authors are guilty—the whole shelf of "dead, white, European males" (abbreviated "DWEMs" in politically correct tracts) who allegedly engraved racism, sexism, classism, and homophobia upon the doorposts of our civilization. You can start with the Bible itself, which, according to deconstructionist critic Jonathan Culler, must be understood "not as poetry or as narrative but as a powerfully influential racist and sexist text." Milton, as Stanford English professor Linda Paulson assesses him, is "an ass ... a sexist pig," while according to University of Pennsylvania English professor Houston A. Baker, Jr., a recent past president of the influential Modern Language Association, the U.S. Constitution is a racist document, a "gothic romance." In the neat if rather uncanonical formulation of Stanley Hauerwas, a Duke University professor of theological ethics: "The canon of great literature was created by high Anglican assholes to underwrite their social class."

In trying to topple such DWEM idols as Plato, Aristotle, Machiavelli, and Shakespeare the political correctness movement on campus aims, above all, to overturn the value system under whose aegis blacks and women allegedly were so long oppressed and found inferior. Those who want to preserve the authority of the canon, it is claimed, are not trying to preserve an inheritance of values that are liberating, mind-expanding, ennobling, and life-enhancing. How deluded of black thinker W.E.B. Du Bois, for example, to embrace the Western master-pieces in such terms, when he said (most movingly, to my polit-ically incorrect mind): "I sit with Shakespeare and he winces not. Across the color line I move arm in arm with Balzac and Dumas, where smiling men and welcoming women glide in gilded halls.... I summon Aristotle and Aurelius and what soul I will, and they come all graciously with no scorn nor conde-scension. So wed with Truth, I dwell above the veil."

Efforts to preserve this legacy, campus dogma has it, are only an attempt to preserve the "hegemony" of the traditional oppressors and their unjust system. Charges Catharine Stimp-son, dean of the Rutgers graduate school and another recent past president of the Modern Language Association: "Under the guise of defending objectivity and intellectual rigor, which is a lot of mishmash, they are trying to preserve the cultural and political supremacy of white heterosexual males." Says Harvard University English professor Henry Louis Gates, Jr., who is black: "The return of 'the' canon, the high canon of Western master-pieces, represents the return of an order in which my people were the subjugated, the voiceless, the invisible, the unrepre-sented, and the unrepresentable. Who would return us to that medieval never-never land?"

It was in this spirit that the widely publicized crowd of pro-testers against Stanford University's required Western civiliza-tion course followed the Reverend Jesse Jackson in chanting, like a parody of the barbarians at the gates, "Hey, hey; ho, ho; Western culture's got to go." The aim of the long demonstra-tions that led to the junking of that course in 1988 was, in one protester's words, to overthrow a requirement that is "not just racist education; it is the education of racists."

Not only at Stanford but on campuses nationwide, teaching of the humanities has taken on this explicitly political mission. Says one prominent English professor, Gerald Graff of North-western University: "Speaking as a leftist, I too find it tempting to try to turn the curriculum into an instrument of social trans-formation." Short of the whole curriculum, he says, at least his own courses can be such an instrument. Influential University of Virginia philosopher Richard Rorty notes approvingly that "a new American cultural Left ... would like to use the English, French, and Comparative Literature Departments of the universities as staging areas for political action." Boasts Annette Kolodny, the University of Arizona's humanities dean and a proud veteran of the Berkeley protests of the sixties: "I see my scholarship as an extension of my political activism."

The new requirement that Stanford authorities substituted for the old course is a model of the kind of humanities courses now rampant on elite campuses, taught by professors like these. Flying the colors of the reigning ideology of victimization, guilt, and reparations, today's multitrack requirement at Stanford embodies what might be called curricular affirmative action, making sure that students study at least one non-European culture, get indoctrinated in the race, gender, and class analysis of texts, and study such nonwhite, nonmale, or non-European figures as Frantz Fanon, Zora Neale Hurston, and Rigoberta Menchu alongside—and equal in importance to—Aristotle, Euripides, and Shakespeare. The very name of the new sequence, "Cultures, Ideas, and Values"—the plurals betokening pluralism—announces the cultural and moral relativism, the unwillingness to make judgments between one culture or value and another, that informs this obliteration of universal standards of value. Since no culture, class, gender, or sexual preference has any more authority or value than any other, every point of view, every "perspective," is equally essential for a complete and representative picture.

But ultimately all the texts, monumental or ephemeral, are made to teach the same dreary basic lesson of Western civilization's malfeasance and the martyrdom of the usual array of victims. For example, Rigoberta Menchu, mentioned above, is an illiterate Guatemalan whose autobiography, dictated in Paris to a French feminist, records her alleged victimization by racism, sexism, and colonialism. As an Indian, she's even victimized by the majority Latino culture within her already victimized land. "Thus," as Dinesh D'Souza trenchantly observes, "she is really a mouthpiece for a sophisticated left-wing critique of Western society, all the more devastating because it issues not from a French scholar-activist but from a seemingly authentic Third World source—now further confirmed by the Nobel peace prize."

The Western mouthpieces are made to utter the same lesson. They are unmasked and demystified: Milton, as we've seen, is construed as a sexist ass. Or they are turned into mere grist for the ideological mill: Shakespeare's *Tempest*, for instance, is studied for what it purportedly shows about the relations between colonizer and colonized in the New World. In the many other universities that have similarly twisted the curriculum, the masterpieces suffer the same ignominious fate. At Duke (a political correctness hotbed), one professor assigns Shakespeare's plays "to illuminate the way 17th century society mistreated women, the working class, and minorities."

For good measure, Cultures, Ideas, and Values also administers a dose of Marx and Freud to students, making explicit the intellectual underpinnings of the deterministic worldview the course purveys. The debt to Marx is self-evident throughout the new requirement's assumption that literary texts are only reflections of more fundamental economic and social power relations, and Freud as usual is made to back up the Marxian determinism with a different determinism that similarly frees individuals from personal responsibility. As one professor approvingly described Freud's basic lesson in a paper first delivered at a Stanford University conference: "[P]sychoanalysis radically undermines notions about autonomy, individual choice, will, responsibility, and rationality, showing that we do not control our lives in the most fundamental sense."

Humanities professors like to boast that what they do is "subversive." And truly, their deepest aim, negative rather than creative, is to discredit Western values and standards by unmasking them as mere human creations, upholding a particular class interest and without objective validity. The mere act of "demystifying" these values, the professors believe, will liberate the oppressed from their power. As Duke University's Stanley Fish puts it: "Once you realize that standards emerge historically, then you can see through and discard all the norms to which we have been falsely enslaved." You would be left, of course, with nothing, for this kind of criticism is a universal solvent, which no idea or belief can withstand.

Yet what more manifests the humanity of mankind than its ability to conceive such ideas as justice, mercy, loyalty, self-sacrifice, honor, freedom—and to give them reality by living according to them? One would think that if humanism means anything, it means the belief that man has cloaked his life with meaning and dignity through his ability to live by ideals he himself has made. Surely, the humanities are the study of those ideals, and it is an astonishing development to see the humanities now animated by the spirit of antihumanism, in the most literal sense.

How literally antihumanistic that spirit really is became apparent in deconstruction, academe's trendiest fashion in literary theory between the late sixties and the late eighties. Deconstruction is the most extreme expression of the new orthodoxy's urge to leave Western values and standards in tatters. Boasting of his movement's subversive intent, English professor J. Hillis Miller defines a deconstructionist as "a parricide. He is a bad son demolishing beyond hope of repair the machine of Western metaphysics."

But first, a word about how the theory works. Deconstruction attempts to accomplish its subversion of Western values by asserting that any text, carefully examined, contains not one message but at least two, and those messages are always so mutually contradictory that they cancel each other out and leave the text empty of any determinate meaning whatsoever. The contradiction normally is found between the text's surface, apparent meaning and its rhetorical structure, which in its use of imagery or metaphor or philosophical categories discloses assumptions that subvert the surface meaning.

Thus the work of deconstruction is, usually gleefully, to debunk texts by showing how authors, despite what they think they are saying, are in reality "the unwitting mouthpieces for a reigning ideology," as David Lehman puts it in his absorbing *Signs of the Times: Deconstruction and the Fall of Paul de Man*. Lehman wittily dramatizes how a deconstructionist might disembowel the great opening of the Gettysburg Address, for example, showing how sexist that purportedly equalitarian document really is. "A deconstructionist," he writes, "might pause over 'our fathers brought forth' and 'conceived,' characterizing this trope as an attempt to appropriate for the patriarchal authorities the procreative power vested in the female body. 'All men are created equal,' but the deconstructionist might point out that 'men' excludes women and other 'marginalized' figures and that therefore the document promotes something other than full equality.... The critic must expose the text as one would expose a scam or a sham." It is this approach that allows the professors to impeach Milton as a sexist, the Bible as sexist and racist to boot. Riddled with bad faith, all the texts that embody Western values—indeed, all texts period—are incoherent and meaningless. This goes for those texts we call laws, too; indeed deconstruction is a key progenitor of "critical legal studies" in the law schools, where the latest literary theories are currently all the rage.

Where there are many culturally constructed truths, there is no Truth. So Harvard English professor Sacvan Bercovitch can write: "Individualism, self-reliance, and liberal democracy are no more or less absolute, no more or less true to the laws of nature and the mind, than the once-eternal truths of providence, hierarchy, and the divine right of kings." And, going one rhetorical step farther, an American Council of Learned Societies paper called *Speaking for the Humanities* asserts that while "we may wish to argue that a commitment to democracy is *not* ideological but a recognition of a universal truth, disinterestedly achieved, ... we should not equate truth with our own political ideology." Nothing in democracy is objectively better than authoritarianism.

Into this mist of intoxicating academic rhetoric, reality shockingly intruded. In 1987, four years after the death of the celebrated humanities professor Paul de Man, courtly chairman of Yale's French and comparative literature departments and one of deconstruction's two chief exponents, it came to light that he had never been a member of the Resistance in his native Belgium during World War II, as he had led people to believe. Instead, he had been a willing writer of blatantly anti-Semitic, pro-Nazi articles for Belgium's principal, and hated, collaborationist newspaper. Moreover, his personal life turned out to have been as squalid as his public writings had been evil. A shady, failed business project in Belgium earned him, says David Lehman, "a local reputation for dishonesty," and he had abandoned his three Belgian children and their mother to marry (perhaps bigamously) one of his Bard College students once he arrived in America.

Small wonder that the writer of texts with such unmistakably vicious meaning would have preached years later that texts have no determinate meaning and that there are no absolute values. Dismayingly true to form, his deconstructionist confreres met the revelations by saying that you couldn't tell where his anti-Semitic essays really stood on the Jewish question, and that everything in them and in the whole situation was the opposite of what it appeared. Those who condemn de Man, asserted his Yale colleague Jacques Derrida, in fact "reproduce the exterminating gesture" of the Nazis in doing so. As the object of so much bigoted prejudice from his unmaskers, asked deconstructionist Richard Rand, "are not, indeed, Paul de Man and his deconstruction somehow overwhelmingly Jewish—as Jewish as anyone, perhaps, in our multi-national 1980s, can be?" So the real Jewish victim is the non-Jewish de Man himself.

However much this shameful response tries to deny that de Man's Nazi-collaborationist writings have an inescapably plain meaning, the vehemence of its denial discloses the pretense behind the new campus orthodoxy's central claim that no universal standards and values exist. Notwithstanding their relativist ideology, these professors clearly have no problem knowing that Nazism is evil. They know that there really is an ascertainable distinction between good and evil; that standards exist by which we can judge Nazism and those standards are a matter not of cultural choice but of moral values.

According to the thirty-years-long cultural revolution outlined over the course of this book—a revolution that has made the condition of the poor and the black the measure of American society—ours is a racist, oppressive culture that dooms minorities to failure and judges their failure by unjust standards that perversely hold society's victims responsible for their own victimization. In fairness, the society owes reparations to its victims, reparations based on race-consciousness, not race-blindness; for group rights and group representation—as opposed to democratic individualism, with its emphasis on individual rights, achievement, and meritocracy—form the heart of true democracy.

In college, political correctness begins with indoctrination sessions, like Haverford College's "Social Justice Requirement," which makes students take one of a menu of courses outlining the grievances of this or that group of approved victims, or like Harvard's annual racism consciousness-raising week, whose keynote is struck by the slogan on its posters: "I don't want to be a racist . . . but I think I might be."

Once students know the correct line, colleges try to enforce it through censorship codes and harassment policies. Above all, their effort is to forbid questioning of the new orthodoxy's central dogmas, even in jest. The University of Connecticut, for example, subjects students to punishment even for "conspicuous exclusion from conversation," "inconsiderate jokes," and "misdirected laughter."

The University of Michigan's code makes male students liable to punishment for saying in class, "Women just aren't as good in this field as men." A federal judge struck down the code in 1989, observing that it forbids utterances that, however politically incorrect, might be true.

Again and again, the codes prohibit even mentioning alternate views that challenge the new orthodoxy. For example, is it really true that "sexual orientation" is nothing but a question of taste in "life-style?" If you're at the University of Michigan, don't even dream of asking. Confronted in his new dorm room by a wall covered with photographs of naked men, and by a homosexual roommate who explained he would entertain his partners right there, a grad student fled to the authorities to request a transfer. The authorities haughtily told him his moral and religious scruples were *his* problem. At last they agreed to change his room, but only with the warning that if he disclosed why, he'd be hauled up for breaching the code.

Not even a faculty member is permitted to question the dogma of affirmative action. A Berkeley anthropology professor, who wrote in the alumni magazine that Berkeley's affirmative action program discriminates against white and Asian applicants, had his class disrupted and shouted down by seventy-five student protesters chanting "Bullshit." Far from disciplining the students, Berkeley authorities went after the professor: the chancellor solicited student complaints about his lectures, and his department began an investigation of his views. At Harvard, a highly regarded history professor was accused of "racial insensitivity" in the school newspaper for assigning a text mentioning that some dismiss affirmative action as preferential treatment.

At Stanford, residential assistants patrol the dormitories on behalf of the "PC agenda," as one former resident assistant—self-described as "a member of the PC 'thought police' "—calls it. The assistants pressure fellow students to use approved PC language such as "people of color" or "Chicanas"; they put up PC posters, even in the bathrooms, to make the message inescapable; they subtly pressure students to show up for seminars and discussions on PC topics led by, say, a member of "a gay students' speakers bureau." "Attendance wasn't mandatory," says this ex-commissar, "but did we know who wouldn't show? You bet." For its part, Harvard assigns a "designated race relations tutor" to each house, with orders to "monitor the racial atmosphere," denounce "violations of community," and "raise consciousness." The University of Michigan not only forced a hapless student who ridiculed homosexuality to recant publicly in an article in the school paper titled "Learned My Lesson" but also sent him to gay-sensitivity sessions for political reeducation.

Yet at the very moment that the new ideology has triumphed on campus—in affirmative action in admissions and hiring, in required multicultural courses, in sensitivity seminars, "Social Justice Requirements," and black studies and women's studies programs, in race-consciousness that has resulted in black-only dormitories, clubs, lounges, even a black-only yearbook—black students are flunking out, dropping out, or graduating with poor grades in dismaying numbers. The politically correct explanation is white racism; but when colleges have turned themselves upside down to combat racism, that explanation is hard to maintain. The true reason, discussed in the last chapter, is that affirmative action has mismatched students with the institutions in which they are enrolled.

Thus political correctness also prefigures its own unraveling. Colleges have to insist so urgently that students toe the line only because students are growing impatient with what they perceive as humbug. They know it is a lie when they are told that they are responsible for black failure on campus. They resent the double standards and double-talk that surround them. As a University of Michigan senior told Dinesh D'Souza: "Now there are truths that are not socially safe.... I'm tired of being lied to. They're fighting racism with lies." Sadly, the continual pressure to believe untruths, as Thomas Sowell has written, sometimes breeds the very racism it is designed to eradicate, resulting in ugly racial incidents on northern campuses hitherto free of racism.

Nor does political correctness stop at the college level. Spilling over from the universities into the primary and secondary schools, it provides one more part of the explanation of why these schools fail the poor. With families often too troubled to transmit the values necessary for success, the poorest children must look to the classroom as a second-best source. But political correctness has short-circuited that transmission. The schools, no less than the colleges, not only are failing to pass on mainstream, democratic values adequately; they are actively working to delegitimize them by teaching that the whole civilization they uphold is unworthy of respect. This is the main thrust of multiculturalism, education's latest craze in history and social studies courses.

Multiculturalism in the schools started out in the sixties and early seventies with the reasonable goal of including previously neglected groups in the American history books, taking notice of their accomplishments. The idea was that if blacks or Hispanic-Americans, especially, could see themselves as contributing to the making of America, that would put them in touch with a past that would enhance their self-esteem in the present. So the history books properly focused more attention on Harriet Tubman or the black soldiers who fought in the Civil War or the black scientist Charles R. Drew.

Perhaps inevitably, this effort led to some distortion. In the pictures of one leading high school text analyzed in an Educational Excellence Network report, "Texas cowboys, World War I soldiers, and Civilian Conservation Corps surveyors are represented [only] by blacks. In its index, Women's Rights is a longer entry than the Revolutionary War." New York State, possessing an active Iroquois lobby, misinforms its eleventh graders that the Iroquois League was one of the principal "foundations" of the U.S. Constitution, equal in influence to the thought of the European Enlightenment.

But these misrepresentations were benignly intended compared to multiculturalism's next phase. Minority educators grew impatient with an account of American history that assigned their ancestors mere walk-on parts in what remained fundamentally a white, European drama. They wanted equal billing. In the words of a report of a New York State Regents committee on curriculum reform, the day had passed when European culture should be "likened to the master of a house ruling over a dinner table, himself firmly established at the head of the table and all other cultures being guests some distance down the table from the master, who has invited the others through his beneficence." It was time, the 1989 report went on to say, to demote white, Anglo-Saxon culture and its contributions to the making of America to equal status with other cultures, no more important or valuable than they.

Less valuable, in fact. For according to the New York report, whose point of view has become multiculturalist orthodoxy, white, Anglo-Saxon culture has been damagingly oppressive. "African Americans, Asian Americans, Puerto Ricans/Latinos, and Native Americans," the report contends, "have all been the victims of a cultural oppression and stereotyping that has characterized institutions—including the educational institutions—of the United States and the European American world for centuries."

Indeed, if you look at the whole history of Europeans on the American continent from any other perspective than their own and in terms of anyone else's interest but their own, you see mostly violence, expropriation, oppression, and the obliteration of cultures at least as good as, and often better than, the Eurocentric civilization that suppressed them. And that is how history should be taught. Thus, according to a more recent New York State Regents report, elementary school teachers shouldn't discuss Columbus Day or Thanksgiving or the westward migration of settlers without presenting the "perspectives of Native Americans."

The effect, of course, is to make the main current of the nation's history—the bringing of European culture to the New

World, the birth of a new social order based on the individual's freedom of conscience, the founding and expansion of a free, democratic nation on the principles of the European Enlightenment—problematic, especially for minority pupils. Therefore, such pupils are hindered from learning that they live in a uniquely free and open society offering unprecedented opportunity to anyone who will seize it, that they can claim the supraethnic identity of an American and participate in an American community without being false to themselves. Instead, students are taught resentment, along with a militant certainty that they neither can nor should transcend their own ethnicity.

Multiculturalism's final twist is the doctrine of Afrocentrism, the assertion that American blacks do not have an American cultural identity but a superior African one, from which they can draw self-esteem in plenty and which should be taught in schools to white and black students alike. By contrast with Western culture, which is cold, linear, mechanically rational, calculating, selfishly individualistic and materialistic, African culture is warm, emotional, intuitive, sharing, creative, and humanistic, according to Afrocentrist theorists. African culture looks beyond the polarities of fact and fiction or male and female that structure Western thought to a unity where time is irrelevant, and being is more important than doing.

Thus, reason, individualism, industriousness, engagement with the real world, even the distinction between reality and fiction, are rejected as foreign to black pupils. And, multiculturalist theorists claim, this rejection of Western values may be based on genetic differences between blacks and whites—differences in how they process information, even differences in the amount of melanin in their skin, which according to Leonard Jeffries, chairman of City College's black studies department, makes Africans the warm "sun people" and Europeans the aggressive "ice people," who brought "domination, destruction, and death" into the world. These theories that race determines mental functioning, as historian Arthur Schlesinger notes, are in the most literal sense racist.

With extraordinary illogic, Afrocentrists both reject Western culture and assert that it is an African creation. The ancient Egyptians, who according to Afrocentrists were a black African people, invented all Western science and philosophy, which later the Greeks shamelessly plagiarized. Georgia State University urban education professor Asa G. Hilliard, a leading Afrocentrist and the editor of an Afrocentrism textbook that is required or suggested reading for teachers in major urban school systems across the nation, claims not only that Africa is "the mother of Western civilization" but also that Africans discovered America centuries before Columbus was born.

Shouldn't blacks therefore embrace Western culture and values with proprietary fervor? No, because the Greeks and Europeans corrupted Egyptian learning as they stole it. As Wade Nobles, director of a program for troubled black youths in an Oakland, California, high school, exhorted a major national conference of mostly black Afrocentrist high school teachers: "It's like someone drinking some good stuff, vomiting it, and then we have to catch the vomit and drink it ourselves. The Greeks gave back the vomit of the African way.... Don't become the vomit-drinkers!"

So what black children should learn instead is the myth of a vanished African greatness despoiled by the West, first in Egypt, later in the kingdoms of West Africa. They should learn African ritual and music; and all that they learn should be taught in a style consistent with the alleged emotional, intuitive, non-rational—above all, non-Western—values of African culture.

Thus black children are to be educated in a way that puts them in opposition to the Western values they need to succeed and that emphasizes their separateness from mainstream culture and its myriad opportunities. "If some Kleagle of the Ku Klux Klan wanted to devise an educational curriculum for the specific purpose of handicapping and disabling black Americans," Arthur Schlesinger eloquently judges, "he would not be likely to come up with anything more diabolically effective than Afrocentrism."

Multiculturalism, especially in its Afrocentric manifestation, is based on the premise that all cultures are equal in value, but Western culture is less equal than others. Yet while multiculturalists urge Americans to fly apart into separate enclaves of ethnicity, the rest of the world has inexorably moved to embrace what novelist V. S. Naipaul calls "our universal civilization." Based on the Western values of democracy, human rights, and the Golden Rule, it is a civilization that has produced a degree of freedom, personal fulfillment, prosperity, and life-enhancing technological mastery that has dazzled and converted peoples of the entire world—or on occasion, says Naipaul, has left them enraged with a sense of their own impotence in the face of such seductive achievement.

That universal civilization is part and parcel of the globalism toward which the world is irresistibly moving. It is globalism with a Western, not a multicultural, twist. As we increasingly find our fortunes linked to those of the Japanese, the Chinese in Hong Kong, Singapore, and Taiwan, the Koreans, the Latin Americans, the Indians, they become more like us, subscribing to the Western values that underlie Western democratic individualism.

As the world converges on these values, our schools and colleges should be transmitting them to young Americans as a vital heritage. But the Have-Nots remain deprived of the beliefs and values they desperately need for success. And the Haves suffer an impoverishment, too: for between them and what is most precious and sustaining in our common heritage falls an estranging shadow.

CHAPTER ELEVEN

The Poverty of Spirit

The cultural revolution hit the worst-off hardest of all, inflicting catastrophic damage on them. But looking over the wreckage, one can't help but see that the damage was so extensive that it wasn't just the underclass who suffered harm. The Haves who trashed America's culture injured, in addition, their own children—nowhere near as grievously as they injured the worst-off, but enough to leave a discernible scar on the character of the present age.

No one seems to have much good to say about the standard-issue eighties and nineties middle-class youth, especially in his or her yuppie manifestation. Even though the children of the sixties have left cultural mayhem behind them, they can seem generous-minded and life-affirming by comparison with the self-interested opportunism that characterizes so many young people of this age. The usual explanation is that somehow an epidemic of greed set upon these young people, withering away their altruistic or communitarian impulses and leaving little of soul within the hard, unlovely shell of their narcissistic materialism.

In fact, the reverse occurred. The cultural revolution created a spiritual vacuum within them that greedy selfishness could invade and fill. Their parents and teachers, in order to accomplish the liberations they sought, had steamrolled the Western tradition. The sustaining ideals that young people in the past had been able to hold on to, having been deconstructed to smithereens, weren't there for them.

Nor could they readily draw strength from their parents' and teachers' faith that the new culture would regenerate either their own lives or the lives of the poor. AIDS had ended the idyll of hassle-free sex; urban streets full of wrecked homeless and underclass lives testified that the dream of liberation for the Have-Nots remained only a dream. And so young people were emptily receptive when the personal liberation of the sixties, after being debased into the Me Decade narcissism of the seventies, transmogrified itself one more time and reemerged as the Me Too Decade sense of entitlement of the eighties.

Imagine a young person entering into adult life at the start of the eighties boom. He or she looks out over the moral landscape and sees that every value is problematic. Democracy, for instance, though it would seem highly desirable, would be hard to define. Does it mean group rights and discrimination by race or individual rights and nondiscrimination? Does the Constitution say exactly the opposite of what it seems to say, as judges are claiming? Do judges enlarge or abridge democracy when they make social policy based on the authority of that reading?

The more he or she tried to make sense of justice, the fuzzier it would grow. It was impossible to think about the subject without thinking about affirmative action; but was affirmative action an advance, or was it an attempt to make up for past injustice by establishing unfair double standards and committing injustice against the innocent in the present? And was it a refinement of justice or a travesty of it when judges let murderers and other criminals walk away scot-free, reprimanding the cops who arrested them?

What about personal morality? Are actions determined not by free will but by unseen economic and psychological forces that are beyond the individual's control? Driven by such determinism, the poor are bound to behave in pathological ways. As for the rich, if they are good, it is only because they can afford to be: virtue is a luxury of the privileged.

Given such assumptions, the personal responsibility that makes for the moral life becomes illusory. People cannot be ultimately responsible for choices that are beyond their direct control. By the early eighties, even belief in something as basic as Truth with a capital T was already being eroded by the humanities professors' assertions that all moral values are relative. Justice, virtue, reason: the ground was being undermined beneath our worthiest human qualities.

As part of the upheaval, the idea of the family as an institution dedicated to the nurturing of children—whether Mother has a career or not—became demoted to being only one of a number of "life-styles." And the removal of the stigma from out-of-wedlock births, along with the cheerful willingness of the larger culture to support single welfare mothers and their illegitimate offspring, further dissolved the traditional family as a cultural norm.

Today, a decade later, the trashing of values and standards has become almost exuberantly explicit. For example, a typical headline on the *New York Times* arts pages asks, "Is 'Quality' An Idea Whose Time Has Gone?" Evidently so: the story below breezily concludes that applying such a standard to painting is, properly, all but obsolete, since quality is a subjective measure often invoked to "preserv[e] the authority of the heterosexual white male."

Not just the staid daily papers but the venerable museums trumpet the overturning of traditional beliefs and values. The Smithsonian Institution's National Museum of American Art recently mounted a show of paintings celebrating the American frontier, whose point, as expressed in the show's catalog, was that the settling of America should be deplored as a monumental capitalist atrocity. The churches sing the same chorus. The five hundredth anniversary of Columbus's arrival in the New World, says the National Council of Churches, should occasion "repentance," since the European discovery and settlement of the Americas, which produced both "genocide" and "ecocide," was "a historic tragedy."

The only value that hadn't curdled in the new culture was "compassion" or "caring" or "sensitivity" toward the excluded of all varieties. This attitude, for many, became the touchstone of moral worth, displacing considerations of justice and responsibility. But "compassion" or "caring" proved a barren value, for no amount of it made the condition of the lowest of the excluded get better. On the contrary, throughout the eighties the number of homeless increased and the underclass sank deeper into disorder.

The result for many Americans, and especially for a young person starting out in life, was a spiritual desert, in which values were so qualified and contradictory that they canceled each other out. Many popular movies and books of the eighties depict the moral wasteland that the crisis in values created. The setting of the cult film *The Road Warrior* is a world literally laid waste and reduced to tribal barbarism by the failure of modern civilization. Only a saving remnant preserves a scrap—and only a scrap—of anything recognizable as a human ideal; all other individuals exhibit only lust and cruelty. *Terminator* conjures up a similarly ruined world, in which people with feelings and ideals are nearly exterminated by robots who look human but lack feeling or morality. Even an erstwhile superhero like Batman becomes a solitary, obsessed figure, driven to make war on crime not by love of virtue and justice but by workaholism and the irresistible force of psychopathology.

In a more ordinary, realistic setting, the inner lives imagined by a minimalist writer like Ann Beattie are minimal indeed. The title of her novel *Chilly Scenes of Winter* precisely describes its characters' spiritual landscape, where every ideal and value is frozen solid. And by the start of the nineties, the notorious *American Psycho* of Bret Easton Ellis could describe the by-now-familiar spiritual wasteland with chilling explicitness. In this inner emptiness, without ideals of justice or reason or knowledge, individuality itself has died along with individual responsibility, and the most intimate human relations have in consequence become impersonal and mechanical.

For these reasons, the endless editorials bemoaning the "Decade of Greed" have got it all backward. It isn't true that a headlong, intemperate pursuit of wealth has plunged us into a crisis of values. That crisis is the inevitable result of the cultural development that has been traced over the course of this book.

The cultural revolution, not soulless greed, created the vacuum, and during the eighties boom money expanded to fill the emptiness. From his front-row vantage point on the money follies, the former head of the Visa credit card operation, Dee Hock, perceptively assessed this phenomenon: "It's not that people value money more," he remarked in the late eighties, "but that they value everything else so much less—not that they are more greedy, but that they have no other values to keep greed in check." Or as sociologist E. Digby Baltzell succinctly put it: "When there are no values, money counts."

Sure, the eighties displayed a carnival sideshow of greed pure, simple, and ugly, as when insider trader Ivan Boesky sultanically ordered every entrée at a fashionable New York restaurant, took a bite of each, and, choosing one to finish, sent the rest back. But aside from the Wall Street panjandrums, the more ordinary, humble forms of the eighties' money hunger were really three distinct strategies to try to invest life with solidity. One impulse was to use money to make your life look distinguished and distinctive to other people, so that you could persuade yourself of your own worth by buying and flaunting fancy German cars, British raincoats, Swiss gold watches, and all the opulent luxury offered in the shop windows of Madison Avenue or Rodeo Drive throughout the decade. So too the Gatsby-like clothes and advertisements of designer Ralph Lauren had a similar intent of using the outward trappings of a vanished order to appropriate its rootedness and dignity. As Bret Easton Ellis's novel says: "Surface, surface, surface was all that anyone found meaning in."

A second, more unlovely group tried to use the mere making of money, not the spending of it, to assure themselves that their lives had value. "Worth" may be either an economic or a moral quality, and this group measured worth by the easily ascertainable, nondeconstructable standard of dollars. To them, all other values were humbug and money was the only real source of power and therefore respect.

The third, much more sympathetic group includes many eighties yuppies who rejected the cultural revolution's nihilism but had nothing with which to replace it. Many were trying to choose the bourgeois solidity that the cultural revolution had jeered down. But after the mutilation of so many of the values that had undergirded that life, little more than an empty shell was left for them. That's why people restoring old houses, or inhabiting ones they've just restored, are recurrent motifs in such recent movies as *Pacific Heights, Ghost,* and *sex, lies, and videotape.* These young married or almost-married couples are yearning to bring back to life an ideal of home and family; but in the movies, before they figure out how to do so, some disaster overwhelms them.

All through the eighties, the editorialists who harangued these young people to give up their soulless materialism and return to the commitment of the sixties were giving them useless advice. The "commitment" they were recommending was to the ideology of the cultural revolution that had already bled so much of the life and vigor out of our key values.

After thirty years of cultural revolution, we have come to an impasse. How do we get out of it? What is to be done about the underclass, the homeless, and the pervasive sense that these groups are evidence that our national life is fundamentally askew? When people ask this question, they generally ask it out of the belief that we have broken faith with our old commitment to the unfortunate and that we need to return to it.

Take a recent example of such a mind-set, Nicholas Lemann's best-seller, *The Promised Land.* We never *really* prosecuted the War on Poverty, Lemann argues, but instead got sidetracked on misguided community development projects whose spectacular failures persuaded us that government programs couldn't help the poor. But in fact federal government programs can help, Lemann asserts: look at job training, which gives its graduates a higher likelihood of being employed (though, as we've already seen, it is an insignificantly higher likelihood that is no solution to the underclass problem). So now let's seriously commit ourselves to training programs, public works projects, and guaranteed jobs, Lemann suggests, and finally get the task accomplished.

But the reality is that we have made a Herculean effort to rescue the worst-off, an effort that goes far beyond the War on Poverty or any set of government programs. We have turned our entire culture inside out to achieve that end and, heartbreakingly, have only made things worse rather than better.

The first answer to the question of what is to be done, then, is to stop doing what makes the problem worse. *Stop* the current welfare system, *stop* quota-based affirmative action, *stop* treating criminals as justified rebels, *stop* letting bums expropriate public spaces or wrongdoers live in public housing at public expense, *stop* Afrocentric education in the schools.

This is so unorthodox a solution that people quickly dismiss it as unserious, impracticable, diametrically counter to the tide of history. Their response is not to say that you have offered a suggestion that they think won't work, but rather that you haven't offered any suggestion at all. And so they go on searching for the perfect job-training program, the labor camps for underclass men that will somehow bring them into the mainstream economy by taking them out to the country, the magical adjustment to the welfare system, the condom giveaway program in the schools—the ideal program, so fine-tuned that it will at last succeed where all the others have failed.

However, the material structure needed to solve the poverty problem is already in place: an economy that for two decades has multiplied jobs at every skill level; a universal, free educational system from kindergarten to college that spends some $5,500 per pupil each year and needs only to be directed to teach and to discipline; and an open society that allows anyone to better his condition by his own efforts. A Ghanaian cabdriver in New York recently summed it up when he said, after contemptuously bawling out an able-bodied panhandler who'd tried to beg from him at a red light: "They have freedom, and they don't know what to do with it."

It's as if the rich and the poor are under a spell of malign enchantment. The poor already have the strenuous but genuine opportunity for escaping poverty, but they lack the inner resources to embrace their chance. The rich believe that the degraded condition of the worst-off is an indictment of their society and, ultimately, of themselves. But they can't see that the required solution is for the poor to take responsibility for themselves, not to be made dependent on programs and exempted from responsibility. Nor can they see that their own spiritual malaise comes from the erosion of the most cherished mainstream values in the course of the effort to rescue the worst-off.

For the breakdown of the poor to be healed and the moral confusion of the Haves to be dispelled, we need above all to repair the damage that has been done to the beliefs and values that have made America remarkable and that for two centuries have successfully transformed huddled masses of the poor into free and prosperous citizens. The soul of American society isn't an ancient dynasty, or racial homogeneity, or immemorial root-edness in an ancestral fatherland, or welfare paternalism, but an allegiance to a few fundamental ideas. The principles on which our society was built must once again inform our pub-lic life, from social policy to school curricula: that everyone is responsible for his or her actions; that we believe in freedom under the rule of law, and that we enforce the law scrupulously in all neighborhoods; that the public, communal life is a boon, not an oppression; that everyone has equal rights, and rights belong to individuals, not groups; that we are free to shape our own fate.

ACKNOWLEDGMENTS

This book began to take shape in a series of stories on poverty and social policy I wrote for *Fortune* in 1987 and 1988. In reporting those stories, I interviewed homeless and underclass people, shelter operators, public officials, advocates, and dozens of experts, who kindly and patiently helped educate me in the intricacies of the subject, for which I am much in their debt. Among the experts are several I spoke to regularly—Richard B. Freeman, Lawrence M. Mead, Richard E. Morgan, Charles Murray, and Isabel Sawhill—and I am deeply grateful to them for many fascinating and instructive hours. I am indebted, too, to Marshall Loeb, *Fortune*'s editor, for first making the match between subject and willing writer and giving me the opportunity to explore the subject in depth.

Several friends have taken the trouble to help me think through various sections of this book or to comment on the manuscript. I especially want to thank Geoffrey Colvin, Randall Filer, Gertrude Himmelfarb, Johanna Kaplan, Irving Kristol, Starling Lawrence, Elizabeth B. Lurie, Norman Podhoretz, Daniel Seligman, and Fred Siegel. Thanks too to the Manhattan Institute, its staff, its trustees, and its indefatigable president, William M. H. Hammett, for allowing me to write this book as a senior fellow under the Institute's extremely hospitable and stimulating auspices. Harvey Ginsberg, the book's editor, has exercised his inexhaustible skill and vigilance to make the text better in countless ways. And my wife, Barbara Crehan, has as always wisely counseled at every stage.

NOTES

Introduction: What's Gone Wrong?

Page

13   *between 1980 and 1987.* As calculated by economist Martin Anderson, Hoover Institution.

17   *without responsibilities.* Joe Klein, "The National Interest: Ask Not? Don't Ask," *New York* (June 3, 1991).

17   *"... escape from it."* Personal interview.

21   *"... unrelated to the actual problem."* Personal interview.

21   *"... make any other way."* Personal interview.

Chapter One: The Power of Culture

24   *on the waves.* Elie Halévy, *England in 1815* (London: Ernest Benn, 1960), pp. 424–425; E. Digby Baltzell, *Puritan Boston and Quaker Philadelphia* (New York: Free Press, 1979), chs. 1–3.

25   *economic development.* Max Weber, *The Protestant Ethic and the Spirit of Capitalism* (New York: Scribner's, 1958); Martin J. Wiener, *English Culture and the Decline of the Industrial Spirit, 1850–1980* (Cambridge: Cambridge University Press, 1981); V. S. Naipaul, *India: A Wounded Civilization* (New York: Viking, 1991).

25   *require education.* Thomas Sowell, *Ethnic America* (New York: Basic Books, 1981).

26   *"... man in society."* Quoted in Lionel Trilling, *Matthew Arnold* (New York: Harcourt Brace Jovanovich, 1977), p. 381.

31   *The Promised Land.* Nicholas Lemann, *The Promised Land: The Great Black Migration and How It Changed America* (New York: Knopf, 1991); David Whitman, "The Great Sharecropper Success Story," *Public Interest* (Summer 1991).

33   *"... in the sixties."* Personal interview.

34   *"... on our feet."* Personal interview.

35   *and Los Angeles.* New York City Public Schools, *The Cohort Report* (May 1992), pp. 90–92.

35   *had a job.* 1991 average annual earnings. Bureau of Labor Statistics, *Employment and Earnings,* 39, no. 1 (January 1992).

Chapter Two: The Underclass

37   *and school failure.* Kenneth B. Clark, *The Dark Ghetto: Dilemmas of Social Power* (New York: Harper & Row, 1965).

38   *"'... get on welfare.'"* Ken Auletta, *The Underclass* (New York: Vintage, 1983), p. 11.

38   *"... deal with that."* "Street Dealers: In the War on Drugs, Toughest Foe May Be the Alienated Youth," *The Wall Street Journal* (September 9, 1989).

38   *"... tense every day."* Ibid.

38   *"... dead or what."* "How Benji Takes His Cue," *New York Post* (June 26, 1991).

38   *"... be in jail."* "Street Dealers."

38   *"... time to party."* "Holding On to Dreams Amid Harlem's Reality," *The New York Times* (February 5, 1991).

38   *"... know your name."* "For Young Blacks, Despair and Rage," *The New York Times* (August 25, 1991).

38   *"... what to do."* "Dinkins Bid Rekindles Community Hope," *The New York Times* (October 28, 1989).

39   *government officials.* Michael Novak et al., *The New Consensus on Family and Welfare* (Washington, D.C.: American Enterprise Institute for Public Policy Research; and Milwaukee: Marquette University, 1987), p. 5.

39   *the poverty line.* Charles Murray, "According to Age: Longitudinal Profiles of AFDC Recipients and the Poor by Age Group," Working Seminar on the Family and American Welfare (September 23, 1986).

41   *"... bad habits."* Kevin Sack, "The Short Life of 'Little Man,' A 14-Year-Old Drug Peddler," *The New York Times* (November 29, 1989).

41   *as underclass.* Ronald B. Mincy, *The Underclass: Concept, Controversy and Evidence* (Madison, Wis.: Institute for Research on Poverty, University of Wisconsin, 1992), pp. 12–16.

42   *doing even now.* Ibid., pp. 15, 13–14.

43   *to the contrary.* "Study Finds Gains for Black Middle Class," *The New York Times* (August 10, 1991).

45   *pay by 1988.* McKinley L. Blackburn, David E. Bloom, and Richard B. Freeman, "Changes in Earnings Differentials in the 1980s: Concordance, Convergence, Causes, and Consequences" (National Bureau of Economic Research, 1991), table 1.

45   *"... around today."* William Woodside, personal interview.

47   *the underclass.* Richard B. Freeman, "Help Wanted: Disadvantaged Youths in a Labor Shortage Economy" (unpublished manuscript,

1989); Charles Murray, "Here's the Bad News on the Underclass," *The Wall Street Journal* (March 8, 1990).

47   *more immigrants.* Julian Simon, personal communication.

49   *Tan concludes.* Personal interview.

50   *dying in battle.* James Q. Wilson, *Thinking About Crime,* rev. ed. (New York: Vintage, 1985), p. 24.

50   *in college.* According to the Sentencing Project. "Study Shows Racial Imbalance in Who Is Punished," *The New York Times* (February 27, 1990).

50   *for their arrest.* According to the National Center for Institutions and Alternatives. "Going to Jail Is 'Rite of Passage' for Many D.C. Men," *The Washington Post* (April 18, 1992).

51   *being robbed.* "Bronx Man, 69, Slain Waiting to Walk Wife Home," *New York Post* (February 15, 1989), p. 16.

51   *a beast.* Aristotle, *Ethics* 1113b.

52   *shots into him.* "Student Is Slain on Packed IRT After Argument," *The New York Times* (October 28, 1989); "When Violence and Terror Strike Outside the Schools," *The New York Times* (November 14, 1989).

52   *"... the dream."* "A Hopeful Young Life Is Stolen and an Aching Void Remains," *The New York Times* (January 21, 1989).

53   *48 percent in 1990.* William Julius Wilson, *The Truly Disadvantaged: The Inner City, the Underclass, and Public Policy* (Chicago: University of Chicago Press, 1987), p. 26; U.S. Bureau of the Census, Current Population Reports, Series P–20, Number 458, *Household and Family Characteristics: March 1991* (Washington, D.C.: Government Printing Office, 1992).

53   *two thirds. The Truly Disadvantaged,* p. 28; Charles Murray, *Losing Ground: American Social Policy, 1950–1980* (New York: Basic Books, 1984), p. 126; National Center for Health Statistics, *Vital Statistics of the United States, 1989* (Washington, D.C.: Government Printing Office, 1992), vol. 1, p. 190.

53   *family's income.* U.S. Bureau of the Census, Current Population Reports, Series P–60, Number 174, *Money Income of Households, Families, and Persons in the United States: 1990* (Washington, D.C.: Government Printing Office, 1991).

54   *other children.* "Study Finds Severe Effects From Childhood Abuse," *The New York Times* (February 18, 1991).

54   *over a decade.* David T. Ellwood, *Poor Support: Poverty in the American Family* (New York: Basic Books, 1988), p. 148; Committee on Ways and Means, U.S. House of Representatives, *1991 Green Book* (Washington, D.C.: Government Printing Office, 1991), pp. 641–642.

54   *"... what it is."* Leon Dash, "When Outcomes Collide with Desires," *The Washington Post* (January 29, 1986).

Chapter Three: The Hole in the Theory

57 *"... to represent." Losing Ground: American Social Policy, 1950–1980* (New York: Basic Books, 1984), p. 161.

58 *somber phrase.* Ibid., pp. 154, 167.

60 *"... just went along."* Leon Dash, "When Outcomes Collide with Desires," *The Washington Post* (January 29, 1986).

64 *"... a bleak future."* William Julius Wilson, *The Truly Disadvantaged: The Inner City, the Underclass, and Public Policy* (Chicago: University of Chicago Press, 1987), pp. 158–159.

67 *"... in city hall."* Karl Zinsmeister, "Asians: Prejudice From Top and Bottom," *Public Opinion* (July-August 1987).

69 *1200 percent greater.* James Q. Wilson, *Thinking About Crime,* rev. ed. (New York: Vintage, 1985), pp. 20–25.

72 *on the jogger.* Michael Stone, "What Really Happened in Central Park," *New York* (August 14, 1989).

74 *"... available to them."* Personal interview.

75 *academic competitions.* Jeffrey Litt, "Bringing a School Back to Life," *Clipboard* (New York: Center for Educational Innovation, June 1992).

76 *says Gray.* Personal interview.

76 *last four years.* Robert Woodson, "Transform Inner Cities From the Grass Roots Up," *The Wall Street Journal* (June 3, 1992).

Chapter Four: The Homeless

80 *can only intensify.* Jonathan Kozol, *Rachel and Her Children* (New York: Fawcett Columbine, 1988), pp. 10–11, 15.

81 *"... everything in sight."* "The Homeless Issue: An Adman's Dream," *Reason* (July 1987): 22.

81 *to 360,000.* Peter H. Rossi et al., " 'The Urban Homeless: Estimating Composition and Size," *Science* 235 (March 13, 1987): 1336–1341.

81 *" '... plant—white?' "* Personal interview.

82 *dubbed Reaganvilles.* Alvin L. Schorr, "Will We Have Reaganvilles?" *The New York Times* (August 26, 1986).

82 *" '... directly—go I.' "* Personal interview.

83 *"... is a mess."* "In Our Backyard," *The New York Times* (October 26, 1991).

83 *by friends.* Robert C. Ellickson, "The Homelessness Muddle," *Public Interest* (Spring 1990): 47–51.

83 *subsidized housing.* "Families Seek Out Shelters As Route to Better Homes," *The New York Times* (September 4, 1991); Randall Filer, "What Really Causes Family Homelessness?" *NY: The City Journal* (Autumn 1990).

84 *for cocaine.* New York City Commission on the Homeless, Andrew M. Cuomo, Chairman, "The Way Home: A New Direction in Social Policy" (February 1992).

84 *tried to evoke.* "Santa Monica Grows Hostile to the Homeless Who Consider It Home," *The Wall Street Journal* (November 9, 1992);

Richard B. Freeman, *Labor Markets in Action* (Cambridge, Mass.: Harvard University Press, 1989), pp. 135–156; Institute of Medicine, *Homelessness, Health, and Human Needs* (Washington, D.C.: National Academy Press, 1988); R. C. Tessler and D. L. Dennis, "A Synthesis of NIMH-Funded Research Concerning Persons Who Are Homeless and Mentally Ill" (Washington, D.C.: National Institutes of Mental Health, 1989).

85 *another study found.* W. R. Breakey et al., "Health and Mental Health Problems of Homeless Men and Women in Baltimore," *JAMA* (September 8, 1989); E. Fuller Torrey, M.D., *Nowhere to Go: The Tragic Odyssey of the Homeless Mentally Ill* (New York: Harper & Row, 1988), pp. 7–8.

86 *hopelessly defective.* Torrey, *Nowhere to Go,* pp. 55, 57, 67, 77.

86 *with increasing rapidity.* Ibid., pp. 87–88.

87 *"... economies are 'sick.'"* Thomas S. Szasz, M.D., *The Myth of Mental Illness,* rev. ed. (New York: Harper & Row, 1974), p. 267.

89 *"... social world."* Erving Goffman, *Asylums: Essays on the Social Situation of Mental Patients and Other Inmates* (Garden City, N.Y.: Doubleday Anchor, 1961), p. 130.

89 *"... constitute it."* Ibid., p. 168.

90 *"... one's attachment."* Ibid., pp. 305–306.

90 *or inappropriate.* Ibid., p. 363.

92 *they could go.* R. D. Laing, *The Politics of Experience* (New York: Pantheon, 1967).

95 *decade or two.* Torrey, *Nowhere to Go,* pp. 90, 92, 96, 99–101, 108, 118.

95 *71,000 beds.* Ibid., p. 139.

96 *their fellows.* Ibid., pp. 141, 23.

96 *dysfunctional persons.* Ibid., p. 141.

97 *to supervise.* Ibid., pp. 142–143, 147–148, 120.

98 *as inseparable.* Ibid., pp. 122–123, 129; Leonard Duhl, quoted in ibid., p. 125.

98 *"... all of society...."* Ibid., p. 124.

98 *"... healthy individuals."* Ibid., p. 123.

98 *"... attributed to them."* Stanley F. Yolles, quoted in ibid., p. 126.

98 *near a school.* Ibid., pp. 127, 129–130.

99 *a grate one.* Ibid., pp. 201–202.

99 *was too bad.* Ibid., pp. 150–153.

100 *from the asylums.* Ibid., pp. 151–153, 155.

Chapter Five: Homelessness and Liberty

101 *"... damage to people."* Quoted in E. Fuller Torrey, M.D., *Nowhere to Go: The Tragic Odyssey of the Homeless Mentally Ill* (New York: Harper & Row, 1988), pp. 158–159.

102 *refuse treatment, period.* Ibid., pp. 157–158.

102 *few days later.* Ibid., pp. 31–32.

103   *1982 and 1988.* W. R. Breakey et al., "Health and Mental Health Problems of Homeless Men and Women in Baltimore," *JAMA* (September 8, 1989): 1354; "Test Finds High TB Rate at a Shelter," *The New York Times* (April 25, 1990).

103   *". . . shedding his psychosis."* Personal interview.

104   *a national problem.* Robert C. Ellickson, "The Homelessness Muddle," *Public Interest* (Spring 1990): 56.

105   *mental asylums.* Torrey, *Nowhere to Go,* p. 12.

106   *". . . with her axe."* Ibid., p. 30.

106   *his delusional orders.* "Dangerous People on the Street and What to Do About Them," *The New York Times* (July 25, 1986).

109   *or any other.* Jeanie Kasindorf, "The Real Story of Billie Boggs," *New York* (May 2, 1988).

111   *get no treatment.* Torrey, *Nowhere to Go,* p. 10.

111   *house them.* "Twins of the Streets: Homelessness and Addiction," *The New York Times* (May 22, 1989).

112   *feed their children?* Vernon Loeb, "The Shelter Fiasco," *The Philadelphia Inquirer* (March 6, 1988).

112   *disintegration and crime.* James Q. Wilson, *Thinking About Crime,* rev. ed. (New York: Vintage, 1985), pp. 75–89.

112   *of the jungle.* "New York Is Not a Curfew Town," *New York Post* (August 2, 1989).

113   *". . . but some don't."* Personal interview.

113   *either real parent.* Richard B. Freeman, *Labor Markets in Action* (Cambridge, Mass.: Harvard University Press, 1989), pp. 141–142.

114   *listless to cry.* Personal interview.

116   *is liberalized.* Ellickson, "The Homelessness Muddle," pp. 47–51.

116   *and her children.* "Homeless Families Triple in District," *The Washington Post* (August 9, 1986).

Chapter Six: Victimizing the Poor

122   *to replace them.* Karl Marx, *Capital,* trans. Samuel Moore and Edward Aveling (New York: International Publishers, 1967), vol. 1, Ch. 25.

123   *War on Poverty.* Michael Harrington, *The Other America: Poverty in the United States,* rev. ed. (New York: Penguin, 1971), pp. xvi, 212.

124   *". . . progress is misery."* Ibid., p. 13.

124   *". . . the less fortunate."* Kevin Phillips, *The Politics of Rich and Poor: Wealth and the American Electorate in the Reagan Aftermath* (New York: Random House, 1990), pp. 3, 8.

125   *". . . but in justice."* Harrington, *The Other America,* pp. xxi–xxii.

126   *good fortune.* Jean-Jacques Rousseau, *Discourse on Inequality,* in *The First and Second Discourses,* trans. Roger D. Masters (New York: St. Martin's Press, 1964), p. 175.

127   *improved their lot.* Harrington, *The Other America,* pp. 76–77.

127 *"... becomes a taunt."* Ibid., pp. 19, 32, 31.

127 *"... futile universe...."* Ibid., pp. 2, 129.

128 *pleasure lost?* Ibid., pp. 168, 140, 142.

128 *"... and to society."* Ibid., pp. 10, 162, 170, 160, 149.

128 *that breed crime.* "The Jogger and the Wolf Pack," *The New York Times* (April 26, 1989).

129 *the slums, slummy.* Harrington, *The Other America,* pp. 149, 150, 11.

131 *pity, not censure.* Robert K. Merton, *Social Theory and Social Structure* (New York: Free Press, 1963); Allen J. Matusow, *The Unraveling of America: A History of Liberalism in the 1960s* (New York: Harper & Row, 1984), pp. 108–110; Lloyd Ohlin and Richard Cloward, *Delinquency and Opportunity: A Theory of Delinquent Gangs* (New York: Free Press, 1960); James Leiby, *A History of Social Welfare and Social Work in the United States* (New York: Columbia University Press, 1978), pp. 294–296, 280–282.

133 *offered them.* Harrington, *The Other America,* pp. 181, 177.

133 *victimizes the poor.* Ibid., pp. 177–178, 105.

135 *label them.* William Ryan, *Blaming the Victim,* rev. ed. (New York: Vintage, 1976), pp. 4–9.

135 *poor people.* Ibid., pp. 18, 32–33, 37, 54–55, 57, 247–248.

135 *of our institutions.* Ibid., pp. 28–30.

136 *"... care of itself."* Ibid., pp. 246–247, 140.

136 *wealth and power.* Ibid., pp. 140–141, 250.

136 *A Theory of Justice.* John Rawls, *A Theory of Justice* (Cambridge, Mass.: Harvard University Press, 1971).

137 *unjust and illegitimate.* Ibid., pp. 14–15.

Chapter Seven: Race and Reparations

139 *percentage of blacks.* Greg Duncan, Director of the Panel Study of Income Dynamics, Survey Research Center, University of Michigan, personal communication.

140 *purely economic one.* Allen J. Matusow, *The Unraveling of America: A History of Liberalism in the 1960s* (New York: Harper & Row, 1984), pp. 119–120.

140 *have imagined.* Jim Sleeper, *The Closest of Strangers: Liberalism and the Politics of Race in New York* (New York: Norton, 1990), p. 163.

140 *the mid-eighties.* Howard Schuman, "Changing Racial Norms in America," *Michigan Quarterly Review* (Summer 1991): 460–477; Dinesh D'Souza, *Illiberal Education: The Politics of Race and Sex on Campus* (New York: Free Press, 1991), pp. 127–128.

140 *would in 1990.* Daniel Yankelovich, "The Affluence Effect" (unpublished manuscript, 1991), p. 30.

141 *opportunity for blacks.* Schuman, "Changing Racial Norms in America."

141 *"Reparations Now."* Amity Schlaes, "In Brooklyn, Not Just Another

Racial Incident," *The Wall Street Journal* (August 26, 1991); Charles Krauthammer, "Reparations for Black Americans," *Time* (December 31, 1990).

142 *very nearly so.* Stuart Butler, "Guidelines for State Welfare Reform" (Washington, D.C.: Heritage Foundation, 1991), p. 4.

142 *are universal.* Lao Tzu, *Tao Te Ching,* trans. Stephen Mitchell (Harper & Row, 1988), p. 57.

143 *job more dependably.* Judith S. Wallerstein, "The Long-Term Effects of Divorce on Children: A Review," *Journal of the American Academy of Child and Adolescent Psychiatry* (May 1991): 349–360; Nicholas Zill et al., "Developmental, Learning, and Emotional Problems: Health of Our Nation's Children, United States, 1988," *Vital and Health Statistics of the National Center for Health Statistics* 190 (November 16, 1990); Myron Magnet, "The American Family, 1992," *Fortune* (August 10, 1992).

144 *never heals.* Judith S. Wallerstein and Sandra Blakeslee, *Second Chances: Men, Women, and Children a Decade After Divorce* (New York: Ticknor & Fields, 1989).

144 *their ill partner.* "Family Redefines Itself, And Now the Law Follows," *The New York Times* (May 28, 1989).

145 *the nuclear family.* See for instance the 24/31 July 1989 issue of *The Nation* entitled "Scapegoating the Black Family."

146 *welfare benefits.* Sleeper, *The Closest of Strangers,* pp. 91–94; Matusow, *The Unraveling of America,* pp. 263–264.

147 *"... generation of citizens?"* Barbara Ehrenreich and Frances Fox Piven, "Workfare Means Mass Peonage," *The New York Times* (May 30, 1987).

147 *costs will decline.* Judith M. Gueron and Edward Pauly, *From Welfare to Work: Summary* (New York: Manpower Demonstration Research Corporation, 1991).

147 *first year.* James Riccio and Daniel Friedlander, *GAIN: Program Strategies, Participation Patterns, and First-Year Impacts in Six Counties* (New York: Manpower Demonstration Research Corporation, 1992).

148 *within five years.* Charles Murray, *Losing Ground: American Social Policy, 1950–1980* (New York: Basic Books, 1984), p. 38.

148 *too great.* Ibid., pp. 227–233.

151 *and understanding.* Ibid., pp. 178–185.

153 *by collective protest.* Shelby Steele, *The Content of Our Character* (New York: St. Martin's Press, 1990), pp. 14–15.

153 *grew more shrill.* Ibid., pp. 49, 24, 33.

154 *and vulnerability.* Ibid., p. 25.

154 *Nazis and Klansmen.* "Black Poet Says Faculty 'Nazis' Blocked Tenure," *The New York Times* (March 15, 1990).

154 *your own fate?* Jason DeParle, "Talk of Government Being Out to

Get Blacks Falls on More Attentive Ears," *The New York Times* (October 29, 1990).

155 *to identify.* Steele, *The Content of Our Character,* p. 101.

156 *all before him.* Robert Sam Anson, *Best Intentions: The Education and Killing of Edmund Perry* (New York: Vintage, 1988), p. 204.

156 *"... back for class."* Ibid., p. 93.

Chapter Eight: Rebels with a Cause

160 *"... change the kid."* George Cadwalader, *Castaways: The Penikese Island Experiment* (Chelsea, Vt.: Chelsea Green, 1988), p. viii.

160 *"... given up on?"* Ibid., pp. ix–x.

161 *its foundation.* Jean-Jacques Rousseau, *The Second Discourse,* in *The First and Second Discourses,* trans. Roger D. Masters (New York: St. Martin's Press, 1964), pp. 154–160.

162 *political society.* Thomas Paine, *The Rights of Man* (New York: Dent/Dutton Everyman, 1969), pp. 163–164, 31–33.

163 *"... diseased environment."* Michael Harrington, *The Other America: Poverty in the United States,* rev. ed. (New York: Penguin, 1971), p. 136.

163 *"... is responsible."* Ramsey Clark, *Crime in America: Observations on Its Nature, Causes, Prevention and Control* (New York: Simon & Schuster, 1970), p. 51.

163 *Clark concludes.* Ibid., pp. 29, 43.

163 *in the suites.* Ibid., pp. 37–38.

163 *"... expect violence."* Ibid., pp. 42–43, 144.

164 *"... this assertion?"* Sigmund Freud, *Civilization and Its Discontents,* trans. James Strachey (New York: Norton, 1961), p. 58.

165 *of the governed.* Edmund Burke, *Reflections on the Revolution in France,* together with Thomas Paine, *The Rights of Man* (Garden City, N.Y.: Doubleday Anchor, 1973), pp. 180, 240.

168 *"heart" and "guts."* Richard Cloward and Lloyd Ohlin, *Delinquency and Opportunity: A Theory of Delinquent Gangs* (New York: Free Press, 1960).

168 *"... instinct stifled."* Norman Mailer, *Advertisements for Myself* (New York: Putnam-Berkley, 1959), p. 312.

169 *"... life [is] war."* Ibid., pp. 313, 321, 314.

169 *American society....* Ibid., p. 313.

169 *"... not altogether cowardly."* Ibid., pp. 313, 320–321.

170 *from restraint.* Nathan Glazer, "On Subway Graffiti in New York," *Public Interest* (Winter 1979).

172 *"... left in us."* John Edgar Wideman, *Brothers and Keepers* (New York: Penguin, 1985), p. 57.

173 *"... so corrupt?"* Ibid., pp. 58, 90.

173 *"... settle for less."* "As Many Fall, Project's Survivors Struggle On," *The New York Times* (February 6, 1991).

174 *the shootout.* "Larry Davis Convicted in Killing of a Drug Dealer," *The New York Times* (March 15, 1991).

174 *". . . man and man."* William Ryan, *Blaming the Victim,* rev. ed. (New York: Vintage, 1976), p. 217.

176 *two to one.* Richard E. Morgan, *Disabling America: The "Rights Industry" in Our Time* (New York: Basic Books, 1984), p. 76.

176 *rates quintupled.* FBI Uniform Crime Reports.

176 *". . . of the state."* Rita Kramer, *At a Tender Age: Violent Youth and Juvenile Justice* (New York: Holt, 1988), pp. 65–67.

177 *would be entitled.* Ibid., pp. 68–70.

177 *". . . no conscience."* Selma Fraiberg, "The Origins of Human Bonds," *Commentary* (December 1967).

178 *". . . serious offenders."* James Q. Wilson, *Thinking About Crime,* rev. ed. (New York: Vintage, 1985), pp. 5, 119, 123–124.

178 *too often get.* Kramer, *At a Tender Age,* p. 195.

178 *serious crime.* Wilson, *Thinking About Crime;* Wesley G. Skogan, *Disorder and Decline: Crime and the Spiral of Decay in American Neighborhoods* (New York: Free Press, 1990).

179 *" '. . . any police officer.' "* Morgan, *Disabling America,* pp. 114–116; *Papachristo* v. *City of Jacksonville,* 405 U.S. 156 (1972).

180 *or "fascist" variety.* Morgan, *Disabling America,* pp. 118–121.

181 *jungles of Vietnam.* "Homicide Rate Up For Young Blacks," *The New York Times* (December 7, 1990).

181 *half of them fatally. New York Post* (April 26, 1991).

182 *". . . blows your brains out."* "Caught in Crossfire: Rising Toll in Streets," *The New York Times* (April 19, 1991).

182 *". . . human existence."* "Wild Shooting on Street Hits Girl, 9, in Car," *The New York Times* (July 23, 1990).

182 *". . . Only a murder!"* Kramer, *At a Tender Age,* p. 92.

Chapter Nine: The Living Constitution

184 *law professor.* H. L. McBain, *The Living Constitution* (1927), cited in William H. Rehnquist, "The Notion of a Living Constitution," *Texas Law Review* (May 1976): 694.

185 *". . . general interest."* "Why Judges Act," *The New York Times* (May 13, 1991).

187 *in any way.* See Richard E. Morgan review of C. A. Lofgren, *The Plessy Case* in *Constitutional Commentary* (Winter 1988): 256–261.

188 *". . . not a democrat."* Personal interview.

189 *we might.* Ronald Dworkin, *Taking Rights Seriously* (Cambridge, Mass.: Harvard University Press, 1977).

190 *the case's meaning.* Raymond Wolters, *The Burden of Brown: Thirty Years of School Desegregation* (Knoxville: University of Tennessee Press, 1984), pp. 4–6; Lino A. Graglia, *Disaster by Decree: The Supreme Court Decisions on Race and the Schools* (Ithaca, N.Y.: Cornell University Press, 1976), pp. 29–30.

190 *racial discrimination.* Wolters, *The Burden of Brown,* p. 5.

191 *racial imbalance.* Graglia, *Disaster by Decree,* pp. 46–49.

194 *"... is incalculable."* Personal interview.

195 *civil rights.* Richard E. Morgan, *Disabling America: The "Rights Industry" in Our Time* (New York: Basic Books, 1984), pp. 64–73.

197 *no longer necessary.* Thomas Sowell, *Preferential Policies: An International Perspective* (New York: William Morrow, 1990), p. 120.

198 *this movement.* Charles Murray, *Losing Ground: American Social Policy, 1950–1980* (New York: Basic Books, 1984), p. 251.

198 *"... in admissions."* Dinesh D'Souza, *Illiberal Education: The Politics of Race and Sex on Campus* (New York: Free Press, 1991), pp. 42, 36.

199 *from employers.* "'Race Norming' Tests Becomes a Fiery Issue," *The New York Times* (May 19, 1991).

199 *will not be random.* Sowell, *Preferential Policies,* pp. 128–135.

200 *prestigious colleges.* D'Souza, *Illiberal Education,* p. 296, n. 56.

200 *years since then.* Robert Klitgaard, *Choosing Elites* (New York: Basic Books, 1985), p. 15.

200 *fellow students.* Thomas Sowell, "The New Racism on Campus," *Fortune* (February 13, 1989), pp. 115–120.

200 *down the line.* Ibid.

200 *after matriculating.* Ibid.; D'Souza, *Illiberal Education,* p. 39; Shelby Steele, *The Content of Our Character* (New York: St. Martin's Press, 1990), p. 116.

202 *of failure.* Steele, *The Content of Our Character,* pp. 87, 116, 118.

203 *"... dominant group."* Alan Charles Kors, "It's Speech, Not Sex, the Dean Bans Now," *The Wall Street Journal* (October 12, 1989).

203 *"... for whites."* D'Souza, *Illiberal Education,* pp. 52, 4.

Chapter Ten: Trashing the Culture

208 *of the story.* Gertrude Himmelfarb, *The New History and the Old: Critical Essays and Reappraisals* (Cambridge, Mass.: Harvard University Press, 1987).

209 *parents having sex.* Steven Marcus, *Dickens: From Pickwick to Dombey* (New York: Basic Books, 1965), pp. 358–378.

211 *said you'd find.* Lionel Trilling, *Beyond Culture* (New York: Harcourt Brace Jovanovich, 1979), p. 18, in an otherwise superb essay by our finest critic.

215 *"... begun in earnest."* Quoted in Dinesh D'Souza, *Illiberal Education: The Politics of Race and Sex on Campus* (New York: Free Press, 1991), p. 18.

216 *"... sexist society."* "Initiatives for the Race and Gender Enrichment of Tulane University of Louisiana" (June 4, 1990).

216 *"... whites are racist."* "It's Speech, Not Sex, the Dean Bans Now," *The Wall Street Journal* (October 12, 1989).

216 *"... measure is privilege."* Quoted in D'Souza, *Illiberal Education,* pp. 176, 153.

217   *of performance.* Joel Segall, "When Academic Quality Is Beside the Point," *The Wall Street Journal* (October 29, 1990).

217   *". . . Canon went too."* Quoted in Roger Kimball, *Tenured Radicals: How Politics Has Corrupted Our Higher Education* (New York: Harper & Row, 1990), p. 5.

217   *". . . sexist text."* Quoted in David Lehman, *Signs of the Times: Deconstruction and the Fall of Paul de Man* (New York: Poseidon, 1991), p. 265.

217   *". . . a sexist pig."* Quoted in D'Souza, *Illiberal Education,* p. 83.

217   *"gothic romance."* Quoted in Kimball, *Tenured Radicals,* p. 20.

217   *". . . social class."* Quoted in Arthur M. Schlesinger, Jr., *The Disuniting of America: Reflections on a Multicultural Society* (Knoxville, Tenn.: Whittle, 1991), p. 73.

218   *". . . above the veil." The Souls of Black Folk,* quoted in ibid., p. 51.

218   *". . . white heterosexual males."* Quoted in ibid., p. 66.

218   *". . . never-never land?"* Quoted in John Searle, "The Storm Over the University," *The New York Review of Books* (December 6, 1990), p. 35.

218   *". . . education of racists."* Quoted in Kimball, *Tenured Radicals,* p. 27.

218   *an instrument.* Searle, "The Storm Over the University," p. 35.

219   *". . . political action."* Quoted in Kimball, *Tenured Radicals,* p. xii.

219   *". . . political activism."* Quoted in John Taylor, "Are You Politically Correct?" *New York* (January 21, 1991), p. 36.

219   *". . . Nobel peace prize."* D'Souza, *Illiberal Education,* p. 72.

220   *the New World.* George Levine et al., *Speaking for the Humanities* (New York: American Council of Learned Societies, 1989), p. 20.

220   *". . . class and minorities."* D'Souza, *Illiberal Education,* p. 162.

220   *". . . fundamental sense."* Nancy Julia Chodorow in *Reconstructing Individualism,* quoted in Kimball, *Tenured Radicals,* p. 47.

220   *". . . falsely enslaved."* Quoted in D'Souza, *Illiberal Education,* p. 175.

221   *". . . Western metaphysics."* Quoted in Lehman, *Signs of the Times,* pp. 40–41.

221   *the Fall of Paul de Man.* Ibid., p. 54.

222   *". . . or a sham."* Ibid., pp. 57–58.

222   *". . . right of kings."* Quoted in D'Souza, *Illiberal Education,* p. 159.

222   *than authoritarianism.* Levine et al., *Speaking for the Humanities,* p. 10.

223   *arrived in America.* Lehman, *Signs of the Times,* pp. 191, 133, 171–180, 187–190.

223   *de Man himself.* Ibid., pp. 243, 240.

224   *". . . I might be."* "Politically Correct," *The Wall Street Journal* (November 26, 1990); D'Souza, *Illiberal Education,* pp. 215–216.

224   *"misdirected laughter."* Quoted in D'Souza, *Illiberal Education,* pp. 146, 143.

224   *might be true.* Quoted in D'Souza, *Illiberal Education,* pp. 143–144.
224   *breaching the code.* Ibid., pp. 8–9.
225   *of his views.* "Taking Offense," *Newsweek* (December 24, 1990),
p. 50.
225   *preferential treatment.* Taylor, "Are You Politically Correct?,"
pp. 32–34.
225   *"... You bet."* Marcus Mabry, "A View From the Front," *Newsweek*
(December 24, 1990), p. 55.
225   *"raise consciousness."* D'Souza, *Illiberal Education,* p. 217.
225   *political reeducation.* Taylor, "Are You Politically Correct?," p. 35.
226   *"... with lies."* D'Souza, *Illiberal Education,* p. 131.
227   *European Enlightenment.* Schlesinger, *The Disuniting of America,*
p. 54.
227   *"... his beneficence."* Task Force on Minorities, "A Curriculum of
Inclusion" (July 1989): iv.
227   *"... for centuries."* Ibid., p. 6.
227   *"... Native Americans."* New York State Social Studies Review and
Development Committee, "One Nation, Many Peoples: A Declaration of Cultural Interdependence" (June 1991): 43, 41.
228   *more important than doing.* Schlesinger, *The Disuniting of America,*
pp. 31, 34; Andrew Sullivan, "Racism 101," *The New Republic*
(November 26, 1990), p. 20, quoting Wade Nobles.
228   *literal sense racist.* Schlesinger, *The Disuniting of America,* pp. 33–34,
44.
229   *Columbus was born.* Ibid., pp. 35–36, 42; Irving Kristol, "The
Tragedy of Multiculturalism," *The Wall Street Journal* (July 31,
1991).
229   *"... the vomit-drinkers!"* Quoted in Sullivan, "Racism 101," p. 20.
229   *"... than Afrocentrism."* Schlesinger, *The Disuniting of America,*
p. 52.
230   *seductive achievement.* V. S. Naipaul, "Our Universal Civilization,"
The New York Review of Books (January 31, 1991).

Chapter Eleven: The Poverty of Spirit

233   *"... heterosexual white male."* "Is 'Quality' An Idea Whose Time Has
Gone?" *The New York Times* (July 22, 1990).
233   *capitalist atrocity.* "Pilgrims and Other Imperialists," *The Wall Street
Journal* (May 17, 1991).
233   *"a historic tragedy."* Dorothy Rabinowitz, "Columbus and His Controversial Legacy," *The Wall Street Journal* (October 7, 1991).
235   *"... money counts."* Personal interviews.
235   *the rest back.* James B. Stewart, *Den of Thieves* (New York: Simon &
Schuster, 1991), p. 82.
235   *"... found meaning in."* Bret Easton Ellis, *American Psycho* (New
York: Random House, 1991).

236 *The Promised Land.* Nicholas Lemann, *The Promised Land: The Great Black Migration and How It Changed America* (New York: Knopf, 1991), pp. 344, 350–351.

236 *task accomplished.* Ibid., pp. 219, 344, 350–351.

INDEX